W9-CAN-827

Strategic Management for Academic Libraries

Recent Titles in
The Greenwood Library Management Collection

The Smaller Academic Library: A Management Handbook
Gerard B. McCabe, editor

Operations Handbook for the Small Academic Library
Gerard B. McCabe, editor

Data Bases for Special Libraries: A Strategic Guide to Information Management
Lynda W. Moulton

Time Management Handbook for Librarians
J. Wesley Cochran

Academic Libraries in Urban and Metropolitan Areas: A Management
Handbook
Gerard B. McCabe, editor

Managing Institutional Archives: Foundational Principles and Practices
Richard J. Cox

Automated Information Retrieval in Libraries
Vicki Anders

Circulation Services in a Small Academic Library
Connie Battaile

Using Consultants in Libraries and Information Centers: A Management
Handbook
Edward D. Garten, editor

Automation in Library Reference Services: A Handbook
Robert Carande

Planning Second Generation Automated Library Systems
Edwin M. Cortez and Tom Smorch

Strategic Management for Academic Libraries

A Handbook

Robert M. Hayes

MORTON COLLEGE LIBRARY
CICERO, ILLINOIS

THE GREENWOOD LIBRARY MANAGEMENT COLLECTION
Gerard B. McCabe, Series Adviser

GREENWOOD PRESS
Westport, Connecticut • London

Library of Congress Cataloging-in-Publication Data

Hayes, Robert Mayo.
  Strategic management for academic libraries : a handbook / Robert
M. Hayes.
    p. cm.—(The Greenwood library management collection, ISSN
0894–2986)
  Includes bibliographical references and index.
  ISBN 0–313–28111–4 (alk. paper)
  1. Academic libraries—United States—Administration.
  2. University of California, Los Angeles. Library—Administration.
I. Title. II. Series.
  Z675.U5H35 1993
  027.7'0973—dc20   92–40775

British Library Cataloguing in Publication Data is available.

Copyright © 1993 by Robert M. Hayes

All rights reserved. No portion of this book may be
reproduced, by any process or technique, without the
express written consent of the publisher.

Library of Congress Catalog Card Number: 92–40775
ISBN: 0–313–28111–4
ISSN: 0894–2986

First published in 1993

Greenwood Press, 88 Post Road West, Westport, CT 06881
An imprint of Greenwood Publishing Group, Inc.

Printed in the United States of America

The paper used in this book complies with the
Permanent Paper Standard issued by the National
Information Standards Organization (Z39.48–1984).

10 9 8 7 6 5 4 3 2 1

Contents

MORTON COLLEGE
VERITAS
1924

LIBRARY

Illustrations

TABLES

Preface

This professional reference is intended to serve both practicing academic library managers and students in schools of library and information science. It is written generally, at a level that requires intellectual commitment but no specific technical skills. Chapters 9 and 10, however, do involve accounting and mathematics to an extent that makes it valuable to have skills in their use.

The contents of chapters 3 through 6 are based on assessments of the strategic situation for academic libraries during the years leading up to publication. While it is likely that the issues in these chapters that are identified as important will continue to have an impact for some time, it must be recognized that strategic situations do change. In the same vein, the contents of chapters 7 through 10 are based on current theory and techniques for strategic management. While they are likely to continue to be valuable, the ideas therein presumably will also develop over time, both within business management contexts and in their application to libraries. As a result, while it is hoped that the basic structure and philosophy presented in this reference will have continuing validity, its content is rather specific to the situation that academic libraries face currently.

THE COUNCIL ON LIBRARY RESOURCES PROJECT

This book is an outgrowth of a project, conducted under the sponsorship of the Council on Library Resources (CLR), on strategic planning for libraries and information resources in the research university. The project was undertaken at the University of California at Los Angeles (UCLA), from the beginning of 1987 through the end of 1990, and was designed to explore the means by which a major university could carry forward such planning, with an emphasis on faculty involvement.

Genesis

The project was stimulated by a conference, held at the UCLA Lake Arrowhead Conference Center in December 1981,[1] which brought together university administrators, academic librarians, and library educators to identify the effects of technology on the future of universities and the research libraries within them. One vital element was missing from that conference, however: the community of research scholars, the persons depending on libraries and information resources for their responsibilities in instruction and research.

During the ensuing years, discussions between the staffs of the CLR and UCLA led to the project as an effort in planning that would directly involve the research faculty as well as librarians and administrators. The intent was to initiate a series of studies of future information needs and, based on the results, to identify issues of importance in strategic planning for the university with respect to libraries, specifically, and information resources throughout the university, more generally.

Strategic Management Rather than Strategic Planning

One point, though, became evident at the outset: Planning in this area cannot keep pace with developments as they actually occur. The most dramatic evidence of this was the initiation, about six to nine months after the start of the CLR project, of a planning effort for the entire UCLA campus academic program. Suddenly, the primary element for planning information resources—the academic program—had become the focus of a vastly greater effort.

Furthermore, the UCLA Library itself is a highly dynamic organization, which is constantly at the forefront of developments of every kind. The planning effort was faced repeatedly with the reality of implementing services and facilities within the library, not at some planned future time, but today. Conversely, the very means used by the project stimulated demands and presented the university library management with immediate operational problems.

It became clear that something more than "planning" was necessary if this kind of dynamic environment was to be properly dealt with. The answer is evident and is represented by a simple, though vital, change in one word. Rather than planning, we must concern ourselves with strategic *management*, within which planning may play a role, but at most, only a supporting one.

Campus Context

It is important to note that at UCLA strategic management, and planning within it, are facts of campus policy, long embedded in procedures of both the campus and the library administrations. The CLR strategic planning project was therefore at most an ancillary support: a means for providing data that would be of potential value in the ongoing management and planning efforts.

It is also important to note, however, that the campus commitment to this kind of management provides a context within which the CLR strategic planning project could be initiated not as an isolated activity, but rather, with the full commitment of the campus and library administrations. The timing, in fact, was especially fortuitous, given the initiation by the UCLA administration of its campus-wide academic planning efforts some months after the initiation of the CLR project. The result was that the two efforts could be mutually supportive.

Methodology

The proposed methodology involved four interrelated activities:[2] First, disciplinary task forces were to be established in as many areas of the total campus academic program as was feasible; they were intended to be a primary means for identifying future needs for information resources in their respective academic areas. Second, small-scale studies were to be carried out, as appropriate, to support the work of the disciplinary task forces. Third, research investigations were to be initiated based on results arising from the work of the task forces or from the identification of problems by individual faculty from throughout the university. Fourth, to carry forward this work, a small administrative structure was to be established, consisting of an advisory committee and a program of communication existing both within and outside UCLA.

Was the methodology successful? Overall, it was not; however, in specific respects, perhaps it was.[3] On the negative side, there were difficulties in accomplishing the objectives of the disciplinary task forces. While many were established, only a few actually became effective; consequently, the primary methodology simply was less successful than had been hoped. On the positive side, the small-scale studies and research projects were very successful and did indeed provide a rich picture of current and future needs for information resources on the campus.

Results

Perhaps the most important result, especially as a long-term effect, was the establishment of the position of assistant vice-chancellor for library and information services planning. In a very real sense, it institutionalized the means for carrying forward this kind of planning effort. Another result was the establishment of an ad hoc administrative committee that involved faculty from throughout the campus in monitoring federal activities, such as copyright legislation and executive branch policies, that affect the university's academic programs. A number of preliminary databases were created covering persons, academic programs, facilities, projects (both within the scope of this project and beyond), and external environments. They provide a starting point for continuing maintenance of the data necessary for effective planning.

The subprojects themselves served as means for identifying real, rather than hypothetical, needs for information resources. Several led to funding by external agencies of substantial projects for continuation of the work initiated as a small study.

Finally, the CLR project provides the Graduate School of Library and Information Science with a heightened visibility on campus. It also had an impact on the school's faculty and program of instruction. Finally, given the experience with the CLR-sponsored study, it seemed valuable to summarize here the knowledge gained from it.

ORGANIZATION

The book is organized into three parts: (1) concepts, (2) contexts, and (3) techniques for assessment. The first section provides definitions, emphasizes the importance of vision on the part of library management, provides a structure for strategic management, and discusses specific key issues in applying strategic management to academic libraries. The second part discusses issues of current importance, both within the academic institution and from the external environment; the former, of course, reflect the immediate situation, in which universities throughout the country are facing immense pressures of all kinds and, as a result, are experiencing unprecedented change, while the latter represent both immediate and long-term effects, with which library management must deal. The third part provides a set of technical tools and procedures by which the process of strategic management can be supported, especially with respect to the assessment of the internal and external situations.

ACKNOWLEDGMENTS

There are persons to whom I wish to convey my deep gratitude. Whatever value this book may have is in large part due to them, while any deficiencies are due solely to me. Central among these people is W. J. Haas, president of the Council on Library Resources during the time of the UCLA project. His vision and strategic perceptions have been of vital importance to the development and progress of academic librarianship for the past two decades, and his leadership of the CLR has been of unparalleled effect in maintaining a high level of excellence. He has served as an inspiration to me in many ways, so I wish to express my thanks to him.

Within the UCLA community, there are persons who have been of special significance for the development of this book. Dr. Russell Shank was director of the UCLA University Library System during the progress of the UCLA project and his enthusiastic support and participation were essential to its accomplishments. Professor Andrea Rich, now executive vice-chancellor at UCLA, has brought to academic management on exceptional awareness of the wide range of information resources that are essential parts of university research and education today; her example has been an inspiration for me. Chancellor Charles Young has maintained a continuing commitment to information resources, represented by the University Library especially, but also including the development of computing, the Film Archives, and numerous other specific activities; his academic leadership has represented to me the best of university traditions.

The UCLA Senior Fellows constitute now a group of nearly one hundred top-level managers of academic libraries. Any value that the program may have had to them was equaled for me by the opportunity to work with remarkably capable persons. The Senior Fellows managed to teach me about the realities of the problems they face and the means by which they overcome them.

Finally, I want to thank my colleagues at OCLC—especially Rich Van Orden, Kate Nevins, and Clarence Walters—who have provided me with the opportunity to see strategic issues from a truly national scope.

NOTES

1. Hayes, Robert M., (ed.), *Universities, Information Technology, and Academic Libraries: The Next Twenty Years. The Report of the CLR Sponsored Frontiers Conference, Lake Arrowhead, December 1981* (Norwood, N.J.: Ablex Press), 1986.

2. Hayes, Robert M., "Strategic Planning for Information Resources in the Research University," *RQ* 25(4) (Summer 1986): 427–31.

3. Hayes, Robert M., "Long-Range Strategic Planning for Information Resources in the Research University," in *Advances in Library Administration and Organization*, ed. Gerard B. McCabe and Bernard Kreissman (New York: JAI Press, 1992). This reprinted the final report to the Council on Library Resources on this project.

Abbreviations

AAAS	American Association for the Advancement of Science
AAP	Association of American Publishers
AAU	Association of American Universities
ACLS	American Council of Learned Societies
ACRL	Association of College and Research Libraries
ALA	American Library Association
ARL	Association of Research Libraries
BCG	Boston Consulting Group
bit	*Binary digIT*
BLRDD	British Library Research and Development Department
CARL	Colorado Association of Research Libraries
CD-ROM	Compact Disk–Read Only Memory
CIT	Critical Incident Technique
CLR	Council on Library Resources
CONSER	*Cooperative Online Serials*
E-mail	Electronic mail
G&A	General and Administrative
IAIMS	Integrated Academic Information Management System
IBM	International Business Machines, Inc.
IEG	Information Exchange Group
IFLA	International Federation of Library Associations and Institutions
ILL	Interlibrary Loan

ISO   International Standards Organization
LAN   Local Area Network
MARC   originally, Machine-Readable Cataloging, but now a word in itself
NCCP   National Cooperative Cataloging Program (also NACO)
NCIP   North American Collections Inventory Project
NCLIS   National Commission on Libraries and Information Science
NIH   National Institutes of Health
NREN   National Research and Education Network
OCLC   originally, Ohio College Library Center, but when the organization
           became a national service it adopted OCLC, Inc. itself as its name.
           Then, when purists insisted on an acronym, the phrase Online Com-
           puter Library Center was coined; OCLC is still the name, however.
OPAC   Online Public Access Catalog
PC   Personal computer
RLG   Research Libraries Group
RLIN   Research Libraries Information Network
SGML   Standard Generalized Markup Language
UCLA   University of California, Los Angeles
WLN   Washington Library Network
WORM   Write Once, Read Many

PART I

Concepts

1

Definitions, Objectives, and Alternatives

This chapter defines *strategic management*, provides a conceptual framework, identifies major concerns, and discusses the relationship of strategic management to tactical and operational management. The concepts of strategic management derive largely from its application in the commercial and industrial environments. Consequently, to apply it to academic research libraries requires changes in the definitions of *product*, *market*, and *performance criteria*.

LEVELS OF MANAGEMENT

Definitions

Strategic management is a concept of increasing importance in modern industrial management.[1] The purpose of this book is to demonstrate the value of applying it to academic libraries and to provide useful tools.[2] The following is a definition of the term as it will be used here:

> *Strategic management* is that part of the general management of organizations that emphasizes the relationships to external environments, evaluates the current status and the effects of future changes in them, and determines the most appropriate organizational response.

Strategic management is oriented toward long-range institutional goals and objectives. It is concerned with identifying them, creating a political consensus concerning their validity, establishing priorities among them, determining the necessary resources, and creating the environment within which those resources can be marshaled. The time frame of concern may be quite short—even less than a year—especially if organizational goals and objectives are in a state of change, uncertainty, or controversy; it can also be quite long—perhaps five to twenty years—if there is institutional stability and the environment is reasonably predictable.

A distinction is made between such long-range, externally focused management and that which is internally focused, which will be characterized as either *tactical management* (concerned with the most effective deployment of resources within the organization) or *operational management* (concerned with assuring maximum effectiveness in the use of available resources).[3]

> *Tactical management* is oriented toward implementation of the means for meeting goals and objectives, either as defined on strategic bases or as may be needed to meet immediate needs. It must assure that the necessary resources are allocated consistent both with the goals and with what, in fact, are at hand or can be obtained. The time frame of concern is likely to be quite immediate: on the order of months to, at most, a year.

> *Operational management* is oriented toward the most immediate needs in maintaining an effective operation. It is concerned with using the resources at hand in the most effective and efficient manner to meet those immediate needs. The time frame of concern is usually days to weeks.

Relationships among Levels

The crucial point, given these definitions, is that if they are to be effective, the three levels of management must be in close interaction. While one might conceptualize long-range goals in the abstract, especially in the context of speculations and enthusiams about such resources as information technology, the fact is that such speculations are far removed from reality. The future must be built on what is happening today, and the needs that will be of paramount importance are those that will be evidenced in current development. Strategic planning must deal with that fact.

The evident disadvantage of this approach is that it ties planning to what is currently known, and thus may fail adequately to recognize potentials that depart radically from present trends. It tends, therefore, to be conservative in nature and constrained by traditional means for dealing with information resources. Despite that disadvantage, though, I will argue that strategic management should identify goals, objectives, external developments, and internal pressures by examining current academic programs and proposed changes in them rather than by speculating on future developments that are divorced from actual faculty concerns. This means that current faculty perspectives and projects serve as the starting point for determining needs.

The result, however, is that perceived needs inevitably become reflected in demands for immediate capabilities. It would otherwise be a disappointment if faculty were encouraged to consider means for meeting their needs, only to find that the campus information facilities—the libraries, computers, archives, and others—were incapable of their implementation.

As a result, at the same time that strategic objectives are identified from the academic programs, individuals who are concerned with tactical implementation must be completely aware of their implications. Moreover, in most cases, there will be operational requirements to meet as well.

A specific example in this respect is the role of the on-line public access catalog of the library. Developed as a full-service support to technical processing, it is a capability with exceptional importance, both strategically and tactically. In itself, the database can serve the needs of individual faculty and projects requiring catalog data to be downloaded for their own special bibliographic purposes. Beyond that, though, in principle the associated software can provide the basis for creating and maintaining "private databases," handling acquisitions, cataloging, maintaining databases, and searching and retrieving from files for individual faculty or research projects, with access available to those individuals whom the creators identify.

Furthermore, the catalog can serve as the technical means for creating single-point access to campus-wide information resources. By establishing MARC formats as the standard for the inclusion of data records for holdings of databases, films, and other media, the public access catalog contributes directly to that strategic goal. Beyond that, though, the use of the catalog system by individual faculty and projects aids in bringing their files into formats and structures that are compatible with their eventual integration into generally accessible files, if and when this is desired.

The tactical implications are also exceptionally important, since use of software for online public access catalogs (OPACs) requires a high level of expertise, placing a burden on the library for training users and making the technical additions necessitated by user demands. The operational implications are important as well, since the ability to meet user needs depends on having adequate hardware, storage facilities, and access terminals. The library and the computing facility must cooperate to assure that these needs can be met.

STRATEGIC MANAGEMENT IN ACADEMIC LIBRARIES

Considering the overall character and quality of the management of libraries, both now and as it has been for decades, it is clear that strategic management has been of paramount importance. In a real sense, in fact, the academic library embodies the very objective of the concept, since to fulfill its most fundamental imperative, preservation of the records of the past, it must continually assess the value of information in meeting future needs. As a result, the perspective of the academic library is essentially

long-term and strategic, and it is not surprising that academic library directors have been highly effective in strategic management, dealing with
problems through long-term solutions rather than immediate quick-fixes.

The growth of collections, as identified by Fremont Rider and examined
by Herman Fussler for their relationship to usage, has been a strategic
management issue and has been recognized as being crucial nationally as
well as to individual libraries.[4] In that context, the need for cooperation
in collection development and management has been handled strategically
by the profession, from the days of the Farmington Plan to today's Research
Libraries Group (RLG).[5] The development of automated systems in academic research libraries was treated as a strategic management problem,
leading to development of the cooperative bibliographic utilities. The preservation of brittle books has also been recognized as a strategic management issue. Moreover, the current crisis in the pricing of journals is a clear
example of a strategic management issue with which the academic library
community is struggling.[6] The effect of technology on changes in the means
of publication, information distribution, and access is another issue of
importance, both historically, in the adoption of computer-based reference
services, and currently, in dealing with electronic media.

These are only a few of the great number of issues that academic library
directors have recognized and dealt with strategically. The point is that the
academic library community has been among the most effective users of
strategic management concepts and methods. It requires only the recognition of what we have been doing and its placement into a general frame
of reference.

However, to apply an industrial management approach to libraries requires some necessary changes in the definition of such concepts as "product," "market," "competition," and performance criteria. The concerns
in strategic management (goals and objectives, administration, constituency and market, sources and resources, competition and cooperation,
politics, technologies, economics, social policy, and sources for staff) all
need to be reinterpreted and applied with a clear knowledge of the nature
of the community being served and the library within it.

Overall Academic Library Strategy

The overriding strategic concern must be with the academic library as a
whole: its mission, its relationship to the university and the faculty, and
its means for dealing with other libraries and cooperative arrangements.
Most of this work will focus on this scope of concern, and chapter 3 will
explicitly identify the issues (tactical and operational as well as strategic)
that are involved in overall academic library strategy.

The mission to date has been embodied in two imperatives: preserving
the records of scholarship and providing access to those records and their

contents. The primary issue of overall importance for the academic library is whether the two imperatives are still the focus of its mission, the basis of its role in the institution, and a valuable resource to the faculty and students it primarily serves. The strategic answer of the academic library to that issue has been a resounding "Yes."

Strategies for Individual Products and Services

In implementing that strategic answer, however, the academic library has faced some critical decisions with respect to individual products and services. One arises in balancing the relative importance of the two imperatives. The choice between "acquisition" and "access" is so central to strategic decisions that the final chapter in this book, chapter 10, will be totally focused on a model for it.

Another set of critical decisions lies in balancing the relative importance of the traditional printed forms of information with the newer electronic ones. The array of potential records, of course, has been greatly expanded, and the traditional tools of reference have been augmented by a variety of electronic tools. Consequently, we must decide which of them should take priority in the future.

Specific assessment of individual products and services of the academic library, aside from their roles in meeting overall objectives, is also necessary in strategic management. Chapter 3 will consider in detail the array of products and services that characterize the academic library today. The strategic issue with respect to specific products and services is whether each will continue to be essential in the coming decades. Does the market for any of them justify continuing it? Will the electronic forms of records and means for access require instituting new services? Finally, should the academic library provide services other than simply preserving and providing access?

Academic Library Markets

Chapter 5 will consider in detail the needs of communities of users who today are the market for the products and services of the academic library. They are primarily the communities that are self-evident in the mission of the institution within which the library operates: faculty and students. To those internal markets, however, the academic library must also consider adding a number of external ones, including other libraries, business and industry, and government.

It seems unlikely that there will be a substantial change in this array of markets, but the strategic issue is whether there will be changes in their needs. It is primarily this question that is addressed in chapter 5.

Academic Library Competition

It is perhaps strange to think of competition for academic libraries, since their position in the academic institution is so accepted and has such a momentum of investment. Competition there is, however, if not for the library as an institution then at least for many of its products and services. There is a variety of alternative means for access to information. In fact, almost any survey of users of academic libraries will show that the library is somewhere between fourth and seventh in the order of priority of sources for information. The faculty member's own library, colleagues down the hall, telephone calls to colleagues elsewhere, the departmental reading room and file of preprints, and electronic mail: These channels are each likely to be considered before turning to the library. Today, a number of commercial services are being added to those traditional sources, especially database access and document delivery services; the potential for significant competition from them is a very real threat to academic library services for information access.

Beyond the functional competition, though, is the competition for resources. The academic library competes with the computing facility, communications, media facilities, and various archives for resources within the institution.

The strategic challenge, of course, is to deal with the competition in ways that will best maintain the continued viability of the academic library. That may mean the necessity of strategic decisions about specific products and services in ways that will maintain the overall viability of the academic library as a whole.

OBJECTIVES IN STRATEGIC MANAGEMENT

There is a large range of objectives that, individually and combined, can serve as the motivation for strategic management.

Management for Change

The most dramatic objective surely is the need to deal with an accelerating rate of change and to increase the ability of management to anticipate crises. In this respect, strategic management, as a continuing process, provides the basis for the organizational response to the environment.[7]

Historically, the picture of management in any organization was one of careful, considered assessment in specific decision-making contexts. The role of the manager was to identify problems, determine what information was needed to deal with them, initiate whatever action was needed to assemble the information, and then make a reasoned decision based on an analysis. The good manager was seen as someone who was virtually a technician in the application and use of information resources and methods for scientific management, such as operations research.

Today, though, there is a different picture of management, one that is consistent with reality and also highlights the role of strategic planning. In this newer picture, the manager is seen as someone who responds to situations with rapidity and decisiveness. The reality underlying this picture is the fact that problems requiring management decision are likely to have immediate importance and must be dealt with in a context of uncertainty, without the time to acquire the information that is so necessary to the more technical picture.

Support to Decision Making

If this newer picture has any substantial validity, it requires that the manager continually monitor the environment, whether consciously or subconsciously. The good manager is likely to be constantly talking with people at every level of operation, internally and externally, thus assuring an understanding of what is happening and what the effects of change in that environment will be. The result is that decisions will be made that prevent problems, rather than having to solve them, because there is an intuitive grasp of what is happening. When a problem cannot be prevented, the same intuitive understanding provides the basis for immediate, effective decision making because necessary information already is embedded in that understanding. This truly is what strategic management is all about.

In that respect, then, strategic planning has the supporting role in such management by providing the formal basis for continually acquiring, analyzing, and integrating information into systematic decision making.

Provide a Basis for Accountability

Strategic management also serves as the means to integrate planning with operations and to provide a basis for accountability. Expectations must be communicated, and individuals must be motivated to meet them. In this way, management can assure that the accomplishments are directed to organizational objectives.

Encourage Creativity

A somewhat different set of objectives for strategic management is to encourage innovation and creativity. By its nature, strategic management must identify new opportunities and call for the generation of new ideas.

Assess Individual Products and Services

An objective may be simply to assess one or more academic library products or services for the purpose of determining costs, markets, competition, needed resources, and relative priorities. Such an objective might arise from a proposal to implement a new product or service, from a concern about the value in an existing one, or from a need to reallocate resources.

Improve System Operations

The ultimate objective, perhaps, is to improve library operations, and many of the issues discussed in subsequent chapters will focus on aspects of this objective.

ALTERNATIVE STRATEGIES FOR MEETING OBJECTIVES

The literature for strategic management has generally been focused on business, commerce, and industry. Can meaningful alternatives in those contexts be applied in academic libraries? To explore that question, three major categories of alternatives will be identified: those that build on the core business, though perhaps with changes in the way in which it is conducted; those that involve substantial change in the core business; and those that involve change in environmental contexts. For each category, examples will be provided to illustrate the application to strategic alternatives for academic libraries.

Build on the Core Business

If the core business is essentially successful, alternatives that maintain it (though possibly with modification to meet new opportunities) would seem to be the ones that are most important to consider.

Maintain the Status Quo

The most conservative option, as represented by the traditional adage "If it ain't broke, don't fix it," is to preserve the status quo. In the case of the academic library, this may well be the option of choice, given the long history of successful integration of the library into the academic program, the overall quality of strategic management exhibited to date, and organizational stability and existing momentum (or, perhaps the equivalent, inertia).

Innovate and Diversify

The most popular strategies, of course, are those that innovate by expanding the core business and by implementing new kinds of services, new ways of doing things, and relationships with the constituencies served. Certainly, these options underlay efforts to automate library services and internal operations. This option, in fact, will be the one most evident in this work as it considers issues faced by the academic library in serving its institution and its users, and also in dealing with the external environment. During the past couple of decades it is the strategy that has been followed in academic libraries, with great success.

Concentrate

A reverse option is concentration, a narrowing of focus and of objectives to specific library roles. An academic library might consider focusing acquisitions and collection development on identified areas of strength, rather than continuing an effort to cover the entire range of academic disciplines. Alternatively, it might consider focusing its attention on specific academic objectives, such as support to teaching. Finally, it might concentrate on specific media or eliminate some existing services.

Retrench, Divest, or Liquidate

The extreme options in this respect must also be considered, negative though they may seem: retrenchment, divestment, and liquidation. To an extent, these may be necessary results of concentration as the means for dealing with the residual activities not included in the focus. However, they may also be more deliberate options, through reflecting a conscious decision to close down operations. There is nothing really new or threatening about this option, unpleasant though it may be. Academic libraries have eliminated branches, sold collections, reduced staff, and contracted out for replacement services.

Reconceive the Core Business and Innovate

Another set of options involves substantial change in the core business through movement into new and different kinds of activities.

Horizontal Integration

One strategy is horizontal integration: an active effort to encompass a wide range of academic information activities within a single organizational structure. For many individuals, this option is a natural consequence of the perception that computers, audiovisual media, database archives, film, and television, as well as the library, are essentially similar. By bringing these activities administratively together, there could be economies of scale, efficiencies in performance of common functions, and sharing of resources and facilities. This option is by no means new or revolutionary. Academic libraries indeed have incorporated media centers within services; moreover, they are acquiring databases of various kinds, and they include computer facilities within their operations. The current options for horizontal integration, though, appear to be substantially larger and more complex.

The most dramatic example of horizontal integration is found in the various consortia and cooperative arrangement among academic libraries. These have been especially effective in the coordination of collections, in the provision of reciprocal borrowing privileges, and in the sharing of resources. In addition, there have been fewer and less successful examples of sharing processing and computing services.

Vertical Integration and Joint Ventures

A related strategy is vertical integration, in which additional functions are added to those that are traditionally seen as the responsibility of the library. This option is one with which academic libraries have less experience, but there are those who have suggested that they should expand services into areas of commercial information brokerage, academic publishing, or indexing and abstracting. Several of the national on-line reference and bibliographic services have experimented with some academic libraries in such ways. In that respect, the development of joint ventures, whether with other libraries or with other information agencies, represents a component strategy and an approach to vertical integration.

Modify the Environment

A final set of strategies turns to the larger frame of reference, the environment, considering alternatives that change the environment or its relationship with the academic library. It must be said that by their nature, these alternatives appear to be meaningful for the entire set of academic libraries of the country, rather than for individual libraries.

Expand the Societal Role of Information

It is now well recognized that the United States, along with other highly industrialized nations, has moved from an economy that was focused on the production of physical goods and services to one in which information is dominant. It has been estimated that well over 50 percent of the nation's work force is engaged in information work, and that percentage is growing. The problem, though, is that national policies and national economic accounts have not kept pace with the times. Those policies and accounts need to be changed to reflect today's reality.

If that kind of change can be made, the role of libraries and contributors to economic success will be made more evident, providing an added basis for the commitment of resources to their services.

Modify the Political, Legislative, and Legal Environments

The library community generally has been reasonably effective in lobbying, but the specific interests of academic libraries have not been well represented. Political decisions are being made about intellectual property rights, the availability of information from the federal government, privatization of government activities, and the development of the National Research and Education Network (NREN); these decisions vitally affect the operations, the services, and even the mission of academic libraries. The need is to develop means for the academic library community to influence those decisions.[8]

Change the Nature of Sources

Academic libraries for decades have had a stable set of sources for the materials and technologies that they acquire: the publishers, distributors, and booksellers, and also the computer manufacturers, database services, and local systems vendors. Now, though, those sources are themselves in a turmoil of change as they try to absorb the technologies, and the opportunity is here, in principle, for academic libraries to influence the changes that are occurring.

Indeed, academic libraries have been doing just that. The creation of the bibliographic utilities as a partnership among libraries is one evident example. Another has been the role of libraries in the development of computer systems, in which they have, in many cases, become the vendor of processing systems and software. There is also the potential for libraries themselves to become publishers; preservation microfilm can serve as an example.

The major force arguing for this kind of impact is the important role of libraries, given the magnitude of investment and their history of success in meeting institutional objectives. The major differences from the past in that respect is the effect of the information technologies in stimulating change, but with the academic library as the crucial component in the delivery of electronic services. The implications are clear: There is an opportunity for academic libraries to be dominant players in shaping the future of the delivery of information in all forms.

Change Relationships with the Environment

To an extent, this alternative is represented by approaches to vertical integration. By combining with other agencies in broadening the scope of joint responsibilities, the academic library changes its relationship to the environment from that of a recipient to that of a participant.

EVALUATION OF ALTERNATIVE STRATEGIES

Each of these strategic options must be evaluated for its effectiveness, likelihood of success, level of resulting performance, and cost. In the context of systems analysis and evaluation, the relevant encompassing measure would be efficiency (i.e., cost-effectiveness).

Criteria for Evaluation

To assess these several alternatives and choose among them, the strategic manager should consider a range of criteria.

Internal

Is the alternative congruent with the mission of the library and the institution that it serves? Does it draw on existing skills? Is there the potential for sharing resources within the scope of management? Will the results be measurable? Is the alternative aimed at the prevention of problems or as a cure?

External

Will the alternative appeal to groups that will be affected by it, and will it gain their support? Is it fundable, and will there be funding stability? What is the size and concentration of the client base implied by the alternative, and will it grow? Is there resistance on the part of existing or future clients? Are there barriers to change in the alternative, once it has been chosen? Is the alternative one in which the library can be self-sufficient or will it be dependent on other agencies?

Competitive Position

Is the library well located and logistically capable of handling the alternative? Is there loyalty to the library's interests on the part of those with a stake in the outcome? Is there a history of prior funding: a track record of fund-raising ability and performance to justify confidence? What is, and would be, the market share? Is there momentum derived from prior performance? Is there a basis for assessing likely quality? Are there advocates for the option, and who are they?

Program Position

Are there adequate policies: programmatic, client, costing, and funding? Are there adequate internal procedures for the control of funds and management of staff? Is there demonstrable leadership capability? Are the requisite skills—technical, organizational, and research and development—at hand? Will the option be cost-effective?

Strategic Positions and Associated Options

Chapter 7 will present the range of issues involved in the assessment of strategic positions, together with several models that can assist in the evaluation of alternative strategies.[9] One among them seems especially valuable and applicable to evaluation in academic libraries.[10] It is based on an overall assessment of three variables: (1) the relative value of services provided by the academic library, (2) the relative strength of the academic library's position, and (3) the relative strength of the competition faced by the academic library. The cells of the resulting three-dimensional matrix then provide contexts in which to identify the strategic options of choice. The ones identified here are derived from conventional wisdom for the not-for-profit context, and they appear to apply with great force to academic libraries. It is important to note that the assessments of position and options apply both to the academic library as a whole and to individual products and services.

High Value: Strong Position, Strong Competition

This option appears to be applicable to most strong academic institutions. Their libraries are in strong positions within the institution; the library's services are valued; and there is strong competition from other means for information access—especially campus computing facilities but also including other libraries and commercial information services. The primary strategy for not-for-profit agencies is *cooperation with the competition*, leading to an efficient division of responsibilities. That indeed is the strategy that has been generally followed by academic libraries. The potential secondary strategy is to dominate and shut out competition; that does not appear to have been generally followed.

High Value: Strong Position, Low Competition

In cases in which the competition is weak, the primary strategy is to consolidate and to expand aggressively the library's position. This might occur on a campus on which computing and other information facilities are poorly managed.

High Value: Weak Position, Strong Competition

This applies if the academic library is in a poor position (underfunded, badly managed, or plagued by bad relations to faculty and administration) but there are other strong information structures on campus. The recommended primary strategy is to transfer programs to the strong competing services. For example, responsibility for computer support of library operations might go to the computing facility; for data archives and database access services, to separate units tied to academic departments; and for media, to an instructional facilities center.

High Value: Weak Position, Low Competition

Under these conditions, the institution itself clearly faces a severe problem. The recommended primary strategy must be for the institution to commit its resources and to build strength as rapidly as possible. As a secondary strategy, consideration might be given to selling out.

Low Value

Fortunately for academic libraries, most have high value. These conditions are therefore not likely to apply to the academic library as a whole. However, individual products or services may not be valued, of course, and so should be individually assessed. The strategy generally would be to get out of any undervalued products or services, whatever the position of the library or the competition may be.

NOTES

1. There are literally dozens of standard texts for courses in strategic management for business, and all are roughly equivalent in organization and substantive content. The following is a brief sample of half a dozen that will serve to illustrate the generic approach and, in later chapters of this work, the coverage of specific models: Aaker, David A., *Developing Business Strategies*, 2nd ed. (New York: Wiley, 1988); Boulton, William R., *Business Policy: The Art of Strategic Management* (New York: Macmillan, 1984); Certo, Samuel C., and Peter, J. Paul, *Strategic Management* (New York: Random House, 1988); Glueck, William F., and Jauch, Lawrence R., *Business Policy and Strategic Management* (New York: McGraw-Hill, 1984); Hax, Arnoldo C., and Majluf, Nicolas S., *Strategic Management: An Integrative Perspective* (Englewood Cliffs, N.J.: Prentice-Hall, 1984); Justis, Robert T., Judd, Richard J., and Stephens, David B., *Strategic Management and Policy* (Englewood Cliffs, N.J.: Prentice-Hall, 1985).

2. In addition to the business-oriented references, the following works focus on not-for-profit organizations and, therefore, are especially relevant to academic libraries: Koteen, Jack, *Strategic Management in Public and Nonprofit Organizations* (New York: Praeger, 1989); Macmillan, Ian C., "Competitive Strategies for Not-for-Profit Agencies," in *Advances in Strategic Management*, vol. 1, ed. Robert Lamb (Greenwich, Conn.: JAI Press, 1983), pp. 61–82.

3. The identification of these three levels of management and their definitions are specific to this text and do not seem to be part of the general vocabulary of strategic management.

4. Rider, Fremont, *The Scholar and the Future of the Research Library* (New York: Hadham Press, 1944); Fussler, Herman H., and Simon, J. L., *Patterns in the Use of Books in Large Research Libraries* (Chicago: University of Chicago Press, 1969).

5. Association of Research Libraries, *Farmington Plan Newsletter*, nos. 1–31 (Washington, D.C.: Association of Research Libraries, March 1949–May 1970); Vosper, Robert, *The Farmington Plan Survey: A Summary of the Separate Studies of 1957–1961* (Urbana: University of Illinois, Graduate School of Library Science, 1965); Williams, Edwin Everitt, *Farmington Plan Handbook, with a Bibliography of the Farmington Plan, 1953–1961* (Ithaca, N.Y.: Association of Research Libraries, 1961); Association of Research Libraries, *Qualitative Collection Analysis: The Conspectus Methodology*, SPEC kit 151 (Washington, D.C.: Association of Research Libraries, Office of Management Studies, 1989); Ferguson, Anthony W., Grant, Joan, and Rutstein, Joel S., "The RLG Conspectus: Its Uses and Benefits," *College and Research Libraries*, 49 (March 1989):

197–206; Gwinn, Nancy E., and Mosher, Paul H., "Coordinating Collection Development: The RLG Conspectus," *College and Research Libraries* 44 (March 1983): 128–40; Holt, Brian G. F., and Hanger, Stephen, *Conspectus in the British Library* (London: British Library, 1986).

6. Okerson, Ann L., "Periodical Prices: A History and Discussion," in *Advances in Serials Management*, ed. Jean G. Cook and Marcia Tuttle (Greenwich, Conn.: JAI Press, 1986), pp. 101–34; "ARL Consultants' Reports Likely to Widen Serials Rift," *American Libraries*, June 1989, p. 489; "Journal Publisher Sues Author of Price Study," *American Libraries*, Sept. 1989, pp. 717–18; Okerson, Ann L., "Report on the ARL Serials Project," *Serials Librarian* 17(3–4) (1990): 111–19; Okerson, Ann, and Stubbs, Kenneth, "The Library 'Doomsday Machine,' " *Publishers Weekly* 236(8) (8 February 1991): 36–37; Ford, Kenneth W. (executive director, American Institute of Physics [AIP]), Personal letter: "Refuting Gordon & Breach," *American Libraries*, March 1990, p. 192; "Serials Survey Linked to Gordon & Breach," *American Libraries*, March 1990, p. 173; "Gordon & Breach Sues Again," *American Libraries*, April 1990, p. 286; "A Response from Gordon & Breach," *American Libraries*, May 1990, p. 405.

7. Pettigrew, Andrew M., *The Management of Strategic Change* (Oxford, U.K.: Blackwell, 1987); Reimann, Bernard C., *Managing for Change* (Oxford, Ohio: Planning Forum, 1987); *The Changing System for Scholarly Communication* (Washington, D.C.: Association of Research Libraries, 1986).

8. "ARL, Cause, Educom Form New Information Resources Coalition," *Manage IT* 1(2) (April 1990): 1–2.

9. The following references are more than simply textbooks for courses in strategic management; in addition, they provide a range of philosophical perspectives and technical tools: Checkland, Peter, *Systems Thinking, Systems Practice* (Chichester, U.K.: Wiley, 1981); Hax, Arnoldo C., (ed.), *Readings on Strategic Management* (Cambridge: Ballinger, 1984); Hofer, Charles W., and Schendel, Dan, *Strategy Formulation: Analytical Concepts* (St. Paul, Minn.: West Publishing, 1978); Lamb, Robert, and Shrivastava, Paul (eds.), *Advances in Strategic Management*, vol. 1–3 (Greenwich, Conn.: JAI Press, 1982–1988); Macmillan, Ian C., "Competitive Strategies for Not-for-Profit Agencies," *Advances in Strategic Management*, vol. 1, ed. Robert Lamb (Greenwich, Conn.: JAI Press, 1982), pp. 61–82; Macmillan, Ian C., and Jones, Patricia E., *Strategy Formulation: Power and Politics* (St. Paul, Minn.: West Publishing, 1986); McNamee, Patrick B., *Tools and Techniques for Strategic Management* (Oxford, U.K.: Pergamon, 1985); Naylor, Thomas H., *Corporate Planning Models* (Reading, Mass.: Addison-Wesley, 1979).

10. Macmillan, "Competitive Strategies."

2

Top Management Responsibility

This chapter discusses the strategic responsibilities of top management. It identifies the need for a vision of the role and importance of the library, of information resource management, and of the profession. In that context, it discusses the mission of the academic library; its relationship to institutional objectives; and the resulting commitments, goals, and objectives. It then discusses alternative scopes for strategic management: internal to the library, internal to the institution, national and external to the institution. It then discusses requirements and generic issues related to the needs of users.

VISION, MISSION, AND PROFESSIONAL COMMITMENTS

Vision for the Individual Library

The primary responsibility of top management must be to have a vision of the library's role.[1] Is that role seen as minor and supportive at best, or is it seen as central and critical, as essential and of vital importance? Is the intent to emphasize the excellence and breadth of the collection, or is it to be a focal point for access to information? Is it to be a major source within the national library system, or primarily a user of other sources? Is it to focus on the traditional media, or is it to be a leader in the use of new ones?

Of course, each institution, and each library within it, doubtless has high levels of aspiration, but vision is not merely aspiration. Is top management able to obtain resources (money, facilities, and staff) and willing to commit them to the vision, bringing aspirations to reality? The point, of course, is that strategic management of information resources is determined both by the vision held by the institution and by the degree to which resources can be, and are, committed to the fulfillment of that vision. It is the commitment of resources that constitutes leadership.

National Vision

Strategic management of libraries, though, involves a perspective wider than merely the individual institution. There has been a history of vision for the profession as a whole, a perception of the entire set of academic libraries as a resource for the nation, and even the world. That vision has established a basis for grand strategies, as exemplified by the national bibliographic utilities Research Libraries Information Network (RLIN) and OCLC, by the national efforts in preservation, and by the collaboration in sharing resources.

The result is a hierarchy of objectives, from the individual library to the institution, the nation, and the world. Underlying them all is the vision of the academic library as the institution for information resource management to meet the needs of society at every level. It is wonderful to see the extent to which academic library management has embodied that vision in the full range of contexts.

Institutional Mission

Historically, the mission of the library has been twofold: to preserve the record of knowledge and to provide access to that record and its contents. In the past, the two aspects of mission have been mutually supportive, since the primary concern was with access to the individual library's own collection by its primary constituency. Today, however, while they are still largely mutually supportive, there are growing tensions between them. Increasingly, libraries are facing a crisis in determining their mission and are being forced to make a choice in the commitment of resources between collection development, on the one hand, and information access, on the other.

It is this dilemma that today makes the context for strategic management so crucial. Does the individual library focus its mission on the needs of the institution, perhaps emphasizing collection development in order to serve a vision of excellence, or does it see its mission in the context of the "nation's library," perhaps emphasizing information access and sharing of the wide range of national resources?

Of course, the choice is by no means so dichotomous, and every institution will surely balance collection development with the means for information access. However, choices must be made when resources are committed. Do they go to capital investment in maintenance of the collection to serve needs directly, or do they go to operating costs in obtaining information only when needed, from wherever it may be available?

Professional Commitments

There have been evident corollary commitments by the library: to open availability of collections, without essential barriers, to free service (at least as far as the individual user is concerned), and to cooperation (since it has long been recognized that no library, however large, can encompass the full range of recorded knowledge). Increasingly, though, these commitments are becoming burdens. Libraries are faced with conflicts between meeting needs of their primary constituency and meeting the needs of others, with increasing costs in access to commercial information services, and with complications as well as costs in participating in national cooperative programs. As a result, they must consider imposing restrictions on use, payment by users for special services, and fees for interlibrary lending.

ALTERNATIVE CONTEXTS

The point, in any event, is that high-level managers must set the context for strategic management. What are the priorities among the several scopes to be considered? Should emphasis be given to external factors that are related to politics, social policy, legislation, and legal aspects? Alternatively, should management emphasize cooperation and competition with other institutions; internal, institutional issues; information sources and resources; economics; the needs of the constituencies for services and the mix of services provided to them; technology; or improving the management of operations, production, personnel, and finances?

The first step in dealing with these questions should be the identification of the opportunity or need for change. Since change is a fact of life, this step may seem to be superfluous, but it is important that top management continually emphasize its importance, identify the relevant policy problems, and establish the means for effecting and managing change.

The second step is setting the objectives for planning and management. Are the objectives (aside from dealing with change per se) to be growth; improved efficiency; better resource utilization; or greater levels of contribution to the students, the faculty, and the community?

Third is the assignment of responsibility. Strategic management itself clearly should be at the highest levels of administration in both the university and the library, but who is to do the associated planning? Moreover, where will they be in the administrative hierarchy?

Identification of Scope

Strategic management in general must consider a range of contexts, both internal and external and at various levels of detail. With respect to libraries and information resources, in particular, one must simultaneously deal with at least three levels:

- the *library*, taken narrowly as the traditional collection of books, journals, and a wide range of other media, with its inherent set of facilities, operations, and services;

- the *library of the future*, taken broadly as the entire set of information resources and facilities, including libraries taken narrowly, but also adding to them computing centers, media centers, film and data archives, museums, and telecommunication networks;

- the *national library network*, consisting of the entire set of libraries and other kinds of information resources acting as a cooperative and integrated whole.

It is not easy to keep these levels separate, and it is easy to slip from one to another, sometimes without realizing that this has occurred.

If boundaries are not set, the entire process of analysis will be based on shifting sand. Requirements will reflect mixed and varying perceptions of context; functional components and their relationships to one another will be unclear; and the criteria for evaluation will be amorphous. Of course, having set boundaries for the scope does not prevent their subsequent change. However, the important point is that, at any given time, the focus is clearly defined and known to all participants and that, if changes are made, it is made evident that such has happened.

The Hierarchy of Strategic Contexts

These can be viewed as a sequential hierarchy of strategic contexts. For purposes of description here, that structure will be restricted simply to three levels (although it should be evident that, additionally, the hierarchy will extend both outward and inward to many levels).

As figure 2.1 shows, the strategic focus will fall within a number of contexts. Principal among them are the one or more administrative contexts, reflecting the hierarchy of reporting. Others include the sources of funding, the various groups of users (i.e., the market or constituencies served), the sources of information and services, the suppliers of technologies, the political environment (including aspects of social policy, legislation, and legal decisions), and the potentials for cooperation, and perhaps competition, with other libraries.

Within the strategic focus there are components of various kinds, and in any future alternative there will be similar ones. Some represent issues

Figure 2.1
Sequential Hierarchy of Strategic Contexts

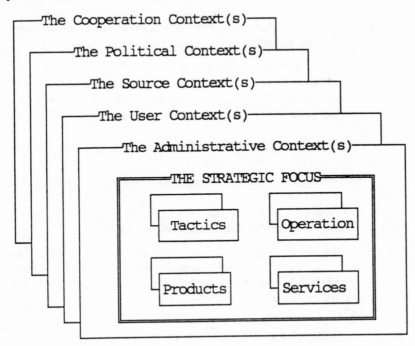

of tactical significance, such as administrative structures within the strategic focus that provide the means for management. Others are of operational significance, such as the matching of expectations with performance.

Some of the components are individual products or services of the academic library. Strategic management will frequently need to assess them, whether in terms of their contribution to the overall effectiveness of the academic library in meeting its objectives or of their individual effectiveness.

The Objectives of the Strategic Focus

As the figure should make evident, the objectives of the strategic focus are derived from the complex interaction of a variety of interests: those of the focus itself, those of the several contexts, and those of the constituent components. The objectives can be categorized into three groups—strategic objectives, tactical objectives, and operational objectives, reflecting perhaps the three major categories in the hierarchy of systems: context, strategic focus, and components. We will examine these in more detail later in this chapter.

Political Factors

The objectives are rarely in complete congruence but rather must be balanced among one another by a political process of reconciling divergent views, priorities, and needs. The following factors can each be operative:

- *Personal Politics*: reflecting personal ambition, personal animosities, and personal characteristics;
- *Administrative Responsibilities*: reflecting the defined functions of the position of each individual in the hierarchy of systems and administrative structures;
- *Professional Perspectives*: reflecting the focus of commitment, societal responsibility, and educational orientation;
- *Capital Commitments*: reflecting the existing status of resources and the effects of alternatives upon them; and
- *Personal Perspectives*: reflecting the differences in perception of risks, the effects of problems, and the relationships among priorities.

The first factor, personal politics, is the most difficult to deal with, though perhaps ultimately it may be the most significant. The other four, though, are vitally significant and must be carefully considered. They each have a profound impact on the assessment of alternatives.

THE MANAGEMENT OF STRATEGIC PLANNING

Strategic management is clearly the responsibility of the director of the academic library. Within strategic management, however, planning is an essential element, serving as the means for acquiring, analyzing, and presenting the data needed to make effective decisions.

Management Style

The style of library management is determined in part by the institutional environment, in part by personal views and philosophy and in part by the demands of the management task. The style may be directive or controlling, in which the library manager unilaterally determines policy; such management has been characteristic of entrepreneurial enterprises, but it also has been the style in many academic libraries with strong directors. It may be analytic or objective, in which management draws on means for measurement and formal assessment; such management would use tools of scientific management, such as operations research. The style may be participatory or political, in which the library manager involves others in the decision processes; such management was fostered during the 1970s and 1980s. Finally, the style may be conceptual or behavioral, in which decision making derives from perceptions of the purposes of the library; the library director who is a renowned book man may well adopt this style. Each style has its own advantages and disadvantages, but strategic management is consistent with any of them.

In particular, it is critical to success, whatever the management style may be, to be able to foresee and even to avert or prevent problems. In itself, this adds importance to the strategic approach to management since it requires a continuous monitoring of the environment in order to maintain an awareness about potential problems that will trigger decisions when subsequent events occur.

Also critical is the proper perception and use of time. The focus should be on the present and the future. The style should allow sufficient time to generate alternatives, without the need to hurry the processes in evaluation and selection. One must be able to deal with problems decisively and rapidly, however. This, too, adds importance to the strategic approach to management since it requires that the information and other bases for decision have been developed before, and not after, problems occur.

The management style must provide means for the translation of problems into challenges and opportunities: means for handling complexity. There must be a tolerance for ambiguity and uncertainty, a willingness to accept dissonance and inconsistency in available information, an ability to separate facts from opinions and judgments, and an understanding of how to handle conflict.

The Locus for the Planning Effort

Strategic planning requires a substantial dedication of effort on the part of any responsible person. It requires an ability to establish working relations with employees at many levels—technical, administrative, professional, and in a wide range of academic contexts. It requires continual discussion with everyone who has a stake in the outcome; it requires both technical skills and political awareness; and it requires some degree of vision about the planning issues and their relationships, both existing and potential, to the strategic management of the library.

What is the suitable locus for such planning? In one project, that locus was in a school of library and information science, but with the stated intent that it should serve as the agent for the campus at large.[2] An alternative locus would be the university library itself, and there are good reasons for eventually moving responsibility there, however the effort may have been initiated. Another would be the campus administration, and again there are good reasons for such a choice, given the increasing importance of broadly defined information resources to the academic program.

MORTON COLLEGE LIBRARY
CICERO, ILLINOIS

The Process of Strategic Planning

Information Gathering

Strategic management depends on a continuing environmental scan to acquire information, not so much to provide a basis for response to specific problems as to provide awareness of the strategic situation. Strategic planning, therefore, must implement that process and make the resulting information files usable for strategic management. Chapter 7 will consider the means for providing management with this kind of support.

Assessment of Current Strategy

Strategic management requires an objective assessment, at periodic intervals, of the status of the current situation. Chapter 7 will provide a set of techniques and models for current strategy assessment focusing on the collection, the operational performance, and the value to the institution. Chapter 9 will present details of a costing model to support that part of such an assessment for both the current situation and potential future circumstances. Finally, chapter 10 will present an allocation model intended to assist in the assessment of one of the most central strategic decisions for academic libraries.

Forecasting Future Needs

Strategic management must be long term in its perspective and therefore requires the means for assessing likely futures. Chapter 8 will provide a set of techniques for assessing the future: the needs of the markets served by academic libraries, both quantitative and qualitative, and the several external environments. It will also discuss some means for determining political positions and their effects.

Analysis and Evaluation of Alternatives

The set of descriptive models and associated techniques for assessing alternative options presented in chapters 7, 9, and 10 can then be applied as well to decisions about moving from the current strategic positions into the future.

Planning Studies

Beyond the formalized tools presented in chapters 7 through 10, planning studies can serve as a means for identifying specific faculty needs and operational effects. Two levels of planning studies should be considered: supporting studies and research projects. There could be a large number of the former, and probably only a few of the latter. For each level, the responsibility should be assigned to the faculty member or information professional submitting a proposal for such a project. The result is that strategic planning gains substantial leverage in furthering its data-gathering objectives through the participation of many individuals.

In each case, the objectives in identifying information needs should be defined by the responsible faculty member or information professional rather than by the strategic planning manager. It is the former individuals who are aware of information developments as they affect their own interests. The result, though, is that faculty generated projects are likely to relate to the broad definition of the library, not the narrow one; they will focus on the use of information and means for its creation and access rather than on needs in selection, acquisition, cataloging, and preservation of the records from which that information is derived. The result is that, from the library's standpoint, the strategic planning process must generalize from the specifics of the individual projects. However, there should be clear evidence of generic problems, ones that should provide the basis for university-wide strategic planning.

DETERMINATION OF REQUIREMENTS

We turn now to the more specific and concrete issue of requirements. They fall into the following categories:

- Performance Expectations: high performance, frugal, or subsistence;

- Boundary Conditions: funding, staffing, equipment, and acceptable (and prescribed) alternatives;

- Functional Requirements: identified functions to be provided by the system; and

- Parametric Requirements: amounts of activity, response times, and measures of quality and quantity.

Performance Expectations

Strategic management should identify the performance expectations. At one extreme is high performance: the expectations of the engineer, the economic "developer," the military-industrial complex, or the highly industrialized world in general. At the other extreme are subsistence expectations, as represented by peasant societies. In the middle are frugal expectations. Libraries in the past would seen to have been characterized as frugal systems, reflected in their operation and their role in society as the preservers of the records of the past. The strategic management question of course, is whether they should continue to be so.

Boundary Conditions

Strategic management should also identify boundary conditions, especially as represented by available resources. Of course, parallel with the picture of expectations is a comparable spectrum of resource requirements, which must be congruent with the expectations:

Subsistence	Resource balance
Frugal	Resource creation and conservation
High performance	Resource exploitation

Subsistence economies live essentially in balance with the available resources, consuming only at the rate at which the resources are renewed. Frugal economies also limit the use of resources, but they attempt to create and conserve capital as the organization of excess resources, beyond those strictly necessary for simple subsistence; thus, there is an element of saving that is not characteristic of the subsistence economies. High-performance expectations lead to the intensive use, exploitation, and consumption of resources, frequently without regard to cost, in order to meet performance objectives.

Functional Requirements

Four levels of formalization of functional requirements can be distinguished. The first is represented by an ad hoc requirement, which is taken as a specific and dealt with as such. At the second level, a formalization of the requirement may be needed to assure that the means for handling it are appropriate, economic, effective, and generalizable beyond specific events. The third level involves formalization in reporting of and about the requirement. Requirements of this kind can then be monitored, accounted for, and perhaps controlled. At the fourth level, operational procedures are established. Clearly, this level implies that the frequency of occurrence or, perhaps, the importance of the situation are great enough to warrant its coverage by normal operations rather than ad hoc arrangements or even standard reportings.

Problems in Determining Requirements

With every method for determining requirements, one faces the problem of reliability. In questionnaires and interviews, one cannot guarantee that the respondent is honest, that the memory of events is correct, that there has not been confusion between different events or different sources, and that the description of outcomes is not just wishful thinking. Even with usage logs, there may be inaccuracies. Even if the data are reliable, one still faces the question of whether they represent valid user needs.

Another problem is the extent to which the results can be generalized beyond simply the specific respondents, time periods of monitoring, and specific events observed or described. Suppose that one has identified, with reliability and validity, the fact that a particular group of respondents had an identified set of needs, and that the activity on the system demonstrated particular characteristics during a specific time. Does that mean that other users at other times will have the same needs and experience the same results? Many of the problems of generalizability reflect the underlying statistical problems of sample size and representativeness.

FACTORS AFFECTING USER NEEDS

Chapter 5 will provide a detailed discussion of various specific needs; we will summarize here the aspects of those needs that are of generic importance to strategic management responsibilities.

Nature of Users

Demographics of User Groups

It is generally assumed that demographic factors affect the needs of users, the extent to which individuals will use an information resource, and the ways in which they will do so.[3] Age, sex, education, social or economic class, ethnicity, geographic location—these have all been considered as potentially relevant demographic variables. Indeed, most surveys of public library users will acquire such data and correlate them with the levels of use. The results are not surprising: The better educated an individual, the greater his or her use of the library; the middle class uses the library more than the poor or even than the very wealthy; men and women use the library differently; and the very young, the very old, and those in between all use the library differently.

The counterparts in the academic, professional, or industrial communities would be the category of user (whether student, faculty, physician, engineer, or manager) and academic or professional discipline, as well as variables listed above for the public library community. These are easy to determine and can be as easily correlated with variables of use.

The point about demographic variables is that they can be treated statistically. Data are readily available on their distributions within a community (from the U.S. Census for public libraries, for example), and those data can be correlated with actual usage as the basis for decisions within the library on the best means for serving the community. Such management decisions as branch library location, local collection policies, staffing needs, hours of opening, and services provided can all be made with at least a statistical basis in the demographics of the population served.

Individual Differences

Aside from the demographic characteristics, which are easy to determine and measure on a statistical basis, individuals will differ in other ways that are much more difficult to assess: motivation, level of knowledge and experience, and psychological attitudes such as persistence, orderliness, motivation, willingness to accept help, facility with languages. These clearly affect the nature of needs, the kinds of usage, and the services that will be needed.

Purposes in Use

Goal-oriented users (exemplified by science, technology, and management professionals) will differ from education-oriented users (students and teachers) and personal-interest users. In talking about the user of information, we generally interpret that to mean the consumer of the information, but the producer and distributor of information are, in a real sense, also users insofar as they use information to achieve specific objectives.

Kinds of Use

Reading and Circulation Use

This is the most self-evident use of a library. After all, books and journals are intended to be read. Whether for recreation, amusement, education, self-development, or more goal-oriented uses, books and journals will be taken from the library and read. Their content will, to whatever extent, be absorbed by the reader and become part of the individual's own knowledge, to be used in any of a number of ways.

Reference

In some cases, one needs specific information, such as a date, a name, a fact of some kind, or the identification of a source of information: These all represent reference use of a library or other information source.

Browsing

In this use, books are selected by the patron in a more or less aimless, almost random fashion; walking down the stacks of books, picking out a book because it looks interesting, glancing at it, only possibly deciding that it is worth reading, and then continuing on in this rather aimless manner with the aim of identifying books of interest and those to be used either by circulation or in-house. In such usage, many books may be examined and discarded for every one that is actually used. Serendipity serves as the means by which books relevant to needs may be found, which is accomplished virtually by accident. A purpose of the classified shelf arrangement may well be to facilitate such use by bringing together books that are likely to be related to each other.

Support of Decision Making

It has been said that "information is the crucial ingredient in decision making." Clearly, this is one of the crucial uses for information. However, it is more true than not that "decision makers don't use information to make decisions; they use information to support decisions they have already made." It is a result of the fact that many decisions are essentially political, reflecting orders of priority rather than facts. Any of the alternatives can be supported by data, almost equally, if the decision context is truly complex. The formula that serves as the means for assessing data becomes the embodiment, not of the decision process, but of political views about what is important.

Intensive Research

Among in-house uses is intensive research use, in which books are successively examined in a process of formulating and testing hypotheses. In such usage, data found in one book may lead to a hypothesis that can be tested by data found in other books. In each case, the books are not being read in the usual sense of the word. Instead, specific data (using that word in the broadest sense) are found (or perhaps not found) and used to test the hypothesis. A special case of the intensive research use is chained reference, in which the successive references are followed by rapid access from book to book. Examples of this kind arise in all kinds of research—whether economic, historical, literary, scientific.

Processing

Finally, the use of an information resource may represent the need not only to acquire information but also to process it. It is this use that makes electronic information so valuable. (In chapter 5 we examine specifics related to it.)

Barriers to Use

A critical barrier is the differential use made of any kind of information resource. Some faculty, recognizing the value of information to their research and teaching, will be heavy users of libraries, computers, and other kinds of information resources; other faculty will make no use of them, instead depending solely on their own work.

Inertia will always be a barrier for the individual. The resource may be there, but it takes effort to use it, and many individuals will not make that effort. In part, that is due to very real commitments on the time of faculty members. The seventy to eighty hours per week that the typical faculty member devotes to teaching, research, and administrative duties are quite thoroughly committed to the necessary activities, and it is easy to focus attention upon them.

In particular, developing new applications of technology is enormously time-consuming, quite risky, and lacks a clear payout in terms of advancement and tenure decisions. The technologies are complicated to use and require knowledge and facility. That facility, even once gained, is easy to lose unless there is continual use; for most faculty, usage will be sporadic, with the result that the technology must be repeatedly relearned.

CHARACTERIZING PARAMETERS

These different kinds of usage differ significantly in several respects, both quantitative and qualitative.

The Distribution of Activity

First is the amount of activity that each type represents. Reshelving data generally suggests that in academic libraries (which is where in-house use is really a critical issue), in-house uses range from two to three times circulation uses. However, what do reshelving statistics measure? Which of the usages listed above are involved?

This parameter is important to strategic management because it affects the decisions concerning *access allocation*: the level of access to be provided to information materials. This decision problem will be the focus of chapter 10, in which a specific model for distribution of use will be presented and then applied.

Users will differ in their view of the value or importance that information has to them, so there will be differential use of any information resource. Those who know the value of an information resource will use it heavily, while those with little or no experience will not even think of it. However, the great majority of potential users will use it minimally, if at all.

Calvin Mooers, an early pioneer in information science, formulated a law stating that an information system will tend *not* to be used whenever it is more painful and troublesome to have information than not to have it.[4] Indeed, it appears that individuals in general do not want information, even though they may pay lip service to it. Scientists would prefer to do an experiment themselves rather than find out what others have done; business managers would prefer to make decisions based on intuition; and politicians would prefer to respond from their own perception of priorities.

This means that "market forces," representing decisions of individuals, are not a suitable basis for the strategic management of libraries and other information activities. For the good of the community, decisions should be as informed as possible. While the effect of a wrong decision for an individual may be minimal, the cumulative effect of wrong decisions by many individuals may be catastrophic for the organization or the society. Thus, information, at least as far as the library is concerned, is a societal investment rather than an individual one.

The Effects of Distance

Distance and the frequency of use of an information resource are inversely related, and apparently determined by the cost of transportation.[5] If the cost of transportation is a linear function of distance, then the rate of decay is exponential; if the cost of transportation is logarithmic, the decay is inverse square. The logarithmic case, to some extent, represents the situation in which there is a large start-up cost followed by a lower linear rate (as exemplified by short-distance automobile travel). Perhaps the distance a person is willing to go in order to obtain information is a measure of the value it has. That does not result in a "dollar" measure, but it may provide a means for avoiding the reduction of all measures to dollar terms.

The Effects of Response Time

It is clear that it takes time to acquire information, whatever the source. If the information is to be acquired from primary sources, such as personal observation and validation, it will probably take the most time. Similarly, if it is to be acquired through surrogates—others who will acquire and validate it—it will take time to train them, time for them to acquire it, and time for the user to confirm their reliability. Furthermore, time involves both money and delay.

Beyond that, however, in at least some of its applications, information has value as a direct function of immediacy and currency. Historical anecdotes (such as the Rothschild information, obtained through carrier pigeon, of the results of the battle of Waterloo) illustrate the importance of immediacy in such commercial contexts. Of a somewhat different nature, but of equivalent impact, are the various scientific races to discovery, in which immediacy of information played a crucial role.

Another phenomenon related to time is what is called the *half-life* of information. On the one hand, one expects to see an exponential rate of decay in use. On the other hand, there does seem to be a steady state at a minimal level of use for material, on into the future; such a steady-state condition suggests a continuing value for information over time. Of course, any specific item may either never be used or be very heavily used; consequently, such patterns are characteristic of the entire group.

A related phenomenon is the fact that the accumulation of information creates value beyond the mere arithmetic sum of the individual values. That value added is almost certainly a function of the reduction in time for access from one item of information to another. Such chained reference is feasible only with large accumulations of information at one place, with sufficient organization and means for access to support chained reference.

Currently, for most investigators, chained reference ultimately leads to the exhaustion of local resources, and recourse must then be made to an interlibrary loan. The cost in time is severe, but the evidence shows that if the material is needed, the user will be prepared to pay that cost. In return though, the user does want some kind of guaranteed response time. In fact, he or she may well be prepared to trade more rapid but less certain response time in favor of less rapid but more certain turnaround.

This parameter is important to strategic management because it affects the decision concerning access allocation, especially as it relates to the needs of the user for rapid response.

The Effects of Cost

The phrase "free access to information" has been traditionally used to describe the commitment of the library community, but there are two quite different issues that the term *free* confuses: "Who pays for the information?" and "How available is it?" The issue of availability is complicated by ability to pay, so the two issues, while different, are not independent. Both issues, of course, are central to information policy (at the institutional as well as the societal level).

NOTES

1. Each of the standard texts for strategic management in business, as listed in note 1 of chapter 1, emphasizes this point, evident though it is in principle. In addition, the following reference may be of interest: Zaleznik, Abraham, *The Managerial Mystique* (New York: Harper and Row, 1989).

2. Hayes, Robert M., "Strategic Planning for Information Resources in the Research University," *RQ* 25(4) (Summer 1986): 427–31.

3. Thompson, Donald D., *Use of Library Services, by Category of Patron and/or Funding Source* (Berkeley, Calif.: University of California, 15 June 1979).

4. Mooers, Calvin, *Zator Technical Bulletin* 136 (December 1959).

5. Hayes, Robert M., and Palmer, Susan, "The Effects of Distance Upon Use of Libraries," *Library and Information Science Research* 5(1) (Spring 1983): 67–100.

3

Strategic Focus on the Academic Library

This text assumes that the strategic focus is on the academic library, with the larger contexts to be considered for their effects upon that organization. This chapter, therefore, discusses strategic, tactical, and operational concerns of library administration: organization, personnel policies and numbers of staff, space, finances, expenditures and revenues, internal operations and quality of service, and the contributions of individual products and services.

TACTICAL ISSUES IN STRATEGIC MANAGEMENT

At the risk of stating the obvious, library management must be concerned with tactical issues related to the library's organizational structure, with personnel management, and with financial management.

Administrative Structure

Paramount among the tactical concerns is the nature of the library's administration. In part that is reflected in the administrative structure: divisions between and within public and technical services, between central and branch library operations, and between operations and central management services (finance, personnel, procurement, research and development, and management information systems). In part it is represented by the management style: Is it responsive to the environment? Is it flexible and effective for internal communication and control? Does it aid in attracting and retaining creative people? Is it able to handle changing technology and to deal with inflation and other financial crises?

The administrative structure is represented in part by the library's administrative hierarchy and in part by a matrix of functional relationships.[1] Should the existing structure be changed to provide a better response to the strategic environment? To an extent, this question represents the *tactical* response to strategic objectives, since it provides the primary basis for the allocation of internal resources. However, it may also be a strategic response, especially as it results in improved relations with the university administration, faculty, and students.

Technology provides the potential for new approaches to administrative structures. Electronic systems for information support to management have led to a current debate in management theory (which is as important to academic libraries as it is to commercial and industrial companies) about the appropriate size of the middle management staff. Should the structure be based on the traditional concepts of span of control, which result in the typical pyramid, or do modern management information systems permit a much flatter structure, eliminating the middle manager and coming to a cusp at the highest levels of management?[2]

With all due respect to the current wisdom about the presumed effects of automated management information systems, is the elimination of middle management a realistic approach? There is a need for awareness that absolutely requires day-to-day knowledge of what is happening, as represented not by data accumulating in a file but by personal observation; that requires middle-level managers who can function close to operations.[3] There is also the need for a process of testing and evaluating people. Where are the future managers to come from if the positions through which they currently advance are eliminated? What will be the means for participatory management if the mechanisms for communication are reduced simply to the processing of data?

A second effect of the technology is provided by the electronic linking of locations. How does the resulting structure relate to the constituency being served? Moreover, how does it affect the centralization or decentralization of functions?

Personnel Management

Another strategic concern with tactical implications relates to development of both professional and nonprofessional personnel. The university library depends largely on educational programs in "library and information science" for its professional staff; those programs serve a much broader set of constituencies than just the academic research library, however. The quality of those programs, the numbers and quality of graduates, and the skills and attitudes they bring to their work must be of concern to strategic management.

Strategies for human resources are implemented tactically through policies of personnel management. They should deal with needs for cultural and ethnic diversity, forecast employment needs, determine the means for recruitment and retention, identify the measures for staff effectiveness, determine the basis for the distribution of staff in professional and support functions, and determine the structure of compensation.

A crucial element of strategy for human resources is the appropriate means for training staff and for the educational development of library administration. In particular, what percentage of library resources should be allocated to staff development: for staff to train trainers, for staff doing training, for supervision, and for staff being trained? What is the appropriate level of commitment in management planning? Data from the industrial context suggest that it should be at least 2 percent of the total staff budget, and preferably as much as 4 percent.

Financial Management

A dominating concern today is the economics of academic libraries. These strategic concerns affect the tactical management of finances: the sources and distribution of funds, control and accountability, and cash flow.

Effects of Technology

In part, this concern is related to technological change. Libraries have been forced to make major investments in automation of operations and services, programming, installation of equipment, conversion of catalogs and other files, and training of staff and the students and faculty being served. Those costs have been of great magnitude, both as capital investments and for operating expenses; moreover, they will continue to grow in the future as obsolescent and even obsolete equipment and related software must be replaced.[4]

Libraries have been forced to deal with costs incurred in purchasing new means of data access, the on-line computer databases. They must respond to the demand for new media, such as optical disk stores, that are acquired to serve the needs in instruction and research. Indeed, the pressures on the acquisition budget are almost certainly the most pernicious economic problem faced by academic research libraries. They are creating conflicts within the library in fighting the diversion of funds from books and journals to databases and external services. They are creating conflicts between the library and the faculty and even among faculty members, as different choices adversely affect different disciplines.

Effects of Inflation

The past decade has seen rates of inflation in journal prices, especially those from foreign commercial publishers, that threaten every other commitment of the acquisition budget. Moreover, those price increases, since they largely focus on journals, affect not merely today's budget but also force commitments of resources for the indefinite future. Compounding inflation, though, has been the nearly catastrophic collapse of the dollar in foreign exchange: a direct result of monumental, almost unbelievable federal deficits during the 1980s.

Effects of Charges for Use

The emerging issue is to determine which costs the users will bear and which users will bear them. At many academic institutions, special student tuition surcharges have served as means for funding libraries, and especially for the development of automated services. Implementation of a full-cost charge-back program on many campuses is becoming a high-priority option, especially for charging private-sector users for special services, the use of electronic resources, reference and user intermediation services, and document delivery services. At other institutions, the option has been considered of charging departments for the inflation in costs of serials.

Effects of Interlibrary Loan (ILL)

The costs of resource sharing and remote access are becoming critical, as interlibrary loan is being buried under an avalanche of requests. Libraries throughout the country, public as well as private institutions, are therefore being forced to reconsider the issue of charging for ILL services.

Outsourcing of Operations

The decision to have operations performed outside an organization rather than within it is called outsourcing.[5] It is a tactical decision, since it determines how resources will be allocated, but it is one with vital strategic implications as well. In businesses today, about 25 percent of information activities overall—in data processing, accounting, software development, computer hardware facilities, even libraries and research and development—are being outsourced.[6] The likelihood is that the proportion of outsourced information work will gradually increase over time. The reasons are multiple, including access to specialized capabilities, sharing of costs with other businesses, focusing resources on core business needs, and expectations of efficiencies in operation.

The concept of outsourcing can be fearful for librarians, but it is well exhibited in libraries already. The most central example is the choice between acquisition or access; if access is chosen, clearly, the library has decided to outsource some portion of its services, and to that extent will depend on other libraries or commercial document delivery services to meet patron needs.

A similar example is in reference, where a typical outsourcing decision might be to replace local printed collections of indexes and abstracts by on-line database services. Another example is in cataloging, in which the decision has been made by virtually every library to outsource to central bibliographic services for the majority of its catalog data. Many libraries have decided to outsource to their campus computing facilities for the management of the hardware and software to support their local systems. In some cases, even the function of systems work in the library has been outsourced in that way.

OPERATIONAL ISSUES IN STRATEGIC MANAGEMENT

During the 1970s and 1980s, the automation of library internal operations has been perhaps the single most dominant strategic issue in academic libraries. Today, though, it has become simply a normal part of operations.[7] Essentially, every major library in the United States now has a local automated system operating in support of its internal operations in cataloging and technical processing. This is changing the ground rules for production planning and for the measurement of production effectiveness. It is changing the mix of professional, nonprofessional, and student staff. What changes are required, therefore, in management of the production and delivery of services? This question represents the *operational* response to the strategic environment.

The traditional functions of the library—selection and acquisition, intellectual and physical organization, storage and preservation, access and retrieval—are all changing. The classical imperatives of collection development and access to the information records are beginning to conflict instead of being mutually supportive; the tools for intellectual access are changing as on-line public access catalogs become universal tools and there is pressure to change the very nature of the catalog records to accommodate new needs and new methods; the problem of preservation is rapidly becoming one of monumental magnitude; and the relationship of the library to other means for information access is becoming increasingly complex. In other words, across the board of academic library management responsibilities, change is the order of the day. Strategic management needs to assess each of these functions, both for its contribution to the mission of the academic library as a whole and for its individual viability.

COLLECTION MANAGEMENT

The collection is the central tool of the academic library. The strategic concerns are with the changing methods of publication and distribution as they relate to research needs and programs, instructional needs, and public service needs.

The Range of Information Media and Technologies

Operational management must be concerned with the full range of media that may be of value to academic programs: printed books and journals, manuscripts and archives, microforms, films, video- and audio tapes, computer hardware and software, computer databases, optical disks and cards, and means for communication.

Print

An issue of current debate is whether print form publications will continue to be viable and an important means for information distribution. Some have claimed that we will become a "paperless society," with electronic means for communication replacing print.[8] Most of that speculation, though, has been generated by the enthusiasts for "computer-based publication," with little attention paid to the paramount importance of the decisions made by publishers about what will be published and about its format. Others have pointed to the fact that the effect of the computer, fax machines, and other new media has been to *increase* the role of paper, not diminish it.

The position of this text is unequivocal: Print is still the *essential medium* for scholarship and scholarly communication. It will continue to be so for at least the next two decades. However, it is also evident that the information technologies and the new media must be considered, not only in their own right, but also as essential adjuncts and supplements to the printed formats and as means for their production.

It is important to provide some basis for projecting the likely rates of print publication and library acquisitions of these publications. For the moment, the available estimates (which are largely based on industrialized countries) are that print publication internationally will grow at a rate between 3 and 4 percent per annum (in constant dollars).[9] The great unknown lies in the Third World; there could be an explosive growth in publication in those developing countries, or, on the other hand, there could be stagnation.

Historically, as shown in the study by Fremont Rider in 1944 and the Purdue studies starting in 1965, the collections of major academic libraries had, for well over one hundred years, increased at exponential rates, doubling every fifteen to twenty years.[10] Such growth rates, in fact, were quite consistent with a 3 to 4 percent annual increase in publication.

Will that continue to be the case? Recent updates by Warren Seibert suggest it will not.[11] In fact, they show that during the years since the early 1970s, the historic trend has changed dramatically. There has been virtually a "steady state" in the rate of addition for medium to large ARL libraries (ranging from 100,000 to 150,000 volumes per year), and an actual decline in the rate of addition for the smaller ARL members (steadily going down from about 80,000 to about 60,000 volumes per year). The decline for the small libraries can be directly attributed to the effects of network sharing of resources, with the smaller libraries depending on the larger ones for guaranteed access. Indeed, the current wisdom is that librarians are now focusing on access, not ownership.

To what can we attribute this change from historic patterns, and is it likely to continue? There are at least five possible explanations, with the likelihood being that all are operative. First, rates of inflation in academic acquisition costs have been substantially greater than the average augmentation of the acquisition budgets, which forces a reduced rate of accession. Second, many large institutions stopped the construction of library buildings for the twenty-year period studied by Siebert, which probably forced librarians to limit their acquisition policies. Third, the great period in which collections were available to be acquired, which made it possible to increase easily collection size, seems to have ended, which means that it is much more difficult to sustain rates of increase. Fourth, the increased dependence on the sharing of resources, which served to drive so many of the technological and organizational developments of the past twenty years, has reduced the dependence on local resources, especially for the smaller institutions. Fifth, the effects of new, technological means for access has led some libraries to use the acquisition budget to fund the costs of these newer means for information access, with the view that they substitute for the need for collection development; this clearly reduces the available funds.

Audiovisual, Multimedia, and Hypermedia

The use of audiovisual materials has, until recently, been limited to the standard array of films and tapes. Now, though, the use of computer-controlled access to a range of instructional materials in systems called *multimedia* and *hypermedia* has dramatically increased the potential range of uses.[12]

Electronic Information

Librarians have seen themselves as the professionals whose position, skills, and commitments make them the natural focal point for management of these new electronic resources. Library schools have virtually preempted the title "information science" to encompass those responsibilities. The new electronic media have very naturally been added to the array of potential acquisitions. CD-ROMs, tape databases, electronic journals, and other forms become grist for the library acquisition mill, as they may appear. All this increases the position and status of the librarians, changing them from mere custodians to dynamic participants in a wonderful new world.[13]

Space

A major operational concern is with storage of the collection and the tools for physical access to it. Major research collections still grow (for good reasons), so buildings must be built to house them—whether on campus or in depository facilities. The capital costs for construction represent fifty- to one hundred–year commitments.

Depository Facilities

These have been a primary strategic response to the space problem during the past two decades, as the construction of new library buildings was severely curtailed.

Compact Storage

This has been a secondary strategic response, despite the rather substantial savings in space that it provides.

Automated Facilities

One academic library (California State–Northridge) has installed a highly automated, computer-managed storage facility; it is based on a system for automated warehousing.[14]

Preservation

The collections of every major research library are in states of disintegration. The result is that a major capital resource of the university system—its library collection—is literally falling apart in our hands.

The Magnitude of the Problem

There have been a number of studies of the deterioration of materials in research libraries, the most important being the one at the Library of Congress.[15] While they vary widely in methodology and analysis, the results are consistent and imply that about 25 percent of printed materials are at risk, primarily due to brittle paper, and an additional .5 percent are becoming at risk each year. Of course, not all may be worthy of preservation, but the risk is so great that every academic library should make provisions for dealing with it as a strategic problem.

Alternative Solutions

The current option of choice for dealing with the preservation problem is *preservation-quality microfilming*. Alternatives would include *preservation photocopying* and *conversion to digitized images*. The option of conversion to digitized text (through optical character reading) is not generally feasible.

Table 3.1
Estimated Costs for Preservation Functions

Function	Staff	Direct Costs	Overhead	G&A	Total
Identification	Student	$ 0.63	$ 0.72	$0.21	$1.56
Decision Making	Technician	2.63	3.02	0.87	6.52
Catalog Work	Technician	7.89	9.07	2.63	19.59
Preparation	Student	3.77	4.34	1.26	9.37
Microfilming	Technician	22.08	29.20	7.36	58.64
Total		$37.00	$46.35	$12.33	$95.68

The National Program

Under the leadership of the Council on Library Resources, the National Commission on Preservation and Access was formed to respond to this problem.[16] The efforts involve joint participation of the research library community, the National Endowment for the Humanities, the three national libraries, and the bibliographic utilities. The bibliographic utilities, in particular, have provided special services for identifying the status of materials being converted to preservation microfilm.[17]

Processes and Their Costs

The functions involved in preservation work are now quite well defined and usually are administered as part of a unit having responsibility for book preparation, binding, and general conservation work. They include (1) identification of materials at risk, (2) assessment of options for their treatment, (3) search and update of the data from the bibliographic utilities, (4) collation and preparation, (5) filming or photocopying, and (6) inspection.[18] Chapter 9 provides data on which the costs of these processes can be estimated (as summarized in table 3.1).

ACCESS VERSUS ACQUISITION

Throughout most of the long history of librarianship, its two imperatives—*preservation* of the records of the past and *access* to those records and their contents—have been mutually supportive. Libraries acquired materials, and access, in the main, was to the resulting holdings of each particular library by the constituency it served; interlibrary loan was a valuable support, but its role was relatively limited and of minor significance overall. In this context, the concept of free access was both meaningful and justifiable; the library, having made the capital investment in its collection, could easily make it freely available at almost no additional cost, aside from wear and tear on the collection and the effects of use on availability. As a result, the library could serve its constituency within its budget and without the need to be concerned about the costs involved in meeting the needs for access. Even the real costs involved in interlibrary loan could be tolerated, given the relatively low level of use, the fiction of reciprocity, and the ability of the established staff to handle the workload.

Resource Sharing

Since the late 1930s, though, increasingly the argument has been made that no library can stand alone and that interinstitutional cooperation, as a basis for the "sharing of resources," should be made a professional priority. At least one of the reasons was that identified by Fremont Rider: exponential increase in collections and the resulting pressure to build ever more library buildings. After World War II, the problems were perceived to be even broader, as each major library faced increasing acquisitions of foreign materials, with the need to not only store but also process them. The immediate result was the creation of cooperative activities; the Center for Research Libraries and the Farmington Plan were specific examples, with the former intended to deal with the problem of space, and the latter, with the acquisition of foreign materials.[19]

For at least the last thirty years, these kinds of efforts have steadily accelerated. The result has been an increased emphasis on sharing, aiming to replace *acquisition* by *access* (meaning not just access to the individual collection, which was the historic emphasis, but access to materials wherever stored, especially elsewhere). Some efforts have resulted in mechanisms to facilitate interinstitutional cooperation, with sharing of resources as a major objective, creating networks and other organizational structures to coordinate the efforts. Some have aimed at developing centralized facilities (with some ideas based on expanding the Center for Research Libraries, and others on replicating the highly successful Lending Division of the British Library) as means to supplement, if not replace, local acquisition. Some were fostered by federal funding explicitly directed at encouraging the development of "multi-type" networks at the state level, with resource-sharing as the watchword. Some created the bibliographic utilities, intended in part to facilitate the process of inter-library lending.

Role of Electronic Access

Today the emphasis on access has reached a near crescendo, as the voices of the purveyors of electronic forms of information access and of some university administrators add to those of the librarians. The enthusiasts present the vision of electronic information as the wave of the future, and at least some administrators see that vision as the solution to the "library problem," as a means to avoid building new libraries to house what they see as ever-increasing collections. The potential represented by the National Research and Educational Network is seen as replacing books and journals with "real information" that is instantly available, current, and readily processible.[20]

What a vision and what a combination of incentives are touted! "Access" means we will not need to spend money on books, journals, buildings, or staff. "Access" also means we will have instant information, with all the technology of computer processing for retrieval, analysis, and presentation. Scholars will be able to communicate directly with "information" as well as with each other, without the need to go to a library and face the problem of finding what they want, and operations will be marked by speed, efficiency, and currency.

Of course, the reality is that libraries are still vitally important to the university, and the gap between electronic potentials and current reality is still so great that librarians must continue to focus their attention on the proper balance today between the benefits and costs of acquisition and access, including those associated with interinstitutional cooperation. The benefits have, in part, been alluded to already: Cooperation implies better utilization of the money spent for acquisitions by reducing unnecessary duplications among libraries. By sharing resources—by treating the major libraries of the country virtually as a single collection—each library (and the constituency it serves) has access to more materials than would otherwise be the case. Growth in holdings at individual libraries can be at a slower pace, so there is less need for constructing new library buildings.

The Costs to the Library

However, the costs of access—of sharing, of interinstitutional cooperation—are not usually discussed by the enthusiasts. It is almost as if the perception were that the benefits are all free. The reality, of course, is that there are very real costs associated with access. Even in earlier, simpler times, when access meant interlibrary loan and use was relatively limited, the major net lenders (especially the prestigious private universities) found the costs and effects on their own constituencies to be burdensome. They argued repeatedly then, and still do today, that there should be some mechanism for reimbursement of at least the direct costs incurred.[21]

The Costs of Access

In that respect, it is relevant to note that libraries generally have underestimated the costs for these kinds of activities. They frequently will consider only the direct costs, ignoring even the most evident of overhead costs (such as salary-related benefits and costs of supervision); that error in itself results in estimates that are half the true costs. The result is a bias in comparisons of access alternatives and of benefits with costs.

In fact, the studies that have been made of interlibrary loan (ILL) costs suggest totals, for both borrowing and lending libraries together, on the order of $30 per transaction. Moreover, commercial document delivery services, which can be used as replacements for the lending library, charge fees that will result in roughly comparable total costs. Given those costs specifically associated with access, even a relatively low rate of use easily justifies a switch to acquisition instead. Indeed, an analysis of benefits versus costs is likely to demonstrate that current acquisition policies of major university libraries are close to optimum, as will be demonstrated in chapter 10.

The Costs of Cooperation

However, beyond the costs directly attributable to access are those associated with the mechanisms of cooperation. Memberships in consortia carry their own costs, indirect as well as direct. Indeed, in many respects, the commitment of upper levels of library management to working with cooperative arrangements represent exceptionally high expenditures of resources. These "general and administrative" costs need to be recognized as decisions are made about access allocations. Furthermore, as increasing numbers of libraries install automated "local systems," each must make decisions concerning input to the national databases in order to maintain those means which are essential to facilitate interinstitutional sharing of resources. Again, costs will be incurred, which are obviously necessary but are also part of the balance in the assessment of benefits versus costs.

The Costs to Users

The elements of costs are, in principle, ones that can be assessed without essential complication. The costs (and perhaps the benefits) to the constituency in the replacement of acquisition by access are much more difficult to assess but also are fundamentally more important. The concern of libraries about maintaining "free access" in the replacement of printed indexing and abstracting journals by database access services reflects some of those issues. The potential of reduced use of library resources, if they are unavailable locally or if the access time is seen as a barrier, is even more important.

Even more intangible, but potentially most significant, is the perception by the university of its own reputation. It is still true that the library is perceived as an important component of that reputation, and any university that aspires to status as a major national research institution needs to have a library collection of national renown. Competition among institutions is real. They compete for distinguished faculty, for the best and brightest students, and for research support from government and industry; the library is crucial in that effort. What is the cost of replacing a reputation for excellence in the collection by an ability, shared with every other institution, to draw on the nation's resources?

REFERENCE SERVICES

Use of On-Line Database Services

During the past two decades, the on-line database services have become increasingly important in academic library operations. That situation, though, appears to be changing. Overall, the predictions are that on-line database services will continue to grow at about 20 percent per year, which covers the entire range of users.[22] Today, libraries are a relatively small portion of the total market. Given the acquisition of many databases in CD-ROM form, the likely addition of the most heavily used ones into public access catalogs, and the increasing direct use of them by the end user, demand for the on-line database access services in libraries is likely not to increase, and indeed may begin to decline during the last half of the decade.

Installation of CD-ROM Databases

CD-ROM databases have now become an evident resource in university libraries. They are standard tools for reference support, and their acquisition will continue to increase. Interconnection among microcomputer servers, in local networks both within the library and throughout the campus, is now standard in academic library operations.[23]

There are increasing amounts of material being distributed in these forms, some as counterparts of prints and some as independent publications. Even government information is now available on CD-ROM (an example being the 1990 census). As a result, libraries of all kinds will face complex decisions about whether to acquire the print versions, the CD-ROM versions, other electronic versions, or mixes of all of them. Strategic management calls for a process of evaluation of electronic media and, as part of collection development policies, establishment of criteria for determining what budget allocation should be committed to acquire them.[24]

The levels of use, though, do not suggest that they will replace print as a means for access to even the kind of information that they store. CD-ROMs may sit on the shelf beside one's home computer at home, but it still is easier to turn to the print sources (the encyclopedia, almanac, dictionary, or thesaurus) than to find the appropriate CD, mount it, load the software for it, and then progress laboriously through the menus to find what is wanted. Of course, if such access is needed daily, CD-ROMs will be used far more often, but for their specific values rather than as replacements for print publications.

On-line Public Access Catalogs

Today, on-line public access catalogs are crucial tools for reader services in academic research libraries. They greatly increase the ability of patrons to identify needed materials and effectively utilize the collections. Beyond that, however, they are powerful tools for assembling bibliographies and downloading data into personal files for manipulation, analysis, and incorporation into databases and documents. They also have value as sources of factual data, such as individual biographic data (for example, dates of birth and death).

Enhanced Bibliographic Records

The on-line public access catalog of the local system also serves as a central tool in reference services. Efforts to augment the bibliographic data, therefore, are among the most important means for increasing the level of support. The addition of tables of contents and even book indexes, for example, would greatly increase the ability to guide patrons in access to and use of monographs, especially compilations and proceedings. Increased analytics, identification of tables, and even current contents of serials are all being experimented with by both individual libraries and the bibliographic utilities.[25]

Local Mounting of Databases

The nearly universal implementation of local system OPACs is now making it feasible for libraries to consider using them to provide access to nationally available databases in addition to the institution's own catalog. Subscription pricing arrangements make it possible to offer access to those databases at minimal cost to the users, or even free, and as a result greatly increase the amount of use made of them by factors as much as a hundredfold.[26] Of special value is the provision of interconnection between the records of those databases and the holdings records from the library's catalog; this permits users to quickly identify the local availability of retrieved references.

Document Delivery Services

During the late 1980s, the fax machine became a tool of dramatic importance in business and industry, where it serves as an essential means for both internal corporate communication and external information exchange. For libraries and the academic world, the pace has been somewhat slower, but currently it has started to pick up. The potential of digitized data files of text as the basis for electronic document delivery—on-demand publication, in effect—promises to revolutionize not only that function, but the very role of the library and its relationship to users.

Expert Reference

During the 1990s, expert systems and generalized expert system approaches will become operational in libraries.[27] Developed systems will be easily transportable and widely available for libraries for a variety of in-house local system uses. Of special importance will be the implementation of automated ready-reference; it will be operational in virtually every library, providing microcomputer support to the ready-reference function.

LIBRARY ISSUES IN ELECTRONIC COMMUNICATION AND PUBLISHING

How do electronic forms of communication, including desktop publishing, affect the library's fundamental responsibilities for preservation and access? The answer is clear: There are serious problems in the control of this literature.[28] Historically, the library field has had extensive experience in dealing with these kinds of problems, as exemplified in the entire array of "report" literature and similar ephemera. The tools that have been developed are indeed useful, but they are expensive to maintain and use. The point, of course, is that desktop publishing is merely "report publication," albeit with improved graphic and typographic quality.

Knowledge of the Fact of Publication

There are problems in lack of information about the fact of publication. With formal publishers, *Books in Print* and similar mechanisms for identifying availability sources of materials provide the answer. What will be the counterpart for desktop publications? There is a lack of means for assessment and review, which is essential in deciding about the selection and acquisition of material to be preserved. Perhaps some desktop publications will make their way into the review literature, but for the bulk of them such means for assessment simply will not be available: There is a lack of means for access. Whereas there is a strong mechanism for distribution of books and journals, as yet no counterpart exists for electronic publications. If a library wished to acquire a particular desktop publication, how would it do so?

The Tools for Secondary Access

There is a lack of the tools needed for secondary access: no coverage of desktop publications in the nation's indexes, abstracts, bibliographies, and catalogs. The result is that persons who need information contained in such ephemeral publications have no means for identifying which are of potential value. Even if such material is identifiable, for example through the various citation indexes (resulting from reference to it in some formally published document that covered them), the user has no means for knowing where to obtain it. The problem not only affects the users, though: From an operational standpoint, it places intolerable burdens on librarians who must track down these "citation ghosts." Do they refer to real publications or ephemeral ones?

GOALS

Goals are concrete and specific means for realizing the vision and implementing the mission. Early on in a strategic management program, an effort should be made to identify specific goals that relate information resources to the academic program as explicitly as possible. They should set the stage, guide the process, and serve as the basis for evaluation of results.

Goals and objectives are by no means easy to establish, and indeed, one of the purposes of strategic planning is to determine what they should be. They are likely to reflect a mix of concerns that need to be resolved in a political process, not a technical one.

Institutional Goals

While each university must establish its own goals and objectives for libraries and information resources as the means by which they respond to the external forces, we can identify the following goals for the role of information resources in support of the university's perceived mission:

1. increase the reputation and national visibility of the university, especially as that may depend on or be affected by information resources;
2. expand the role of information resources in obtaining funding for academic programs for both instruction and research;
3. maintain the position of the university at the forefront of developments in the information resources field itself: educational, professional, technical, and technological;
4. increase the level of cooperation with foreign countries and institutions, both generally, and specifically with respect to information resources;
5. increase the effectiveness in use of expenditures, throughout the university, in acquiring, producing, and using information resources;

MORTON COLLEGE LIBRARY
CICERO. ILLINOIS

6. increase the degree of cooperation among academic units in the use of information resources;

7. establish equitable personnel policies for the full range of staff concerned with information resources; and

8. protect the university's interests with respect to external policies affecting its ability to use information resources in support of its academic responsibilities.

Library Goals

More specific are the goals for the library and other information agencies on campus:

1. improve the quality of instruction and enrich the learning environment, at every level, especially as it may depend on or be affected by information resources;

2. increase the research productivity of faculty as it may depend on or be affected by information resources;

3. increase the information literacy (i.e., ability to use information resources) of students and other users;

4. increase the amount of information available to students and other users;

5. develop the means to assure that faculty and students have access to the technical information support needed to use information resources effectively;

6. develop single-point access to the full range of information resources in the university;

7. deliver information directly to workstations and personal computers (PCs); and

8. provide support to personalized database systems for faculty and students.

NOTES

1. The use of a matrix for describing the structure of an organization is a relatively new concept. It is beyond the scope of this text to go into details, but the following references will provide a start: Knight, Kenneth, (ed.), *Matrix Management* (New York: PBI, 1977); White, Anthony G., *Matrix Management/Public Administration: A Selected Bibliography* (Monticello, Ill.: Vance Bibliographies, 1982); Cleland, David I., *Matrix Management Systems Handbook* (New York: Van Nostrand Reinhold, 1984).

2. American Foundation on Automation and Employment, *Automation and the Middle Manager: What Has Happened and What the Future Holds* (New York: American Foundation on Automation and Employment, 1966); Fulop, L., "Middle Managers—Victims or Vanguards of the Entrepreneurial Movement?" *Journal of Management Studies* 28(1) (1991): 25–54; Lewis, D. W., "8 Truths for Middle Managers in Lean Times," *Library Journal* 116(14) (1 September 1991): 315–16; Harris, C. L., "Columbia University Library's Staff Development Seminar," *Journal of Academic Librarianship* 17(2) (3 May

1991): 71–73; Toffler, Alvin, *Power Shift* (New York: Bantam Books, 1990; see especially pp. 172–77 and 221–22); Toffler, Alvin, "Toffler's Next Shock," *World Monitor*, November 1990, pp. 34–44.

3. Connors, J. L., and Romberg, T. A., "Middle Management and Quality Control," *Human Organization* 50(1) (Spring 1991): 61–65.

4. DeGennaro, Richard, *Libraries, Technology, and the Information Marketplace* (Boston: G. K. Hall, 1987).

5. Conatser, Kelly R., "In or Out—A Simple 1–2–3 Model Reveals Whether Outsourcing Is for You," *Lotus* 8(8) (August 1992): 36–40; Platenic, Suzanne, "Should I or Shouldn't I?" *Beyond Computing* 1(1) (1992): 26–33.

6. Siegel, Donald, and Griliches, Zvi, *Purchased Services, Outsourcing, Computers, and Productivity in Manufacturing*, Working paper no. 3678 (Cambridge, Mass.: National Bureau of Economic Research, April 1991; see especially table 1).

7. Flanders, Bruce, "Spectacular Systems!" *American Libraries*, Oct. 1989, pp. 915–22.

8. Lancaster, F. Wilfrid, *The Dissemination of Scientific and Technical Information: Toward a Paperless System* (Champaign: University of Illinois, Graduate School of Library Science, 1977); Lancaster, F. W., "Whither Libraries? or, Wither Libraries," *College and Research Libraries* 39(5) (Sept. 1978): 345–57; Lancaster, F. W. "The Paperless Society Revisited," *American Libraries*, Sept. 1985, pp. 553–55.

9. *Predicasts* (1990).

10. Rider, Fremont, *The Scholar and the Future of the Research Library* (New York: Hadham Press, 1944); Dunn, Oliver C., et al., *The Past and Likely Future of 58 Research Libraries, 1951–1980: A Statistical Study of Growth and Change* (West Lafayette, Ind.: Purdue University, 1965–72); Drake, Miriam A., *Academic Research Libraries: A Study of Growth* (West Lafayette, Ind.: Purdue University Libraries and Audio-Visual Center, 1977).

11. Seibert, Warren, et al., *Research Library Trends, 1951–1980 and Beyond* (Bethesda, Md.: Lister Hill Center for Biomedical Communications, March 1987); Seibert, Warren, et al., *Research Library Trends II: 35 Libraries in the 1970s and Beyond* (Bethesda, Md.: Lister Hill Center for Biomedical Communications, January 1990).

12. Greenberger, Martin, (ed.), *Technologies for the 21st Century: On Multimedia* (Santa Monica, Calif.: Voyager Co., 1990).

13. Battin, Patricia, "The electronic library—A vision for the future," *Educom Bulletin* 19(2) (Summer 1984): 12–17, 34; Rice, James G., "The Dream of the Memex," *American Libraries*, January 1988, pp. 14–17; *Information and People: A Campus Dialogue on the Challenges of Electronic Information* (Ann Arbor: University of Michigan, SLIS, 1991); Bosseau, Don L., *After the OPAC, CD-ROM, Hypermedia, and Networking—What Lies Ahead for Libraries and Librarians?* (San Diego: California State University at San Diego, 1991); Brindley, Lynne J., *Libraries and the Wired-up Campus: The Future Role of the Library in Academic Information Handling* (Birmingham, U.K.: British Library Research and Development Department, 1988); DeGennaro, Richard, *Libraries, Technology, and the Information Marketplace* (Boston: G. K. Hall, 1987); Kniffel, Leonard, "Books Made to Order: Libraries as Publishers," *American Libraries*, September 1989, pp. 735–39; Lunden, Elizabeth, "The Library as a Business," *American Libraries*, July/August 1982, pp. 471–72; Gilbert, Steven W., "Information Technology, Intellectual Property, and Education," *Educom Review* 25(1) (Spring 1990): 14–20.

14. "Cal. State's Leviathan II Is a Whale of a Project," *American Libraries*, Oct. 1989, p. 839.

15. *Preserving the Illustrated Text: Report of the Joint Task Force on Text and Image* (Washington, D.C.: National Commission on Preservation and Access, 1992); Online Computer Library Center [OCLC], *1991 OCLC Preservation Needs Assessment Study: Detailed Report* (Dublin, Ohio: Online Computer Library Center [OCLC], February 1991); *Brittle Books: Reports of the Committee on Preservation and Access* (Washington, D.C.: Council on Library Resources, 1986); "The Preservation Challenge: A Sampling of Efforts to Save the Nation's Heritage," *Scholarly Communication* 1 (June 1985): 3.

16. National Commission on Preservation and Access, *Annual Report* (Washington, D.C.: National Commission on Preservation and Access). 1988–.

17. "RLG Contributes to National Preservation Effort," *Research Library Group News* 20 (Fall 1989): 3–8.

18. ARL, *ARL Preservation Statistics, 1990–91* (Washington, D.C.: Association of Research Libraries [ARL], 1992); Merrill-Oldham, Jan, et al., *Preservation Program Models: A Study Project and Report* (Washington, D.C.: Association of Research Libraries [ARL], 1991).

19. Vosper, Robert, *The Farmington Plan Survey: A Summary of the Separate Studies of 1957–1961* (Urbana: University of Illinois, Graduate School of Library Science, 1965); Center for Research Libraries, *Center for Research Libraries Handbook* (Chicago: CRL, n.d.).

20. Gore, Albert, "Remarks on the NREN [National Research and Education Network]," *Educom Review* 25(2) (Summer 1990): 12–16; Roberts, Michael M., "The NREN and Commercial Services," *Educom Review* 24(4) (Winter 1989): 10–11; "Progress toward National Research and Education Network," *Manage IT* 1(1) (February 1990): 4; Issues of *Educom Review* devoted to NREN include 26(1) (Spring 1991) and 26(2) (Summer 1991); Rogers, Susan M., "Educational Applications of the NREN," *Educom Review* 25(2) (Summer 1990): 25–29; Flanders, Bruce, "NREN: The Big Issues Aren't Technical," *American Libraries*, June 1991, pp. 572–74; Kibbey, Mark, and Evans, Nancy H., "The Network Is the Library," *Educom Review* 24(3) (Fall 1989): 15–20; Mosher, Paul H., "A Natural Scheme for Collaboration in Collection Development: The RLG-NCIP Effort," *Resource Sharing and Information Networks* 2 (Spring/Summer 1985): 21–35.

21. Palmour, Vernon E., et al., *A Study of the Characteristics, Costs, and Magnitude of Interlibrary Loans in Academic Libraries* (Westport, Conn.: Greenwood Press, 1972); Williams, Gordon, et al., *Library Cost Models: Owning Versus Borrowing Serial Publications* (Washington, D.C.: Office of Science Information Service, National Science Foundation, 1968).

22. *Predicasts*, 1990 (re CD-ROM market growth).

23. Lowry, Charles B., *Comparative Study of Periodical Literature Indexing: Print versus Electronic Access* (Arlington: University of Texas, 31 July 1992).

24. Case, Donald, *Optical Disk Publication of Databases: A Review of Applications for Academic Libraries* (Los Angeles: University of California at Los Angeles, Graduate School of Library and Information Science, 31 August 1986); Miller, David C., *The New Optical Media in the Library and the Academy Tomorrow* (Benicia, Calif.: DCM Associates, prepared for the Fred Meyer Charitable Trust, August 1986); Miller, David C.,

Moving Information: Graphic Images on CD-ROM (Benicia, Calif.: DCM Associates, prepared for the Fred Meyer Charitable Trust, March 1987); Miller, David C., *Special Report: Publishers, Libraries, and CD-ROM* (Benicia, Calif.: DCM Associates, prepared for the Fred Meyer Charitable Trust, March 1987); Miller, David C., *The New Optical Media Mid–1986: A Status Report* (Benicia, Calif.: DCM Associates, prepared for the Fred Meyer Charitable Trust, August 1986); Paisley, William, and Butler, Matilda, "The First Wave: CD-ROM Adoption in Offices and Libraries," *Microcomputers for Information Management* 4(2) (June 1987): 109–27.

25. "A Proposal for More Informative Abstracts of Clinical Articles," *Annals of Internal Medicine* 106 (1987): 598–604; Pitkin, Gary M., "CARL's Latest Project: Access to Articles through the Online Catalog," *American Libraries*, October 1988, 769–70; Michalak, Thomas J., "An Experiment in Enhancing Catalog Records at Carnegie-Mellon University," *Library Hi-Tech* 31(3) (1990): 33–41; Van Orden, Rich, "Content-Enriched Access to Electronic Information: Summaries of Selected Research," *Library Hi-Tech* 31(3) (1990): 27–32; "RLIN Citations File plus Document Delivery Tapped for Major Expansion," *Research Library Group News* 26 (Fall 1991): 6–7; Lowry, *Periodical Literature Indexing*.

26. Lynch, Clifford, "The Melvyl System: Looking Back, Looking Forward," *DLA Bulletin* 12(10) (Spring 1992): 3–5; Machovec, George S., "Locally Loaded Databases in Arizona State University's Online Catalog Using the CARL System," *Information Technology and Libraries* 8(2) (June 1989): 161–69.

27. Lancaster, F. W., and Smith, Linda C., (eds.), *Artificial Intelligence and Expert Systems: Will They Change the Library?* (Urbana-Champaign: University of Illinois at Urbana-Champaign, Graduate School of Library Science, 1992); Richardson, John, Jr., "Toward an Expert System for Reference Service: A Research Agenda for the 1990s," *College and Research Libraries*, March 1989, pp. 233–48; Sedelow, Sally Yeates, and Sedelow, Walter A., Jr., "Artificial Intelligence, Expert Systems, and Productivity," in *Psychology and Productivity*, ed. Paul Whitney (New York: Plenum, 1989), pp. 51–66.

28. Hayes, Robert M., "Desktop Publishing: Problems of Control," *Scholarly Publishing* 21(2) (Jan. 1990): 117–23 (also published as "Who Should Be in Control?" in *Desktop Publishing in the University*, ed. Joan N. Burstyn (Syracuse, N.Y.: Syracuse University, 1991).

PART II

Contexts

4

The Context of Institutional Management

In this chapter and in the following two, we will expand on a set of issues that are of importance to top management and provide the context for strategic management. The issues of concern fall into three groups, relating to (1) institutional management, (2) the users—the constituencies served—and their needs, and (3) the external environment. This chapter focuses on institutional management.

INSTITUTIONAL MISSION

The most important determinant of institutional policies surely is the perception of its mission—by administration, faculty, students, alumni, and the sources of funding. Some academic institutions—presumably those represented by the largest ARL libraries—see themselves as major national research institutions. They will have large libraries and will see them as crucial to their research objectives and reputations, providing the basis for attracting faculty and research grants. They will also have super-computing facilities and will be major nodes on the national networks with respect to both libraries and computing.

Then, there are the institutions that see their mission in research and graduate education, but while the aspiration may be for a major national reputation, the reality is recognized as more limited. They see undergraduate education as important but by no means the primary basis for their reputation. They will need libraries and computing facilities that support their research objectives, but will be ready to consider access to such resources from elsewhere as an economic alternative. Presumably, most of the ARL libraries, other than the very largest institutions, reflect this level of mission.

Finally, there are institutions that focus on undergraduate and technical education. Their libraries and computing facilities will be oriented to educational requirements, with high levels of dependence on outside resources for research support. Presumably, most of the Association of College and Research Libraries (ACRL) institutions, the community colleges, and the small liberal arts colleges are committed to this mission.

Whatever the mission, information imperatives, commitments, and operational realities, they apply not only to the library (whether narrowly or broadly defined), but with at least equal vigor to the university as a whole. The university's imperative, like that of the library, is based on the view that information is important to both the society and the individual. There is a professional commitment to information that is as deep as the librarian's. It is seen in the traditions of both education and research, with open access to published information playing a crucial role in both.

UNIVERSITIES IN THE COMING DECADES

Universities in the United States will face a number of needs and problems during the coming decades, all of them affecting decisions concerning libraries and information resources. Several issues are paramount as determinants of future development, particularly, changes in the economics of universities, effects of technology, changes in the academic enterprise, and changes in patterns of publication.

Economics

The past two decades have seen a steady erosion in the basis of financial support for academic institutions.[1] In 1992, the trend reached crisis proportions as state budgets throughout the country were decimated due to the recession.[2]

As a result, there are dramatic changes occurring in the basis for funding of universities and of libraries within them. There is an increasing shift from public to private funding, even for the public universities; there is also an increasing shift from federal funding to industrial funding of research. How do we fit strategic management of information resources into such fundamental changes in funding patterns?

In the United States at least, the current perception is that universities face a decade of *decreased resources*, despite a general recognition of the importance of universities to our society. Special problems arise with respect to capital needs, as buildings and equipment are aging and as academic programs generate new requirements. Since information resources generally, and libraries especially, are capital-intensive operations, requiring both buildings and equipment, this becomes a critical factor in predicting their progress during the decade. Furthermore, library automation, academic computing, and telecommunications equipment each represent, not just one-time capital demands, but ongoing commitments in maintenance and replacement. The allocation of diminished resources certainly will delay implementation of even the most evidently desirable services.

Effects of Technology

The effects of technology are dramatic.[3] The continuing increases in functional capabilities, capacities, and speeds of computers, combined with equally spectacular decreases in cost, have revolutionized our entire society, the university as much as any other institution. Today, the microcomputer is ubiquitous in the university, replacing the mainframe in virtually every area of routine and user-managed data processing. At the same time, however, the super-computer is adding new dimensions to research, the conceptualization of problems, and the means for processing overwhelming quantities of data, especially from digitized images.

The capabilities for data acquisition, storage, and display have also spectacularly increased over the past decade. Sensors, scanners, and other means for raw data entry now provide the means for acquiring amounts of data of greater orders of magnitude than ever before. Optical disk formats, such as CD-ROM (Compact Disk–Read Only Memory), and WORM (Write Once, Read Many), and videodisk, have increased our ability to store data, again by several orders of magnitude. Displays now provide resolutions that rival the best of printed pages. Indeed, these areas of technology have recently developed at a pace far greater even than computers.

The growth in telecommunications capabilities has paralleled that of data acquisition, storage, processing, and display. The result is that the data can be transmitted at rates commensurate with the processing capabilities: today, at 100 million bits per second, and tomorrow, even higher.

All this technological development clearly is affecting the university, in regard to both what its faculty and students do and what administrators and librarians must do. What are those effects, and how do we deal with them? To what extent do the objectives of the institution and the units within it depend on each kind of information resource?

Faculty Renewal

There is a strange ambivalence today with respect to faculty. On the one hand, recruitment and retention of faculty is perhaps the most crucial problem faced by universities, both currently and for the coming decade, and especially for the humanities and social sciences; it is exacerbated by the decreased production of Ph.D.s during the 1970s and 1980s.[4] On the other hand, there are increasing incentives for the early retirement of faculty as one response to the current fiscal crisis in the universities.[5] Together, though, they add up to the fact that universities are facing dramatic changes in faculty.

Since libraries, computer facilities, and other kinds of information resources are primary among the means for attracting faculty, the implications are clear: Those institutions that commit resources to collection development, service staff, access services, and information equipment are the ones that will be successful; however, in the context of decreased resources, the tension between these demands and others in the university will be difficult to reconcile.

Student Diversity

There is increasing diversity of students, in age, cultural and ethnic background, and quality of pre-academic preparation.[6] Cultural and ethnic diversity is becoming increasingly important, and universities must respond to it as a major and critical instrument in social response to change. Certainly, as universities respond to this need, new and different demands will be placed on their libraries and other information resources, and they will require new kinds of materials and services.

Academic Program

In the decades following the end of World War II, universities placed steadily increasing emphasis upon research, especially funded research. The result was a shift of institutional priorities from undergraduate teaching to graduate, from teaching at whatever level to research, and from individual research to organized research.

However, that emphasis in academic programs is now undergoing a dramatic change. There has been a reduction in government funding of research, which has not been totally replaced by industrial funding. There are concerns about the quality of undergraduate work and about the incorporation of diversity into the curriculum. As a result, universities face internal pressures in setting priorities among levels of education, undergraduate and graduate alike, and between these levels and research.[7] Indeed, one question is whether graduate education and research will be as intertwined as they have been in the past. Today, however, the balance between undergraduate and graduate education is especially complex, raising questions about what the university is responsible for and what values are contained in what it provides. The implications for libraries and information resources are difficult to assess, but, clearly, they must be considered in future planning.

These tensions are exhibited especially in the reward system for faculty. The almost overwhelming emphasis that has been placed on published research in tenure and promotion decisions is now being questioned, and institutions throughout the country are trying to find means to recognize and reward excellence in teaching.[8]

Changes in the Academic Enterprise

The university itself is continually changing. Even though the labels for departments may be the same today as they were yesterday, the substance is dramatically different. The subjects taught, the means for instruction, and the foci of research all change in response to internal development within each discipline. They also must change in response to external pressures from society—changes in the demography of students, governmental priorities, and the means for funding programs.

Means for Scholarly Communication

Primarily as a result of the impact of technology on publishing, but also in part as a result of changes in the disciplines themselves, changes are occurring in patterns of publication. The new media—including computer databases, on-line database access, electronic mail and facsimile, distribution of data and images in optical disk formats, and desktop publishing—all provide new means for communicating scholarly information. How will they relate to the traditional means? At what pace will they affect the publishers' patterns of distribution? Finally, what changes will they make in the substance of what is communicated?

In this context, some university administrators have felt that publishers, especially of journals, have been making what are perceived as unconscionable profits by selling back to the university information that its faculty has created. However, possessing electronic means for distribution makes it possible for the university to take back the control of scholarly publication.[9]

In a world in which information, in any form, is becoming increasingly important, the university is the institution in which, almost by definition, it is the most important of all. It is the very reason for existence, with the result that it pervades all university operations, demanding an ever-increasing proportion of scarce resources. However, electronic distribution provides a uniform means for control. Instead of dealing with a diversity of forms (print, video and audio, computers, and telecommunications), we can reduce them all to just the one form: electronic.

External Environment

A crucial component of institutional strategic management is the external environment of political, social-policy, legislative, and legal decisions. In chapter 5 these issues will be discussed in detail. Here, we will simply summarize the aspects as they affect institutional management.

Each of these environmental elements is, to some extent, supportive of the interests of the university and research library, but each is also somewhat resistant to those interests. In areas such as copyright, federal policies on access to governmental information, and privatization of government functions, the actions of Congress and the president create the environment within which academic responsibilities must be carried out. These external factors need to be identified, and means must be created by which the university's needs and obligations can be recognized in the political processes that lead to policy decisions at the national and state levels. Recognition should be given in university administration to the need for such strategic planning and political involvement.

However, important though these environmental issues are, universities are unlikely, either individually or collectively, to exert significant influence on them. A most significant generic problem with respect to the external environment is uncertainty resulting from the complex interactions among the factors. The university administrator, the librarian, and the faculty member must make decisions at a time when the technology is rapidly changing, the policies of the publishers are still being formulated, the commitment of library resources has already been largely predetermined, and relevant government policies are subject to the political winds. The result frequently is a "wait and see" attitude and minimal, if any, progress.

ADMINISTRATIVE ISSUES

Administrative Structure

Generally, the university library is well managed, viewed as central to the mission of the university, and possessed of a long history of success. However, the lack of equally strong management control of information resources outside the library should raise, as a paramount strategic concern, the need for an administrative structure for total information resource management. Should the campus establish a czar for information, with operating responsibility for the entire set of resources and facilities? Does the campus subsume the computing facility under library management, or vice versa? Should the film archives, data archives, and the media center be merged into the library?[10]

There are good arguments for any of these alternative and perhaps others. On the one hand, establishing an information czar would be consistent with the view that information resources are essentially substitutable for each other. Placing computing and libraries under one manager makes good sense if the perception is that electronic means for information distribution will become the dominant form in the future. Merging various kinds of libraries and archives makes sense if one looks only at the similarities among media. Indeed, several universities have accepted this view and established positions for vice president for libraries and information resources, chief information officer, or similar titles.

On the other hand, the arguments for distributed management seem equally persuasive. First, the different kinds of information resources require different kinds of management and technical expertise; there is no reason, in principle, to expect that one person will be sufficiently expert in each of them. Second, most information facilities, the library and the central computing facility among them, are already major bureaucracies; there is no reason to expect that there would be returns to scale in combining them. Third, most of the information resources are closely tied to specific academic programs, and the political and operational problems that would be created by combining them in some overall agency far outweigh the advantages to be gained from doing so. Fourth, the acquisition budget of the library must be carefully protected from a wide range of forces that would dissipate it; if the library were to be combined with data archives, film archives, media centers, and the wide range of other resource-acquiring agencies, the result would be a dramatic increase in those pressures.

The facts, though, are that administrative structures reflect the style of the institution rather than the logic of similarities. Where the style is hierarchical, with strong lines of authority, one might expect to find an information czar. However, where the style is distributed decision making, one would expect to find independent administrative units working within a coordinated, cooperative framework.

Among the efforts to deal with administrative structures were those to establish Integrated Academic Information Management Systems (IAIMS).[11] While focused on the medical school, the hospital, and the biomedical library, it also provides a model for the integrated information center concept in academic institutions.

Campus Strategic Planning

Every university should have a continuing process of strategic academic planning. There are innumerable faculty task forces, committees on priorities, and program reviews. There are efforts to obtain data regarding programs and infrastructures, to implement operating policies and processes. Within those efforts, planning for information resources should occupy a central position. Unfortunately, though, all too frequently the library is taken for granted and treated simply as part of the structure.

Personnel Policies

Another concern of campus administration should be appropriate personnel policies. There is a need to assure equity across the range of information professionals: librarians, media specialists, computer staff, and archivists of every kind. The need is especially acute in a decentralized administration, since independent units may otherwise make appointments and promotions that meet the needs of the local unit but are at odds with overall equity, and even with real needs in performance. Some departments will assign tasks to clerical staff and students that require professional competence, while others will use appropriate professional staff. The results are inequity, ineffectiveness, and inefficiency.

Generally, the standards for professional librarians in this respect are quite well established and effectively applied. However, in most universities there are no comparable policies for other categories of information professional. This is an area of administration that needs to be carefully examined in every institution. Important though this problem is, however, few campuses if any will establish personnel policies that deal with it, even though they should.

Investment in Information Activities

Virtually every academic administrator has, at one time or another, seen the library as a fiscal black hole: growing exponentially, needing more and more resources, and requiring new, ever-larger buildings. In some states, construction of new library buildings was absolutely stopped during the 1970s and 1980s, yet university library collections continued to grow. What is to be done?

Now appears the answer to every academic administrator's dream: the promise of electronic distribution of information. Instead of acquiring increasing numbers of books and journals (so many of which appear never to be used), we can get them when we need them, by electronic access. We will no longer need acquisitions budgets, stumble over unused old volumes taking up valuable space, or be forced to build expensive new library buildings.

The facts, though, are that the required investments in technological infrastructure are at least as great as those in the library. Wiring the campus, installing mainframe computers and legions of microcomputers, and dealing with external communications: During the past two decades, these have represented massive investments. Of even greater importance, though, are two further facts: First, the investment in the equipment must be repeated, at about five-year intervals, as it rapidly becomes obsolescent, if not obsolete; manufacturers cease to provide spare parts or adequate maintenance for equipment that no longer is in widespread use. Second, the investment in equipment is only a small percentage of the total costs it engenders (perhaps as little as 20 percent); the remaining 80 percent of costs arise from staff, maintenance, software, application, and space and supporting facilities.[12]

Allocation of Budget

Certainly a primary concern of university management must be the effect of libraries and information resources on the allocation of resources, especially budgets. The proportion of the instructional budget for any given university that historically has been allocated to libraries varies, of course, but percentages around 5–6 percent appear to be typical for public universities in the United States.[13] For the broader context of general information resources, though, estimation is far more difficult since it is not clear what will be included within it; whatever may be included, the actual scope will vary much more widely among universities than it does for libraries, and the budget allocations are less clearly delineated.

Taking information resources most broadly (including libraries, computing facilities, data and film archives, information centers, and telecommunication) the total budgets appear to be about 10 percent of the total university budget, though the allocations are not as clearly delineated nor as easy to determine as they are for libraries. A separate means for estimating the proportionate level of commitment to information resources can be derived from the several grants and contracts to the university; those that explicitly involved creating or directly using information resources as their primary objective are likely to represent over 10 percent of the total number of grants and contracts and nearly 15 percent of the budgets.

What, then, is likely to happen with the percentage of the university budget that will be allocated to information resources during the coming decade? First, with respect to libraries, it seems unlikely that there will be any significant change. The budgets are clearly delineated, easy to see (frequently showing up as the line item second in size only to faculty salaries), and historically subject to tight management control. Even in the face of dramatic inflation in journal prices during the past decade, library budgets have remained at a fairly constant percentage of total budget.[14]

However, with respect to information resources broadly defined, the pressures have become so great that substantial increases are likely during the coming decade. To be specific, consider the following:

- the increasing importance of "information" as a part of society and the economy;

- the specific importance of information resources as a means for attracting and retaining faculty;
- continuing growth in computer use in the university for both research and instruction;
- the need to replace equipment that becomes obsolescent, sometimes within months;
- commitments of expenditures to capital investment in wiring the campus, but with the likelihood of substantial cost overruns, and real increases in operating costs by as much as 25 percent to even 50 percent over initial estimates;
- the need to acquire materials (such as databases, for example) that cannot be covered by the library's acquisition budgets;
- the need for services (such as database access) that cannot be covered by the library's operating budgets;
- growing commitments of staff to running distributed computing facilities and to operations such as desktop publishing; and
- lack of strong management controls and visibility of expenditures for most of the nonlibrary components of information resources.

These all imply substantial increases in commitments of university resources. Estimating the amount is even more problematic, but increases from the present level of, say, 10 percent to as much as 12 percent are likely. Assuming that the library's budget remains at a constant proportion, that would imply nearly a doubling of the percentages for expenditures for the nonlibrary components.

NOTES

1. Research Associates, *State Profiles: Financing Public Higher Education* (Washington, D.C.: Research Associates, September 1991). (See page 92: "Since 1984/85 a steady decline in the percentage of state budgets allocated to public higher education . . . [has been] the chief cause of declining appropriations in real dollars.")

2. Young, Charles, "Unmasking the Budget Crisis," *UCLA Magazine* 4(2) (Summer 1992): pp. 6–7; "With a Large Budget Cut on the Way, UC Weighs All Options for Making Ends Meet," *Notice* (Academic Senate of University of California), 16(8) (June 1992); "Colleges and Universities Are Forced to Make Cuts and Adjustments Due to Harsh Economic Realities," *New York Times*, 3 Feb. 1992, p. A1.

3. Cyert, Richard M. "The Role of Electronic Information in Higher Education," *OCLC Newsletter*, Mar./Apr. 1992, pp. 18–19; Galvin, Thomas J., "Research Library Performance in the Delivery of Electronic Information," *OCLC Newsletter*, Mar./Apr. 1992, pp. 20–21; Garrett, Nina, et al., "Computers in Foreign Language Teaching and Research; A 'New Humanism': Part One," *Educom Review* 25(1) (Spring 1990): 36–49; Garrett, Nina, et al., "Computing in Foreign Language Teaching and Research: Part Two," *Educom Review* 25(2) (Summer 1990): 39–45; Glick, Milton D., "Integrating Computing into Higher Education," *Educom Review* 25(2) (Summer 1990): 35–38; Hockey, Susan, "The Role of Electronic Information in Higher Education: The Faculty

Perspective," *OCLC Academic Libraries Directors' Conference* (Dublin, Ohio: OCLC, 1992); Kiesler, S. B., and Sproull, L. S., (eds.), *Computing and Change on Campus* (New York: Cambridge University Press, 1987); *Technology and the Research Environment of the Future* (Albany, N.Y.: New York State Library, February 1989).

4. Vaughn, Robert C., and Rosenzweig, Robert M., "Heading Off a Ph.D. Shortage," *Issues in Science and Technology* 7(2) (Winter 1991): 66–73; "Ph.D. Supply" (letters), *Issues in Science and Technology* 7(4) (Summer 1991): 22–29; Bowen, Howard R., and Schuster, Jack H., *American Professors—A National Resource Imperiled* (New York: Oxford University Press, 1986); National Research Council, *Biomedical and Behavioral Research Scientists: Their Training and Supply* (Washington, D.C.: NRC, 1989); *The Ph.D. Shortage: The Federal Role* (Washington, D.C.: Association of American Universities, 1990); Hake, R. R., "Ph.D. Supply and Demand," *Science* 249 (1969): 611–12.

5. Lohman, C. K., "Retrenchment, Retirement Benefits, and the Faculty Role," *Academe* 77(3) (May/June 1991): 18–21; Lozier, G. G., "Projecting Faculty Retirement," *American Economic Review* 81(2) (May 1991): 101–5; Walz, T., "Social Work Faculty in Retirement," *Journal of Education for Social Work* 27(1) (1991): 60–72.

6. Astone, Barbara, *Pursuing Diversity: Recruiting College Minority Students* (Washington, D.C.: George Washington University, 1990).

7. Smith, Page, *Killing the Spirit: Higher Education in America* (New York: Viking, 1990); *1992 All-University Faculty Conference on Undergraduate Education* (Berkeley: University of California, February 1992); Pelikan, Jaroslav, "The Storm Breaking upon the University: The University in Crisis," *Key Reporter* 57(4): 2–6.

8. *The Report of the Universitywide Task Force on Faculty Rewards* (Berkeley: University of California Academic Senate, October 1991); " 'Pister' Report Calls for Broader Definition of What Constitutes Proper Work of Faculty," *Notice* (Academic Senate of UC) 16(1) (October 1991): 1, 4; "Many Views, but Little Consensus on Pister Report as Time Nears to Make Decision," *Notice* (Academic Senate of UC) 16(7) (March 1992): 1; "Statewide Senate Cool to 'Pister' Report Proposal," *Notice* (Academic Senate of UC) 16(7) (May 1992); "Agreement Near on Changes in Faculty Rewards Structure," *Notice* (Academic Senate of UC) 16(8) (June 1992): 1, 5–6; "UC Adopts Policy to Place More Emphasis on Teaching," *Los Angeles Times*, 17 July 1992, p. A3.

9. Wilson, David L., "Model Proposed for Management of Information," *Chronicle of Higher Education*, 6 Nov. 1991.

10. Van Houweling, Douglas E., "The Information Technology Environment of Higher Education," *Conference on Information Resources for the Campus of the Future* (Dublin, Ohio: OCLC, 1986); Olsen, Wallace C., *Toward an Integrated Information System* (Ithaca, N.Y.: Cornell University, April 1986); Sidgreaves, Ivan, "The Electronic Campus: Organization Issues," in *The Electronic Campus—An Information Strategy*, ed. Lynn J. Brindley. Proceedings of the Conference in Banbury, England, 28–30 October 1988, pp. 65–80; Brindley, *Libraries and the Wired-up Campus*, "Stanford 'Repositions,' Library Faces Major Cuts," *American Libraries*, May 1990, p. 391; "Budget-Struck Stanford Library Merged with Computer Center," *American Libraries*, October 1990, p. 830; "CIO-Type Positions Meeting Higher Ed Needs for Consolidation," *Manage IT* 1(5) (October 1990): 1, 3–4.

11. *The Management of Information in Academic Medicine*, vol. 2 (Washington, D.C.: Association of American Medical Colleges, 1982); Matheson, Nina W., "Academic

Information in the Academic Sciences Center: Roles for the Library in Information Management,'' *Journal of Medical Education* 57(10) (1982): part 2.

12. Frand, Jason, and Britt, Julia A., *Seventh Annual UCLA Survey of Business School Computer Usage, September 1990* (Los Angeles: University of California at Los Angeles, John E. Anderson Graduate School of Management, 1990; page 9 shows total expenses as divided 26 percent for ''capital investment'' in hardware and 74 percent for operating expenses); Kirwin, William D., *Personal Computing: A Gartner Group Briefing—August 10–12, 1992* (Stamford, Conn.: GartnerGroup, 1992; page 2 shows total expenses as divided 19 percent for capital and 81 percent for labor.

13. *State Profiles*, pp. 202–3. (Combining the data shown in this publication with ARL data for the same year shows a distribution for library expenditures as a proportion of the full instructional expenses strongly clustered around 5 percent to 6 percent.)

14. Gherman, Paul M., ''Setting Budgets for Libraries in the Electronic Era,'' *Chronicle of Higher Education* (August 14, 1991): A36.

5

The Context of Users
and Their Needs

Among the most crucial concerns of strategic management must be the
needs of the community of users. Therefore, in this chapter we turn to
examine the users and their needs, both as individuals and as groups.

GENERAL PRINCIPLES

There is some value in stepping back from the specifics of the academic
library to consider the more generic context of industrial marketing. Any
standard text on marketing will suggest that the start must be an assessment
of the *opportunity* for a potential product or service. Is the environment
appropriate and are there needs to be served? Are there specific strengths
of the organization? Is there customer loyalty and a history of satisfaction?
Finally, is there competition, and is there a potential for market growth?

The General Market for Information

The general picture is one of an expanding market for information services, especially among professionals such as scientists, engineers, lawyers,
medical practitioners, managers, and administrators. It has been estimated
that they spend nearly 60 percent of their time communicating: two-thirds
in talking and listening, one-third in reading and writing.[1]

Twenty percent of the costs they incur are in obtaining documents and
80 percent are in using them, but it has been estimated that direct savings
from use of information are as much as ten times those costs. More important than direct savings, though, are increases in productivity as measured by results produced (reports of research, management publications,

research plans or proposals, oral presentations, consultations, and substantive advice) for the time spent doing the work and preparing such
results. It is clear that professionals who read a great deal are more likely
to have high productivity.[2]

The Role of Libraries

People are using libraries more frequently and intensely now than they
have in the past. They use services now that were not even known in the
mid 1970s, and they are increasingly exposed to new information technology. With better awareness and understanding of information systems,
they are more sophisticated in their expectations and demands on library
and information services. The librarian thus serves as an intermediary,
filling a niche as a source of expertise.

SPECIFICS FOR ACADEMIC LIBRARIES

The academic library supports instruction, research, public service, and,
to some extent, industry. It thus serves an array of constitutencies. The
most important, obviously, are those from within the institution itself:
faculty, students, staff, and administration. Beyond those, however, is a
wide range of external constituencies: commercial information brokers,
industry, the general public, and state and local governments. There are
also commitments to serve other academic institutions, including foreign
universities, other libraries through ILL, and the cooperative bibliographic
utilities (OCLC, RLIN, and WLN [Washington Library Network]). There
are even contractual arrangements to serve publishers, microfilming services, commercial database services, and other sources of information.

As described in discussing the academic enterprise, the communities
being served are continually changing. How should libraries and other
information resources respond to these changes? How do we identify these
programmatic changes and determine what must be done to support them
with adequate information resources? That question has been dealt with
repeatedly—by librarians, administrators, enthusiasts, and even the faculty
themselves.[3]

In this chapter we will consider the perceived needs of the internal
academic users (researchers, teachers, students), both at a pragmatic level,
with emphasis on the most immediate and pervasive kinds of requirements,
and at a speculative level, focusing on the visions of information professionals and enthusiasts. Throughout, there will be a balance of both the
technological tools and the forms of content.

Students

The crucial contribution of academic libraries to students is information literacy: skills in using the library itself, accessing on-line databases, and employing the computer as a tool. In this respect, the university must deal with an increasingly diverse student population. There are complications in their performance and in retention, caused especially by students who have transferred from smaller institutions such as community colleges, which lack the libraries and computing facilities needed for them to gain skills in the use of information resources.[4]

Faculty

The faculty depend on the library as they always have and exhibit the same kinds of differences from discipline to discipline. For the scholar in the humanities, the collection is the laboratory for research, testing hypotheses, and deriving the basic stimulus. For the sciences, it is the source of reference materials and published data.

In the same sense that it may cost $250,000 to set up a scientific lab for a new researcher, it costs to provide library support for a new faculty member. Those costs need to be identified and supported. Indeed, campus administrative policies usually require an assessment of the adequacy of library resources as part of proposals for new academic programs; sometimes, they may ask the same question concerning the appointment of a distinguished new faculty member. Rarely if ever does that assessment conclude that the resources are not adequate; the departments are too anxious to get approval to conclude otherwise. Nonetheless, once the new program or faculty member is in place, the deficiencies begin to appear and the library must respond to the increasing demands.

Now added to the traditional relationships is the increasing faculty interest in searching electronic resources. The library is a major node on the campus network and must provide access to databases that serve faculty needs.

Off-Campus Users

Academic librarians are making access to library information services non-location-specific. This requires a reorientation of staff thinking and a change in job functions and organization. Initial steps to begin, or continue, the transition process in all libraries might include: active promotion of telephone service for reference and document delivery, active promotion of the use of electronic mail for reference and interlibrary loan, and the eventual incorporation of all electronic information services through remote access.

The Problem of Equity

The needs to support faculty research and education differ greatly among fields of study. There are differences among disciplines (including the humanities, social sciences, and physical sciences), between the traditional departments and interdisciplinary groups, and between individual and organized research. Those differences are reflected in the nature of the use made of information resources, the relative importance of monographs and journals, and the relative importance of libraries and computers. The result can be a serious problem of equity among different groups of users, who demand fairness in meeting needs of disciplines.

NEEDS OF ACADEMIC PROGRAMS

Paramount among management concerns is the role of information resources in campus strategic planning. Two major questions to address are: To what extent do the objectives of the institution and of the units within it depend upon each kind of information resource, and What are the needs of the constituencies to be served by the information resources?

Needs for Print Publications

Let us emphasize that print is still an essential medium for scholarship and scholarly communication, but the information technologies and the new media must be considered in planning, not only in their own right, but as essential adjuncts and supplements to the printed formats.

Acquisition of Foreign Materials

In this respect, the acquisition of information materials from foreign nations is a problem that is especially acute with respect to the world's developing countries, which represent large populations and vast geographic areas about which our knowledge is fragmentary at best. Academic interests require active research programs in several areas of concern with respect to developing countries: language and literature, society and economy, agriculture and industry, medicine and health, and the arts and sciences. Furthermore, we should anticipate that the developing countries will become important sources of scientific and technical information, certainly by the end of the decade. The examples of countries like Taiwan and South Korea surely represent what can be expected elsewhere.

The acquisition of foreign materials is of importance within the United States, but it is even more critical in the developing countries themselves. Many governments, businesses, and people in these countries lack adequate knowledge of the information about their own countries and their neighbors, not to mention information about the United States. They have poor or nonexistent means to identify publications, they lack the means for logistical support for modern information technologies, and they do not have a sufficiently large professional information staff to provide adequate information services.

Concentrated efforts need to be undertaken to deal with these problems, especially through cooperative efforts and using the technological tools for acquiring, storing, accessing, and distributing library materials and other forms of information resources.

Beyond Growth, a summary report on language and area studies, identified library and information resources as a crucial problem.[5] It pointed out the shortage of staff with the professional competencies in language plus area studies, on the one hand, and library and information management, on the other. Except for the activities of the three national libraries (the Library of Congress, the National Library of Medicine, and the National Agricultural Library), there is almost no sharing of foreign information resources between government and academic research programs. There is no inventory of foreign materials in library collections, of periodical subscriptions, of federal government information services, nor of the extent to which any of these materials are covered by indexing and abstracting services or online information services. There is no general information concerning availability of foreign information resources from government agencies, nor is there evidence that they use the foreign information resources that are available in university library collections or even are aware of such resources.

Interinstitutional Cooperation

Much of academic research today involves cooperation among multiple institutions. This creates special demands for information support: in communication, use of shared databases, and access to common library materials. Interinstitutional cooperation implies a commitment of resources and, to a significant degree, a loss of independence. It also implies basing some of one's own institutional long-range planning on expectations that others will fulfill their responsibilities.

Interinstitutional cooperation within academic programs will steadily increase during the 1990s. The National Research and Educational Network will play a role, but for some time this will probably be limited to high performance computing. Beyond that, the cooperation largely will depend on the shared use of information resources, through that network perhaps, but primarily through other means such as the interlibrary network.

Some projects will be multinational as well as multi-institutional efforts. Information resources will be important, not only as part of the substance, but also as the basis for the management of such efforts: the development

of international academic computer communication, sharing of library cataloging data, and shared study in specific academic areas. They will draw
on both library and computer resources. This will be significant even in
the humanities, in which such projects have been relatively rare but will
become more and more important.

Project Management

There is a need, therefore, for the means to provide support to the
management of such projects. There needs to be consultant capabilities—
in the computing center, the library, the campus office of contracts and
grants, and the campus administration—to provide support tools for project
management and consultative advice on their use.

Information Resources, Facilities, and Functions

There are needs for activities that will focus on information resources
in support of specific academic programs and, of even more importance,
analysis of the data contained in them. They require professional expertise
in both librarianship and subject-related analyses. These kinds of activities
require support tools in acquisition, in staffing, and in analytical tools. The
result surely will be efforts to establish specialized information centers,
similar to those that were developed, starting in the mid 1960s, in engineering and the sciences but now including the arts, the humanities, and
the social sciences.

Indexing and Abstracting Services

Indexing and abstracting services are the essential support tools for information access, whether in printed form or through on-line access. These
tools are now well developed in the physical and biological sciences, in
engineering, and in the professional fields such as the law and medicine.
They are far less well developed in the humanities and arts.

The production of these tools involves costs greater than a single institution can usually support. The implication is that the community of universities and academic research libraries needs to develop policy positions
that will lead to interinstitutional cooperation or the commitment of national funding to the needs of the humanities and arts.

Library Services

The development of library services as tactical and operational responses
to strategic needs is a continuing requirement. These kinds of activities lie
at the very cutting edge of the transition from planning into implementa-

tion. They are the point at which wishes and hopes are translated into commitments of resources; they are the means by which experiments become realities.

Additional Databases

Several kinds of activities fit within this category of needs. First is the addition of new databases to the on-line public access catalogs, beyond the catalog of the university library itself. Some reflect the addition of data about other kinds of university information resources, while others reflect the acquisition of databases from national producers for ready availability on campus through the OPAC. Each represents the kinds of materials that a single point of access must include.

Reference

There is a need to develop expert systems in reference.[6] They should be easily transportable and made available for libraries for a variety of uses on the in-house local system. There is a need for the conversion of ready-reference files into computer databases at a number of libraries, both on campus and elsewhere.

Inventory of Databases

To the greatest extent possible, the full array of databases available, both through the national networks and on campus, should be identified and the means for access made available through the OPAC. On the campus, these would include databases that are formally acquired, those that are associated with large-scale projects, and those that are maintained by individual faculty members. The strategic objective is to establish the basis on which catalog entries for databases can be incorporated into and made accessible through the on-line public access catalog.

Integration of Library, Computer, and Telecommunications

Libraries, computing facilities, and telecommunications must be integrated with each other, not only on a campus-wide basis, but within the individual major units such as colleges and schools.[7] There is clearly a need within academic programs to ensure that the entire set of information resources works smoothly together. While that does not require, or even imply, single-point management for them, it does require that they each function with conscious awareness of the others, that their parallel development be coordinated, and that policies be established that will encourage effective cooperation. How does one bring together resources with divergent administrative reporting paths? How does one plan buildings and space around coordinated information resources? Finally, how does one manage a diverse array of information professionals in a coordinated set of services?

MORTON COLLEGE LIBRARY
CICERO, ILLINOIS

Fax and Administrative Imaging

It is evident that the fax machine has become a vital tool for communication. If nothing else, it has virtually destroyed policy barriers to international communication. The use of digitized image storage for administrative data files, while outside the narrow scope of academic needs, is worth consideration here as a part of academic strategic planning. The concept is that scanned administrative documents can be stored in electronic form, with automated work assignment and scheduling, automated work-flow control, and automated indexing and file searching.[8] The benefits arise from increased staff productivity, reduced costs for paper handling, improved control, and better response to needs.

This approach is feasible because the supporting technologies are now all in place. The scanners are available and inexpensive; the transmission capacity (now 100 megabit/sec) is operational; the processing power is now widespread, with microcomputers capable of meeting most needs; the software development is well in hand; and the capacity for image storage is available.

The use of this approach is likely when large amounts of data are produced (crowded files, multiple documents, or extensive use of microforms); when data cannot be keyed (for example, drawings, handwritten material, and signatures); when there is a need for frequent access and retrieval (the same information being used by many different people, with frequent inquiries); when extensive processing (multiple-view, complex routing, or decisions) is involved; when the information is critical or errors are costly; and when the organization is amenable (willing to change, able to visualize the benefits, and understanding of the effort required).

EFFECTS OF TECHNOLOGY

The following sections will discuss specifics of the promise of electronic information: for the enthusiast and for the users of information, through digitized imaging and information distribution.

The Promise for the Enthusiasts

In many forums, the enthusiasts have proclaimed, loudly and persuasively, what wonderful changes electronic information will bring, what great new capabilities it will provide, and what an important opportunity it means for the librarian.

The World Brain

Electronic information could bring the concepts of a "world brain" to reality, according to Ted Nelson, with just one record needed for any item of information and with links and pointers among items providing the means for access, assemblage, and use.[9] The enthusiasts think it will provide a new range of opportunities for the use of information technologies, new markets, and new products and services. Indeed, it has been claimed by some that it will completely replace the use of printed paper as a means for the communication and distribution of information.[10] Enthusiasts always conclude, "If the librarian does not grasp this opportunity, someone else will."

Computers in Teaching

Among the most exciting promises for the enthusiast are those related to the potentials for the use of computers in teaching. Several current projects are regarded as both innovative and operational: Perseus (at Harvard), focused on classical Greece; Intermedia (at Brown), on literature; Theoria (at Carnegie-Mellon), on ethics; Chemistry (at Illinois); CIText (in the United Kingdom), on mathematics; Dish (in Glasgow), on history; StrathTutor (at Strathclyde), on bioscience; Leeds (at Leeds), on electrical engineering; and Mens (at Bremen), on nonlinear systems.[11] Much of the rationale for multimedia projects (such as *The First Emperor*, developed by Professor Ching-chih Chen at Simmons, and *Columbus*, developed by IBM) is based on the perception that they will enhance the value of computer uses in teaching.[12]

It must be said, though, that the reality is dramatically different from the hopes and wishes involved in these projects. The investment required to produce an innovative, operational instructional package is far greater than to produce a textbook. The investment involved in multimedia packages, though, is orders of magnitude greater (on the order of entertainment products). The investment by an instructor wishing to use such packages in a course is also very great, far more than it is to use an existing textbook as a required reading and the basis for a syllabus. The problem is that the rewards for those investments simply do not exist, either financially or in academic advancement.

The Promise for the Users

Information Access

Much of the promise of electronic information lies in improved access to information. We see it in the growing use of on-line public access catalogs. That great dying dinosaur, the card catalog (with millions of cards occupying tens of thousands of trays in thousands of square feet of space), is literally disappearing, while banks of OPAC terminals next to it are all fully occupied, sometimes with lines of students waiting.

Given the near-universal use of personal computers, they should be regarded as the means for access that is most readily available and responsive to user needs. As a result, there must be at least minimal standards for interconnection, and availability should be distributed in library facilities. However, it is necessary that operations recognize the sociology of users, the nature of personal computing, the range of work styles, and their need for self-service and self-sufficiency. Specialists and technical consultants are necessary, but expert systems technology may provide the means for supplementing them.

There is an evident need for the ability to produce hard copy, so printers must be widely available. There is also a need for access to centralized library facilities and the means for distributed video output, an optical scanning facility, a fax machine, and optical disk access.

The context in which such interfaces will function is, of course, much wider than the single PC, the local area network (LAN), or even the campus computer network. There are numerous existing multi campus networks, not least being those of OCLC and RLIN, but the future potential lies in the creation of national super networks. Of course, most of the immediate uses will result from the origins of the national network in the interconnection among the super-computer centers and in the applications in large-scale image processing. However, they will create opportunities for collaboration among all kinds of faculty and for access to even larger arrays of resources as well as computing power.

We see it in the steady augmentation of the OPACs with other databases from the individual campuses, ad hoc cooperation among institutions, and national sources. It is the realization of the dream of over twenty years ago, a dream that was temporarily sidetracked by the growth of the national on-line database services but is now becoming economically and operationally a viable alternative: the acquisition of electronic forms of publication by individual research libraries and their use through the library.

Information Processing

The ability to retrieve, analyze, compare and combine, process and manipulate, and communicate is a promise that is far more important than the mere access to information: It is the potential to use it.[13]

There is an increasing use of *personal information managers* that permit the individual to download substantial amounts of data, retrieve those data that are needed most immediately, and establish linkages among them and between them and other sources. We see it in the use of computers by scholars in every discipline for the creation and maintenance of databases intended for data analysis and exploration. The effects of the microcomputer, in particular, have been dramatic in making computer processing an integral part of day-to-day working patterns, even in the humanities and the arts.

Database Development

Throughout the university, faculty are creating databases, but they frequently need help in doing so. Typical needs for consulting support are on features of relevant software, design of database structures, indexing of data files, the availability of source data to be downloaded into personal files, actual downloading of data from external sources, and the copyright and licensing requirements. These clearly represent significant needs which will not only continue, but increase. The use of personal databases, with downloading of data from the national interlibrary network, commercial database services, and CD-ROM files will become standard, with at least 60 percent of faculty using them by the end of the decade.

As we move increasingly into computer-based processing of data, the need to convert existing data sources to digital text (or digital image) form arises across the entire campus. Optical character reading equipment is now well enough developed that it can be used effectively in support of this functional need. Policies need to be established to ensure efficient use of such equipment, including inventory of equipment, announcement of availability, assessment of applicability, and allocation of use.

Expert System Development

Expert systems are defined here as the combination of four component elements: (1) an interface for communication with users in the formulation of queries, (2) a decision tree for determining how to interact between the users and the databases, (3) a generic database to support the decision tree, and (4) a factual database. The evidence of the literature is that this will be an important area of research by faculty of the university in every academic discipline and professional area. The implementation of expert systems in the use of information resources will require professional staff expertise.

Conceptualization

This, in the long run, is the most important promise. It opens up new ways of thinking, conceptualizing, and dealing with needs and with problems. It provides researchers and students with means for stretching the mind, seeing new relationships, and comprehending dimensions far beyond the three or four of our immediate sense of space and time. We will now examine in more detail the promise of digitized imaging, as its role in conceptualization is central.

THE ROLE OF DIGITIZED IMAGES

The increasing use of digitized images in support of research and teaching has created the potential for new means of conceptualization.[14] Insights can be gained from using visual displays, being able to manipulate the images, and having the ability to see many dimensions simultaneously through the use of color, windowing, and multidimensional matrices. The possibility is at hand to provide capabilities for the retrieval of digitized images, individually and as sequences in scenes, based on their visual content.

Uses of Digitized Images

We see an increasing role of digitized images in every discipline, from medicine to engineering, architecture to theatre arts, dance to chemistry, and physics to mathematics. Pictures of the human body, generated by digitized imaging, are now crucial in medical practice as well as in research. Pictures of the earth, generated from satellites, are used in oil exploration, community planning, and agriculture, as well as in geographical research.[15] Pictures of buildings and manufactured parts, generated by computer-aided design, are now part of the tool kit of every kind of creative designer.

Sources of Digitized Images

At least four categories of digitized image data can be identified. The first results from the conversion of source data to digitized image form; this arises in fax transmission, in the preservation of brittle books by conversion to optical disk images, and in the conversion of motion picture film to optical disks. The second derives from the algorithmic production of images, as in computer-aided design, architectural design, and cartooning. The third arises from the use of digitized image storage for administrative data files; while outside the narrow scope of academic needs, it is worth consideration here as part of academic strategic planning. The fourth arises from the monitoring or observation of physical processes; this is illustrated by data from satellites scanning the earth and other planets and includes data from the scanning of persons, as in radiology and neurology.

Operational Problems

The fourth category especially poses monumental problems, as well as having tremendous potential. The problems arise from the amount of data that can be generated in this form: from satellites, instrumentation, publication, and conversion. It exceeds by orders of magnitude the amount that is normally considered a library problem. Nonetheless, all the functional needs (for storage, cataloging, access, and processing) must be dealt with. There should be fundamental research on the organization of such files and on the means for retrieval from them. Almost equally important are administrative concerns about access to the facilities, resources, and equipment needed to acquire such data and to analyze it: spectral analyzers, monitors, super-computers, and communication lines to them. Indeed, primary among the supporting equipment are super-computers, which are needed because the volume of processing required for the use of digitized images exceeds the capacity of even very large mainframes.

THE CHANGES IN INFORMATION DISTRIBUTION

Desktop Publishing

Throughout the university, there is clear evidence of the need to support desktop publishing. From the perspective of a faculty member, there are evident values in the speed of getting material into distribution and in control of the end product. The most significant evidence of need is the dramatic increase in the use of microcomputer-based word processing by faculty. In the late 1980s, perhaps 30 to 40 percent of faculty were using this technology, whereas today, the figure is certainly above 90 percent.[16] In the 1990s, it will be a rare faculty member who does not have and actively use a microcomputer for processing, and all students will be required to do so.

Desktop publishing is by no means as widespread as is word processing, however. Today, perhaps 5 percent of faculty use it. Current estimates are that desktop publishing nationally will grow at about 40 percent per annum. From the existing base of use by faculty, by the year 2000 that kind of growth should make it as universal as simple word processing is today.

There are problems that desktop publishing implies: From the perspective of departmental administration, the management of resources and the potential workload in a highly labor-intensive operation are quite worrisome problems. With all due respect to the virtues of the computer, data entry, formatting and design, editing, preparing for production, and final publication all require major efforts. It can be consuming of faculty time (as long as they find it stimulating enough to do themselves) and consuming of support staff and resources (after the faculty loses interest). From the perspective of a campus administrator, the problems are likely to be monumental.

Beyond these institutional concerns, there are even larger problems in control. Indeed, *desktop publishing* is virtually an oxymoron that confuses the real role of the publisher with that of the printer. There are problems in quality control, ensuring a publishable product, and marketing and distribution. However, most important are the scholarly aspects of control: refereeing, reviewing, and assuring integrity of reference.

In the coming decade, the problems created by desktop publishing will become increasingly severe, with no clear means for solving them, and the pace of its actual use will not increase at the rate currently anticipated.

Electronic Manuscripts

There is increasing importance in the use of electronic manuscripts because of the benefits they provide to publication and postpublication processing. The Association of American Publishers (AAP), recognizing the increasing use by authors of microcomputer-based word processing, carried out a project to establish standards for encoding electronic manuscripts to facilitate the communication between authors, publishers, and printers. In 1985 they reported that the percentage of authors writing manuscripts electronically had increased from 20 percent in 1980 to 60 percent in 1983, and projected a figure of 80 percent in 1985.[17] In fact, even by 1983, over 75 percent of dissertation authors used electronic means. Even the publishers saw increases in the percentage of authors writing in electronic forms, from 10 percent in 1980 to 30 percent in 1983, and projected a figure of 50 percent in 1985.

The purpose of the Electronic Manuscript Project of the AAP was to establish standards and guidelines to facilitate the use of electronic manuscripts. The resulting standards are based on a process of identifying elements of documents (such as paragraphs, headings, and emphases) without specifying the ultimate means by which they will be presented. Standard Generalized Markup Language (SGML) is a formal language for the definition of such document structures.[18]

The standards recognize the requirements at each stage in the process of developing, editing, and publishing: from author to editor and publisher and then to conversion to the printed form. They accommodate the array of document types, structural elements within them (such as equations, tables, graphics), and data needed, not only for publication but for other uses as well (such as bibliographic access).

Electronic Mail and "Invisible Colleges"

There is an increasing use of electronic mail (E-mail), with all its conferences, and even electronic junk, and of fax machines. These are uses that transcend international boundaries, providing the means for instant communication without barriers of time, space, or bureaucracy. They have their problems, but they are nonetheless excellent answers to immediate needs.

It is evident, after even a cursory examination, that electronic mail is becoming a crucial means for communication between researchers in narrowly focused disciplinary areas. For example, most of the debate on cold fusion took place on electronic bulletin boards. However, there is a rather difficult issue, which may be exceptionally complicated, in the increasing use of electronic mail for scholarly communication: More and more of the substance of research may never appear in the journals that heretofore have been the open formal record of the results. It is true that communication from one researcher to another, by mail or by phone, has long been the most direct means for getting immediate results. In the past, however, the journal article was regarded as the essential means for more general distribution. Now we are seeing the on-line electronic journal supplementing, and perhaps even replacing, the printed journal. This has an immediate effect on the library's commitment to open access to information.

From the standpoint of scholarship, this process clearly facilitates communication among a small peer group. A similar effort was carried out by the National Institutes of Health (NIH) from 1961 through 1967 to establish what they called information exchange groups (IEGs) as formalized "invisible colleges" to facilitate rapid communication within those groups. Over 3,600 researchers participated in seven groups, and over 2,500 preprints were distributed among them during the six-year program.[19] Controversy arose around the program, however, as many scientists argued that the improved effectiveness in communication is heavily outweighed by the inherent limitations.[20] The peer group is by no means the only, or even the most appropriate, context for research progress and, especially, evaluation. Research should be of importance beyond the limits of the peer group; it should be subject to evaluation and assessment by other minds and other tests of validity. The cold, clear light of day needs to enter, but the invisible college, by its very mode of operation, prevents that kind of "sunshine" effect.

Another inherent danger in the invisible college, and especially so in the electronic modes of communication (though less so in the printed forms of desktop publishing) is the likely loss of *integrity of reference*. Scholarly communication has built up an important tradition of citation. It reflects the fact that in all areas of research—the humanities, natural sciences, and social sciences—we progress by building on the past. Moreover, we acknowledge our debt to the past by citation to it. By doing so, we assure that our sources can be checked, verified, and validated.

However, that implies that material so referenced and cited must be available for checking, verifying, and validating. What happens if the source data has been erased or, worse yet, altered since it was used? The entire structure for scholarly progress would collapse. That danger is very real when we deal with electronic publication. In fact, changes in distributed databases are common, even among those that are formally published.

On-line Electronic Journals

There is a slow but steady development of scholarly communication through electronic mail. Some has been formalized as electronic journals, though most is still informal. The most recent is the *Online Journal of*

Current Clinical Trials, produced by the American Association for the Advancement of Science, with OCLC serving as the distributor.[21]

NOTES

1. Carroll, Bonnie, and King, Donald W., "Value of Information," *Drexel Library Quarterly* 21 (Summer 1985): 39–60.

2. Ibid.

3. Akers, John F. "Two Visions and the Challenge for Higher Education," *Educom Review* 24(4) (Winter 1989): 12–18; Balestri, Diane, "Educational Uses of Information Technology," *Educom Review* 24(4) (Winter 1989): 7–9; Bok, Derek, "Looking into Education's High-Tech Future," *Harvard Magazine*, May/June 1985, pp. 29–38 (also published in *Educom Bulletin*, Fall 1985, pp. 2–17); Brown, Rowland C. W., "Brushstrokes in Flight: A Strategic Overview of Trends in Technology in Higher Education,"in *The Electronic Campus—An Information Strategy*, ed. Lynn J. Brindley. Proceedings of the Conference in Banbury, England, 28–30 October 1988, p. 22–41; Cyert, Richard M., "The role of electronic information in higher education," *OCLC Newsletter*, Mar./Apr. 1992, pp. 18–19; Galvin, Thomas J., "Research Library Performance in the Delivery of Electronic Information," *OCLC Newsletter*, Mar./Apr. 1992, pp. 20–21; Gardner, Nigel, "Bringing the Electronic Campus to Reality: Opportunities and Challenges in Teaching," in *The Electronic Campus—An Information Strategy*, ed. Lynn J. Brindley, proceedings of the Conference in Banbury, England, 28–30 October 1988, p. 5–12; Gilbert, Steven W., and Green, Kenneth C., "New Computing in Higher Education," *Change*, May/June 1986, pp. 33–50; Lynch, Clifford, "The Melvyl System: Looking Back, Looking Forward," *DLA Bulletin* 12(10) (Spring 1992): 3–5; Machovec, George S., "Locally Loaded Databases in Arizona State University's Online Catalog Using the CARL System," *Information Technology and Libraries* 8(2) (June 1989): 161–69; Morton, Herbert C., and Price, Anne Jamieson, "The ACLS Survey of Scholars: Views on Publications, Computers, Libraries," *Scholarly Communication* 5 (Washington, DC: Office of Scholarly Communication and Technology, 1986); Olsen, Wallace C., *Toward an Integrated Information System* (Ithaca, N.Y.: Cornell University, April 1986); Perrault, Anna H., "Humanities Collection Management—An Impressionistic/Realistic/Optimistic Appraisal of the State of the Art," *Collection Management* 5(3–4) (1983): 1–23; Thompson, James, *The End of Libraries* (London: Bingley Press, 1982); Van Houweling, Douglas E., "The Information Technology Environment of Higher Education," in *Conference on Information Resources for the Campus of the Future* (Dublin, OH: OCLC, 1986).

4. Konopasek, Katherine, and O'Brien, Nancy Patricia, "Undergraduate Periodical Usage: A Model of Measurement," *Serials Librarian* 9(2) (1984): 65–74; Terwiliger, Gloria, "Evaluating the Role of the Learning Resource Centre," *Community and Junior College Libraries* 1(4) (1983): 23–32.

5. Hodge, Stanley P., and Ivins, Marilyn, "Current International Newspapers: Some Collection Management Implications," *College and Research Libraries* 48(1) (1987): 50–61; Lambert, Richard D., *Beyond Growth: The Next Stage in Language and Area Studies* (Washington, D.C.: Association of American Universities, 1984).

6. Lancaster, F. W., and Smith, Linda C. (eds.), *Artificial Intelligence and Expert Systems: Will They Change the Library?* (Urbana-Champaign: University of Illinois at Urbana-Champaign, Graduate School of Library Science, 1992); Richardson, John, Jr.,

"Toward an Expert System for Reference Service: A Research Agenda for the 1990s," *College and Research Libraries*, March 1989, pp. 233–48; Sedelow, Sally Yeates, and Sedelow, Walter A., Jr., "Artificial Intelligence, Expert Systems, and Productivity," in *Psychology and Productivity*, ed. Paul Whitney (New York: Plenum, 1989), pp. 51–66.

7. Frand, Jason L., *The Microcomputerization of Business Schools* (Los Angeles: University of California at Los Angeles Graduate School of Management, 1987).

8. Bair, James H., "The Integrated Future of Image Management," *Imaging and Information Consultant* 1(2) (March/April 1991): 3–5.

9. "Hypertext Update," *SIGOMET Education and Training Newsletter* 1(7) (August 1989): 1, 3; Nelson, Theodor H., *Literary Machines: The Report on, and of, Project Xanadu Edition 87.1* (San Antonio, Tex.: T. H. Nelson, 1987); Kolitsky, Michael A., "Constructing a Science Center in the Age of Hypermedia," *Computers in Life Science Education* 8(2) (February 1991): 9–13.

10. Lancaster, F. Wilfrid, *The Dissemination of Scientific and Technical Information: Toward a Paperless System* (Champaign: University of Illinois, Graduate School of Library Science, 1977); Lancaster, F. W. "Whither Libraries? or, Wither Libraries," *College and Research Libraries* 39(5) (Sept. 1978): 345–57; Lancaster, F. W. "The Paperless Society Revisited," *American Libraries*, Sept. 1985, pp. 553–55.

11. Self, John (ed.), *Artificial Intelligence and Human Learning: Intelligent Computer-Aided Instruction* (London: Chapman and Hall, 1988); Lancashire, Ian, and McCarty, Willard, *The Humanities Computing Yearbook, 1988* (Oxford: Clarendon Press, 1988; this book provides a superb review of all aspects of computers in the humanities, with special emphasis on instructional applications); Ito, Russell, "Big Media on Campus," *MacUser* 5(9) (Sept. 1989): 50 (concerning Intermedia); Ess, Charles, "Intermedia," *Computers and the Humanities* 24(4) (August 1990): 324–30; Van Tuyl, Laura, "To Ancient Greece via Computer (Perseus Database, an Electronic Library)," *Christian Science Monitor* 83(101) (19 April 1991): 13.

12. "Simmons Project Tracks Treasures of Qin Dynasty with New Technology," *American Libraries*, March 1986, p. 215; Chen, Ching-Chih, "CD-Interactive: What is Coming Out from the Pipelines?" *Microcomputer Information Management* 7 (Sept. 1990): 243–52; *The First Emperor of China* (video disk) (Santa Monica, California: The Voyager Company, 1991); "Information Technology: Video Disks Offer a Detailed Portrait of Qin, the First Chinese Emperor," *The Chronicle of Higher Education* 38 (22) (Feb. 5, 1992): 1.

13. Meadows, Jack A., "Higher Education and the Influence of Information Technology: Research," in *The Electronic Campus—An Information Strategy*, ed. Lynn J. Brindley. Proceedings of the Conference in Banbury, England, 28–30 October 1988, pp. 28–31. Table 5.1 reports the distributions for uses made of computers, as outlined in these proceedings.

14. Maguire, Carmel, et al., *Image-based Information and the Future of Academic and Research Libraries* (Sydney, Australia: University of New South Wales, 1991); Lesk, M., "Image Formats for Preservation and Access," *Information Technology in Libraries* 9(4) (1991): 300–308; "Joint Project Sends Images at High Speed," *The Australian*, May 21, 1991; Leeuwenburg, Jeff, et al., "Electronic Imaging: Systems R&D, and Collection Building at RMIT," *Australian Academic and Research Libraries*, September 1991; *ILIAD Newsletter* (ILIAD is the telelibrary pilot project at the Royal Melbourne Institute of Technology).

15. *Survey Report on the Literature of Digital Image Management and Administration*

Table 5.1
Distributions for Uses of Computers

Activity	Physical Sciences	Social Sciences	Humanities & Arts
Word processing	58%	63%	62%
Data analysis	55	53	25
Storage of data	42	48	48
Data collection	40	17	24
Searching	28	15	22
Personal databases	18	30	26

to Preserve the Sense of Earth from Space (Washington, D.C.: National Commission on Libraries and Information Science (NCLIS), August 1984); Miller, David C., *Moving Information: Graphic Images on CD-ROM* (Benicia, Calif.: DCM Associates, prepared for the Fred Meyer Charitable Trust, March 1987).

16. "Data view (percentages of users using the popular PC applications): Word processing, 58%; Database, 48.9%; Spreadsheet, 46.2%; Accounting, 24.3%; Electronic Mail, 13.2%; CAD, 9.2%; Desktop Publishing, 8.7%; Graphics, 7.9%" (*Computerworld*, December 11, 1989, p. 57).

17. *AAP Electronic Manuscript Series: Standard for Electronic Manuscript Preparation and Markup: An SGML Application Conforming to International Standard ISO 8879—Standard Generalized Markup Language*, version 2.0, rev. ed. (Washington, D.C.: Association of American Publishers, 1989), including *Author's Guide to Electronic Manuscript Preparation and Markup, Markup of Mathematical Formulas, Markup of Tabular Material*, and *Reference Manual on Electronic Manuscript Preparation and Markup*.

18. Smith, Joan M., *The Standard Generalized Markup Language and Related Issues* (Dover, N.H.: Longwood Publishing Group, 1986).

19. Albritton, Errett C., "NIH's Former 'IEG' Program of Quick Communication," *Bulletin of the American Physical Society*, ser. 2 13(1) (29 January 1968): 31.

20. Abelson, Philip H., "Information Exchange Groups" (editorial), *Science* 154(3750) (11 November 1966): 727; "Publishing without Review" (letter), *Science* 155(3758) (6 January 1967): 34; "International Statement on 'Information Exchange Groups' " (letter), *Science* 155(3767) (10 March 1967): 1195–96; "Publishing in Valid Media" (letter), *Science* 155(3769) (24 March 1967): 1497.

21. *Guide to Using Graph-Text, a Document Retrieval System for Scientific Journals*, prelim. ed. (Dublin, Ohio: OCLC, August 1986); "New Online Journal to Speed Publication of Peer-Reviewed Reports on Clinical Trials of Medical Treatments," *OCLC Update*, October 1991, p. 1; Jul, Erik, "Graph-Text Project Provides Basis for Online Journal," *OCLC Update*, October 1991, p. 1.

6

The Context of the Environment

Issues of strategic management that are external to the institution are the least controllable, the most uncertain, and potentially the most dramatic in their effects. This chapter provides an audit of the external environment within which the library and the institution function. It reviews elements of the current milieu: social policy (including political, legislative, and legal issues), technology, commercial and industrial issues, suppliers, cooperative networks, and potential competitors.

SOCIAL POLICY

In areas such as copyright, federal policies on access to government information, and privatization of governmental functions, the actions of Congress and the president create the environment within which academic responsibilities must be carried out. These external factors need to be identified and means created by which the university's needs and obligations can be recognized in the political processes that lead to policy decisions at the national and state levels.

Intellectual property rights, accessibility of information, and public sector–private sector interactions all have a dramatic impact on the university's ability to carry out its responsibilities, but the university has minimal effect on them. It is important to note here that they tend to be treated as "problems for the library," but they really are problems for the institution; generally, the library deals with them successfully.

Copyright

Intellectual property rights are of twofold importance to the academic community: as creators and users of copyrighted material. Indeed, the principle of duality is explicit in the constitutional provision (Article I, Section 8) on which copyright legislation is based: "To promote the progress of science and useful arts, by securing for limited times . . . the exclusive rights to their respective writings and discoveries." The development of policies to deal with those rights is a matter of current concern in universities throughout the country. Copyright legislation explicitly exempts libraries from liability for copyright infringement by readers provided notices are posted on the copying machines that alert the readers of their obligations to conform to fair use practices.[1] The impact of technological developments on copyright, though, continues to complicate the strategic situation for libraries.[2]

Model Policies on Copyright

A survey was sent to all ARL and Association of American Universities (AAU) institutions, in each case to both the library and the university's legal counsel.[3] The resulting replies became the basis for a new SPEC Kit distributed by the ARL.[4] Overall, the policies seem to be less protective of the rights to use copyrighted materials than they are intended to avoid litigation. One of the revealing facts was the minimal role played by faculty in the formulation of these policies, despite the crucial effect they have on teaching and research.

Copyright may not be, as it once was, an immediately rancorous issue. The data clearly demonstrated that library photocopying is not, and never has been, a significant factor in the reduction of a publisher's sales. However, for years the library community was subjected to attack, both verbally and through legal avenues. It was used as the "stalking horse" for the publishing community to deal with much more vital and significant effects of industrial photocopying, and the ill will shown by the publishers still rankles.

Leaving aside those residual feelings, though, there are issues of current and future importance in balancing the imperatives of the university—the necessity of open access to information for both research and teaching with needs to protect the economic interests of the publishers and distributors of information packages. How should university policies be determined? If protection from litigation is the determinant, it will seriously erode the ability of the university to fulfill its own mission. These are needs of at least as much import as protection of copyright.

Recent Court Decisions

The "look and feel" decision significantly extended the scope of copyright with respect to software, allowing the coverage of concepts underlying structure and user interfaces as well as the actual realization of those concepts.[5] Action was brought for the infringement of copyright for a computer spreadsheet program. The District Court held that the menu command structure of the computer program, including the choice of command terms, the structure and sequence of those terms, their presentation on the screen, and the long prompts, was copyrightable.

Severe limitations were placed on the fair use of unpublished materials by at least two other court decisions.[6] They arose from the use of such materials in biographies of J. D. Salinger and L. Ron Hubbard, respectively. Bills were thereupon introduced in Congress in 1990 and reintroduced in 1991 to make it clear that Section 107 of Title 17 of the Copyright Law "applies equally to unpublished as well as published works" (from the title to the bill).[7]

Extension in Application

A bill was introduced in the Senate in 1989—S. 1198, The Visual Artists Rights Act of 1989—"to protect the rights of artists who create single copies or limited editions of . . . works" (from the title to the bill). It embodied so-called moral rights provisions that were intended to establish rights to prohibit intentional distortion, mutilation, or destruction of art works.[8] Part of the objective was to bring U.S. copyright law into closer conformity with international copyright law, in which there is such recognition, especially in civil law countries (basically deriving from the Napoleonic Code). The Berne Convention requires its member countries to make available certain minimal moral rights.[9]

Government Information

A most central and critical issue in recent years has been the divergence in views concerning government information. The Public Sector/Private Sector Task Force for the National Commission on Libraries and Information Science examined these issues from 1970 through 1972; recommendations from the report of that task force are still applicable to the situation today.[10]

The principle underlying those recommendations was that information, from any source generally, but in particular from the federal government, should be readily, easily, and widely available. Libraries and private sector companies wishing to acquire and provide access to those data, to market and distribute them, to add value to them in packaging or processing, or to combine them with other data should find it easy to do so. The investment made by the government should be regarded as a national capital investment, with prices set to encourage, rather than discourage, its use. By making government information readily available and by pricing it at the lowest possible level (covering just the cost of access and reproduction), that result could be expected.

In the years since that report, the policies of government have perverted the recommendations. Of special concern are three specific policy directions: One is pricing, the second is reduction in availability, and the third is "privatization."

Pricing

Libraries have seen the prices of government information skyrocket, even when it is obtained directly from the government. Indeed, some forms of data have been priced at levels that make it impossible for libraries to acquire them. In parallel, there have been increasing limits placed on the availability of information, by whatever means and at whatever price, from the federal government.[11]

Restrictions on Open Access to Information

During the 1980s, the policies of the executive branch of the federal government were to reduce the access to and availability of information of virtually every kind: from scientific and technical to economic and demographic. The effects on libraries and other information organizations have been so severe that the professional associations have felt forced to take stands. The Information Industry Association, the Medical Library Association, the Association of Law Libraries, and the Association of Research Libraries have all come out with official policy statements of concern about federal restrictions.[12] The restrictive policies not only affect the information provided, they stifle scholarship as well. The *Handbook of Labor Statistics, International Economic Indicators, Federal Statistical Directory, Vital Statistics of the United States, American Education*, and electronic databases have all been affected.[13] Beyond that have been conscious efforts at the control of information, film censorship, and even efforts at disinformation. The policy has been characterized as "less access to less information by and about the U.S. government" by the American Library Association (ALA).[14]

Governmental Barriers

Import-export restrictions, taxation policies, bureaucratic procedures, and restrictions on access to governmental information are all examples of governmental barriers. Many of these are subject to the winds of politics, but others, such as import-export restrictions, are built into not only governmental policy, but national economic structures.

Privatization

A matter of deepest concern is the pressure to force the privatization of federal government activities of all kinds, and information activities—even federal libraries—in particular.[15] We see the effects in the contracts that make federal government information available only through single-source private sector companies, which can set prices at levels that are totally irrational when compared to the costs of accessing and copying.[16] The result for libraries is a further reduction in the availability of federal government information. At the same time, the commercialization and privatization of government information has led to other means of control, as federal agencies have pressed database firms as well as libraries to curb access to sensitive information.[17]

Library of Congress Licensing

Given the rhetoric about privatization and the importance of private sector interests, the initiatives of the Library of Congress (LC) have been somewhat surprising. The most recent was the attempt to restrict and control access by imposing a licensing requirement on the use of LC cataloging data.[18] It was ambiguously worded, would require extensive record keeping, flew against the principle of free dissemination of government information, and failed to recognize that academic libraries contribute to MARC records via CONSER (the serials data conversion project called Cooperative Online Serials), NCCP (the National Cooperative Cataloging Program), and similar organizations.

National Research and Education Network (NREN)

On the positive side, though, has been the effort to make generally available the National Research and Education Network (NREN).[19] This was created initially to facilitate access to the network of supercomputers throughout the nation. That access, though, required such a high bandwidth for communication that there was more than enough capacity to absorb all present usages for scholarly communication. Hence, the network is intended to make that capacity more generally available. On technical grounds, there are no problems in doing so, though there are potential problems in reliability and response time as the number of users increases. From the political and economic standpoint, though, the problems are almost overwhelming. If the debates of a decade ago about public sector–private sector relationships were difficult, those concerning NREN will be even more so.

From the academic library perspective, connectivity through the Internet, and eventually through NREN, is seen as critical. While there will be problems in reliability and accessibility, for most users of library services, those will simply be part of normal operations in the use of E-mail.[20] On the other hand, for operational services in the academic library, the problems are likely to be far too great to warrant the minor cost savings involved.

TECHNOLOGY

It hardly seems necessary at this point to comment on the role of information technologies in modern information distribution. They pervade
every aspect of library operations and services; computer facilities embody
them; and other kinds of information facilities either use them or represent
them. There is a need to consider the changes occurring with computers,
as they become ever more capable, smaller, and yet less expensive. The
changes occurring in data storage, in data input and output, and in data
communication all need to be considered.[21]

Pace in Development

Figure 6.1 outlines the expected pace in development over the decades
in each of the major categories of technology.[22]

Implementation

Interaction among these technologies is occurring at several different
levels and on a variety of machines to support a variety of user needs.
Likely stages in their implementation would appear to be:

1990–1994: Mainframes still key, but increasing implementation of microcomputer based local area networks; servers supporting use of
local CD-ROM files;

1992–1996: Increasing use of high performance microcomputers as distributed, object-oriented, specialized servers; reusable optical disks
common;

1994–1998: Low-cost, high-resolution flat screens; fiber optics;

1996–2000: Optical disk digital libraries integrated into workstations.

User Interfaces

The number of work stations, especially those that are microcomputer-
based in local area networks, is expected to increase at 40 percent to 60
percent per annum. Furthermore, in the 1990s, the processing power they
provide will be an order of magnitude greater than it is now, as will the
quality of display and print output and the data communication rates.
Moreover, the local storage capacities will be at least an order of magnitude
greater.

The near-universal implementation of local systems means that information services can be available on-line and remotely. Locations for access
to library information services can include the faculty office, the laboratory,
the home, and the student dormitory. This may require a reorientation of
staff thinking and a change in job functions and organization.

Figure 6.1
Pace in Development of Technologies

	1970	1980	1990	2000
Processor Technologies	Mainframes, Minis	Micros, Fault tolerant	Supermicros, Highly parallel, Transputer	5th generation, Optical
Storage Technologies	Mag tape/disk	Winchester	Optical, Video disk, Optical card	Digital audio, Erasable optical, Digital paper
Human Interface	Menu/command	Icons, Pull-down	Common command language, Expert systems	Natural language
Human input	Keyboard, Joystick, Lightpen, Touchscreen	OCR	Intelligent OCR, Specific Voice	Generic Voice
Output	Monochrome	Color	Windows, Graphics, Laser printers	Hologram
Workstations	Intelligent terminal	PC workstations	CAD/CAM station	Expert System
Software	Specialized	Structured design	Application generators, CASE, Very high level languages	
Telecomm	Twisted pairs, COAX, Microwave, Satellite, Fiber optics, Packet networks	LAN	Bypass, Cellular, Metro Area Nets	Packet radio, ISDN, Space platform
Applications	Algorithm	Some heuristics, Networking	Special Expert, Knowledge based, Hypermedia	Machine trans, Non-text retrieve

| 1970 | 1980 | 1990 | 2000 |

To effect such remote service requires that there be easy user interfaces.[23] Too often, local systems, even when acceptable to library staff, are difficult for the user. Expert system intelligence, providing ease of use for the end user, can best be done at the workstation level. *Hypertext* is a prime example, with much speculation about the dramatic changes it will make in the means for access to information (though it must be said that the rhetoric appears to be largely a "hype," with little sense of reality to it).[24]

As a result, more emphasis should be placed on the development of intelligent microcomputer interfaces and microcomputer integration as the foundation for the scholar workstation. Microcomputers should be purchased for new installations and as replacements for existing terminals when required. Library systems or computer center staff should develop local microcomputer-based software for distribution to the campus community to assist users in maximizing the use of available information resources and provide for navigation among both the campus and remote services. Local system vendors should be as concerned about user interface issues as they are about technical aspects of their systems, and systems designers must think of the user as they develop automated systems for libraries.

Problems

Infrastructure

In the developing countries, the lack of an adequate infrastructure, including communications, logistical support, and availability of consultation services, is an almost insurmountable barrier. While this may have less significance for the United States or the United Kingdom, it is important to recognize the problem even in advanced economies.

Standards

Failure to conform to standards or, in some cases, a lack thereof, is a second technological barrier. These are exemplified by departures from international MARC, from standard character codes, and from standard programming languages.

Meeting Goals

Failure to meet stated goals in technological development, with respect to both time of delivery and functional capabilities, has been a continuing problem. Clearly, it presents a barrier to future development that depends on the availability of a particular technology.

Closed Systems

Commitment to closed systems has been a most serious technological barrier. The producers of such systems have the evident objective of creating captive markets, but the result is a barrier to all future development, except that which the producers are willing to implement.

COOPERATIVE PROGRAMS

The library community has a long tradition of cooperation. It is represented by interlibrary loan, the development of cooperative cataloging through the Library of Congress and the bibliographic utilities (OCLC, RLIN, and WLN), the Center for Research Libraries depository center, the preservation program, and a wide range of consortia and networks.

These cooperative enterprises have value, as represented by the sharing of resources through interlibrary loan, but they also have costs, both financial and in the resulting loss of institutional prerogatives.

Management of Cooperative Programs

Primary among the costs are those involved in management. Of course, the largest portion is normal costs of operational and tactical management. However, beyond the normal costs are those involved in management of cooperative enterprises. Each of the bibliographic utilities has extensive mechanisms for input from participants to the management process, some of which are not only expensive directly but also involve exceptional commitments of time from the participants.[25]

Integration of Resources

Cooperative efforts require means for identifying materials. To a major extent, of course, that need is met by the bibliographic utilities, as will be discussed. Frequently, however, independent capabilities have been created, especially to link libraries within states. Examples would be the MELVYL system of the University of California, the Colorado Association of Research Libraries (CARL) system, and the Ohio Network. The increase in cooperation among the academic libraries in each state and the negotiation of statewide contracts were significant results.[26] Some forecasters look toward compilations of larger, regional groups.

Funding for Access and Interlibrary Loan

The historic pattern was for ILL to be treated as a reciprocal good, even though it was recognized that a few institutions were substantial net lenders. As a result, the practice was not to charge for lending services. Beyond that, there are large numbers of reciprocal agreements in which libraries formally agree not to charge the participating institutions for ILL services.

ILL statistics now show increases at about 10 percent a year, however, so there is great pressure to change the historic pattern, given the resulting magnitude of cost.[27] As one step toward that objective, the ARL (in cooperation with the Research Libraries Group [RLG]) has just conducted another survey of costs for ILL operations.[28] While those results are not yet available, estimates (presented in chapter 9 of this book) suggest that total costs are on the order of $30 to $35 per filled ILL request (two-thirds of that being within the borrowing library and one-third within the lending institution).

Where charges have been instituted, a typical charge is $5 per article if there is no reciprocal agreement. It has been suggested that the bibliographic utilities provide an automatic charge, such as $10 per item, for

ILL requests processed through their services, in addition to their own fees and as a credit to the lending institution. As the burden increases, though, even a fee at that level may not be sufficient to control the proliferation of ILL requests. Commercial document delivery may then become the option of choice.

THE BIBLIOGRAPHIC UTILITIES

Changing Roles

Retrospective Conversion

The several bibliographic utilities (OCLC, RLIN, and WLN) were started with several roles in mind but with one—sharing the costs of retrospective conversion of catalog data—as the initial priority. They have served that function well, to the point that use of them for that purpose by U.S. libraries is steadily declining. That role, while not disappearing, is certainly less important than it was.[29]

Access to Current Cataloging

Complementary to that role was to provide access to current cataloging both as available from the Library of Congress (as the primary national center for cataloging production) and from interlibrary cooperation. That role continues to be important, though there is an increasing array of alternative sources: CD-ROM versions, tapes available directly from the Library of Congress for mounting on the local system, and data available from other libraries through a number of ad hoc networks.

Surrogate for Local Catalogs

Another role, at least in the perception of some libraries, was to serve as an interim substitute for a local automated catalog. This surely underlay the motivation for including in some of the utilities records that were library specific rather than generic. Now, though, with local systems operating in virtually every academic library, that role is surely disappearing.

National Union Catalog

Perhaps the most comprehensive role of the bibliographic utilities was to serve as the national union catalog, bringing to reality the dream of Charles Jewett of the mid-nineteenth century.[30] A national bibliographic database greatly improves the capability of libraries to share resources and to make effective decisions concerning the acquisition, storage, and preservation of materials. Today, we see increasing emphasis placed on access instead of acquisition; this functional objective, therefore, becomes one of predominant importance.

Even this role, though, is being questioned, as some argue that net-worked interconnections among local systems can serve as a virtual national bibliography, permitting libraries to bypass the utilities. Such substitution is fraught with difficulties, though, and is unlikely to reduce the utilities' central role.

Support to Reference Services

This has become an added role for the utilities. It is based on the es-tablished relationships with libraries, the communication networks and data access systems that are now available to provide access to a wide range of databases, and the means for easy interconnection between the utilities and the local systems in academic libraries. This role serves as a broad base for maintaining the viability of the bibliographic utilities and for their support, especially when combined with document delivery services.[31]

Electronic Publication

The venture of OCLC into electronic publication, made in association with the American Association for the Advancement of Science, raises the potential for an entirely new and exciting role for this and for the other bibliographic utilities.[32]

Support to Library Strategic Management

Given the ability to bring together data from their own operations and make them readily available to the participating libraries, there is the potential for the bibliographic utilities to provide a set of services in support of strategic management. To an extent, they already have done so in the area of collection assessment, as exemplified by the Conspectus service of RLG and the CD-ROM package distributed by OCLC through Amigos.[33] Furthermore, library directors depend on data from use of the utilities for purposes both of internal management and of assessing differences in costs.

Beyond these existing forms of management support, though, the utilities are in a position to serve as the means for environmental scan. They can identify, organize, and make available on-line the data needed by every library to support its own strategic management.

Duplication of Effort

On the negative side, a problem of significant strategic importance to academic libraries is the duplication of effort and expenditure of resources involved in maintaining multiple parallel bibliographic utilities. Efforts to consolidate them have been fraught with difficulties. Among them is con-cern about the potential restraint of trade under provisions of the Sherman Anti-Trust Act, but there is also a continuing level of emotional and per-sonal commitment to past objectives.

In the early 1970s, when the bibliographic utilities were initiated, there were great uncertainties about the best choice of technical approach, the management capabilities, the pace in technology development, the status of local systems, and a score of other factors. Given that situation, there were good reasons for conducting parallel experiments. Now the situation is dramatically different. Success has been proven, and the need for parallel experiments is long gone.

Maintain the "Commons"

The library community has made a commitment in the creation of the national databases. The needs can be served only if the common database is maintained and effectively used for both common and individual interests. Therefore, an essential criterion for assessment of pricing alternatives must be whether they encourage effective maintenance and use of the "commons."[34]

Note that the issues to be considered in this context not only are contribution to the common database but also use of the database in common interests. Underlying this is the complex, nettlesome questions of ownership of the database, of what kinds of uses may be made of it, and of conditions under which such uses may be made. Any strategy with respect to the bibliographic utilities should deal with this issue in ways consistent with both the economic viability of the utility and the maintenance of the commons as a resource of mutual and individual value.

Provide Individual Equity

For cooperative enterprises to succeed, there must be the feeling as well as the reality of equity. Each participant should feel that contributions are commensurate with both capabilities and values received. Notice that both capabilities and values received are identified, in hope that it is still recognized in our society that both are essential elements of equity, that noblesse oblige still has meaning, and that if possible one should pay for what one gets, but that we are not yet governed solely by the forces of the marketplace.

Let us consider resource sharing: one of the underlying rationales for creating cooperative bibliographic utilities. Who should pay for the costs involved for support to that function: the borrowing library or the lending library? The facts are that each will use the utility, but surely equity calls for the borrowing library to bear most, if not all, of those costs, since it is receiving the value from them. Moreover, aside from the issue of equity, the fundamental basis for making choices between acquisition and access should also be recognized; those making such decisions should do so in recognition of the real costs in access.

Costs and Prices

Costs

Each of the utilities, as well as the libraries participating in them, faces strategic decisions with respect to pricing of their products and services. The bottom line is the necessity that the utilities continue to be economically viable. This means that, whatever alternative may be selected, all their costs must be covered by income received. Of course, there is the potential of risk; therefore, whatever the assessments of expected income may be, there may be shortfalls in the actual income. The concomitant result is that the pricing policy may call for the coverage of more than the actual costs in order to ensure against the potential for loss.

In an obvious way, one can identify three kinds of cost: fixed, variable, and specific. The significant point is that the fixed costs are the basis of the risk for the utilities. The communication networks are essential to effective and reliable operation; the processing hardware and software systems provide the capabilities; and there are continuing operating costs that are largely independent of the levels of use. Certainly, the continuing costs must be recovered from income, but it would be essential for future operations that the investments made to date be amortized (i.e., recovered) as well in order to upgrade and replace equipment as necessary.

In contrast, the variable and specific costs are relatively risk-free, since they are incurred only when there are uses made that justify them and for which recovery of those costs is relatively straightforward. Unfortunately, though, the great bulk of costs in the bibliographic utilities are essentially fixed.

Predictability of Use

Uses of the utilities internal to the library, whether directly or through symbiosis between them and the local system, are inherently predictable and limited by the size of staff. While one can conceive of inefficient or even profligate use, this is inconsistent with library operations. Furthermore, whether inefficient or not, there is a limit to how much a given size of staff can do. Consequently, the risks lie only in possible dramatic increases in use by libraries that are negligible users today, which is potentially controllable within almost any pricing strategy.

The great unknowns arise from enlargements in context and services: to the clientele served by the individual library and to library consortia and their users. Support to reference is in this enlarged domain since the size of the population being served plays such a dominant role, though reference use of the utility is likely to be limited by the size of staff. Document access and delivery services, though, are almost unlimited in magnitude.

Alternative Bases for Pricing Policies

The options for pricing are (1) transaction-based pricing, (2) fixed-fee–based pricing, or (3) various combinations of the two. Transaction-based alternatives were used by the utilities in the early years and continue to be used to some extent. The charge may be based on first-time use, number of searches, connect time, or requested services. The problem, though, is that it impedes rather than encourages use.

The utilities have, therefore, recently begun to move toward fixed-fee alternatives, perhaps under the name of subscription pricing or unlimited use.[35] The fixed fee may be based on prior experience such as the charges in a given year or a running average over a number of prior years (note that underlying any prior experience approach must be a set of one or more transaction-based alternatives from which the prior experience is determined). Such approaches appear to be quite effective.

Other alternatives might base a fixed fee on the number of terminals or size of the using population, but these appear to be inappropriate as bases for the fixed-fee pricing of utility services. The first variable is too subject to irrelevant variability in the use of each terminal and uncontrollable in the technological environment. The second is also subject to variability in patterns, kinds, and amounts of use. (For fixed-fee pricing of the use of other databases, of course, the situation is much different, and subscription pricing based on the size of the using population is likely to be very appropriate.)

In principle, alternatives based on objective measures of the size of the library all appear to be viable. The fixed fee presumably would be derived by dividing total utility fixed costs by some appropriate weighting of the given measure such as (Costs) × (Size of Library)/(Average Size). The problem, of course, is finding a measure of library size that would preserve equity.

SOURCES OF INFORMATION

While the role of the publishers may appear to be self-evident, it is important to recognize that publishing is the primary source of information resources that libraries must acquire. Publishing and information service suppliers determine what they will produce and how they will price it based on their own economic interests; while in principle that may reflect the needs of the market, the university and its library are likely to be minor determinants; indeed, given their dependence on the sources, they represent a captive market with few alternatives.

Changing Methods of Publication and Distribution

Primarily as a result of the impact of technology on publishing, there are changes occurring in patterns of publication. The new media—com-

MORTON COLLEGE LIBRARY
CICERO, ILLINOIS

puter databases, on-line access to them, electronic mail and facsimile, distribution of data and images in optical disk formats, and desktop pub-lishing—all provide new means for communication of information. How will they affect the traditional print means? At what pace will they develop? What changes will they make in the substance of what is communicated? Finally, how do we determine what are real changes in publishing and when those changes will be meaningful to operations of libraries and other information facilities?

Especially difficult for strategic management is predicting the pace at which the suppliers will shift from one mode of distribution to another; the library needs to make plans for acquisition of equipment and facilities largely on the basis of speculation, and the publishers provide little data on which to base those decisions. The well-established relationships for monograph writing, editing, publishing, and distribution have, as yet, no counterparts in the electronic arena, at least as it relates to the academic world. Indeed, the lack of expertise on the part of the publishers in iden-tifying authors as sources for publication, and in marketing, packaging, and distribution, may well be the most significant barrier, one that may take decades to resolve.

CD-ROM

Optical disks clearly will affect the nature of journals and perhaps even of books; they are likely to change the kinds of materials published as well as their format and organization.[36] The library community has been at the forefront in development of new formats. In 1986, about 75 percent of CD-ROM publications were specific to library operations (e.g., abstracts and bibliographic data files); in 1988, it was 60 percent, and by 1990 less than 40 percent.[37] Text files and raw reference data (such as pricing and financial data) are rapidly becoming the dominating kinds of content.

On-Line and On-Demand Publication

Among the potential services is that of an electronic library, with on-demand access and publication. The concept today is largely experimental, promotional, and rhetorical. Still, it represents an important new dimension of private sector services.

The OCLC publication of an electronic journal represents this kind of experiment. Another involves scanning journal articles and providing them as electronic document delivery. Academic publications have been devel-oped for the networks (today, there are perhaps thirty journals, ten re-fereed publications, and one hundred bulletin boards, but all are moonlighting efforts), and others are derivative from paper journals.

Still, though, the mainstream publishers of books and journals are mov-ing into this form of publication very slowly and cautiously. This means that there is much uncertainty about when, or even whether, library materials will be available in this form.

Pricing Policies

The economic pressures felt by libraries during the 1980s have been exceptional, and the pricing policies of private sector information industry have been a major element in the crisis. Libraries are clearly seen as captive markets, so prices can be set by publishers at whatever the market will bear. The result, though, has been forced policies of "de-acquisition," especially of journals. The argument of the private sector companies appears to be that the availability of their publications from libraries depletes their other markets, since users will go to the library rather than purchase their own. This view does not reflect the reality. Libraries in no way diminish the market, so discriminatory pricing will become self-defeating.

Prices for Journals

The pricing policies of journal publishers have such critical importance to strategic planning that we must make note of them. The massive rates of inflation experienced in the price of journals, especially foreign commercial journals in the physical and biological sciences, has produced a catastrophic situation for every major research library of the country. The explosive situation has resulted even in a court case as at least one publisher has tried to counter reports that profits of publishers increased at exorbitant rates.[38]

The implications of this trend for strategic planning are multiple. They get to the heart of allocation of resources among academic programs, as commitments of acquisition budgets to journals valued by the sciences force reductions in purchases of the monographs valued by the humanities. Furthermore, the nature of serial publications is that they represent commitments not just for today, but for the foreseeable future as well.

Pricing of Electronic Services

Pricing policies of electronic services are in such a state of flux today that the library manager really has no basis on which even to estimate what costs will be for various kinds of products and services. *Block pricing, differential pricing*, and *usage-based pricing* are all being used by one or more publishers. When the range of alternatives to be considered—including print, CD-ROM, on-line services, and magnetic tapes acquisition—is added to the mix, the result is chaotic.

Relationships between Publishers and Libraries

Publishers as Sources

With these developments, the information industries are creating potentially different relationships to the university and to the library. Without question, the central fact is that libraries depend almost completely on the private sector for their collections and for the tools for access to them. Their collections come overwhelmingly from commercial publishers, with professional societies a secondary source, and governments of all kinds are really minor in the overall. In this respect at least, the library profession sees the private sector as partners. One need merely enter the exhibit area at any meeting of the American Library Association and observe what the librarians do there.

The tools for access also come overwhelmingly from the private sector. The number of exceptions is almost miniscule in comparison. Indeed, one must search carefully to identify any but the most evident examples. Even the most evident one—the cataloging data from the Library of Congress— is accessed through private sector agencies, not public groups. Of course, there is the example of the products and services that the National Library of Medicine has been mandated by Congressional legislation to provide. And there is the National Technical Information Service (NTIS), which similarly is mandated by Congress to provide distribution of federal government documents.

The views of the library profession concerning the importance of the private sector with respect to these support tools are evident. Indeed, these are their tools, whatever their source. There may be disagreements over rights and privileges and debate over technique and details, but overall, the library profession sees the private sector as an essential partner.

Libraries as Markets

The corollary to the dependence of libraries upon the private sector is the reverse dependence of the private sector on libraries. For a wide range of publications, and especially for scientific, technical, and professional ones, the libraries of this country represent one-third to two-thirds of the total market. Of even greater importance is that those sales represent the break-even point for the publishers, so that "library sales" cover the risks of the publishers. Libraries therefore are a primary market for major categories of publication.

Libraries frequently provide the information industry with the basis for a pilot test of general markets. An example was the development of the CD-ROM as means for information distribution. In the early days of on-line reference database access, libraries (especially U.S. medical libraries) provided the context for a pilot test of such services. Certainly, libraries provide a crucial component of the means for distributing private sector information products and services. With respect to the on-line database services, in particular, they still represent a disproportionate share of total sales.

How does the library profession view this side of the so-called partnership? Frankly, it casts a rather jaundiced eye. The rhetoric of the information industry, of all kinds, has ignored or diminished the importance that libraries have for them. The result is a perception that, if there is a partnership, it certainly is not an equal one. The libraries bear the burdens with little or none of the benefits of partnership. They are merely accepted as simply another market, no more or less important than any other.

SOURCES OF STAFF

The schools of library and information science are the primary sources for professional staff. A matter of vital strategic concern, therefore, has been the closure of library schools during the 1980s. The number has been reduced by over 20 percent, and the output of professionally qualified graduates has declined even more.[39]

Aside from the specific concerns with the status of library schools are the more general ones of qualifications needed for staff.[40] Of special concern is the commitment to imperatives of the profession: preservation of the records of the past, access to those records, equity in access, privacy for the users, and service. Also desired are qualities of leadership.

SUPPORT TO RESEARCH

Research has the general objective of increasing our knowledge of the world, of course, but it has the specific objective of providing the bases for decision making and especially for strategic planning. Currently, research in the field is focused in areas such as effects of different forms of information resources, especially newer forms, on academic research; effects of technology on instruction; interface design and development of expert systems; economic foundations and related information policies; economics of publishing; and changing patterns of scholarly communication. Each is providing both insight and data that will be of importance in future planning and management.[41]

NOTES

1. *United States Code*, 1988 edition. Washington: United States Government Printing Office, 1989. Title 17, Section 107 (pages 34–37), defines fair use, while the following section, 108, defines the rights of libraries to make copies under specific conditions. In particular:

> (d) The rights of reproduction and distribution under this section apply to a copy, made from the collection of a library or archives, where the user makes his or her request or from that of another library or archives, of no more than one article or other contribution to a copyrighted collection or periodical issue, or to a copy or phonorecord of any other copyrighted work, if—(1)

the copy or phonorecord becomes the property of the user, and the library or archive has had no notice that the copy or phonorecord would be used for any purpose other than private study, scholarship or research; and (2) the library or archive displays prominently, at the place where orders are accepted, and includes in its order form, a warning of copyright in accordance with requirements that the Register of Copyrights shall require by regulation.

See also Crews, Kenneth D., *Copyright at the Research University: A Select Bibliography of Secondary Literature, 1967–1986* (Los Angeles: GSLIS, 31 October 1986).

2. Avram, Henriette D., "Copyright in the Electronic Environment," *Educom Review* 24(3) (Fall 1989): 31–33; Griffiths, Jose-Marie, and King, Donald W., *Intellectual Property Rights in an Age of Electronics and Information* (Washington, D.C.: U.S. Congress, Office of Technology Assessment, 1986); *Intellectual Property Rights and Fair Use: Strengthening Scholarly Communication in the 1990s*, proceedings of the 9th Annual Conference of Research Library Directors (Dublin, Ohio: OCLC, 1991).

3. Crews, Kenneth D., *Copyright Policies at American Research Universities: Balancing Information Needs and Legal Limits* (Ph.D. dissertation, University of California at Los Angeles, 1990).

4. Association of Research Libraries, *Copyright Policies in ARL Libraries*, SPEC kit 102 (Washington, D.C.: Association of Research Libraries, Office of Management Studies, Systems and Procedures Exchange Center, 1984); Association of Research Libraries, *University Copyright Policies in ARL Libraries*, SPEC kit 138 (Washington, D.C.: Association of Research Libraries, Office of Management Studies, 1987).

5. The case in point was *Lotus Development Corp., Plaintiff v. Paperback Software International*.

6. The two cases in point were *Salinger v. Random House, Inc.* and *New Era Pubs. Int'l ApS v. Henry Holt & Co.*

7. S521–34, *Fair Use and Unpublished Works* (Washington, D.C.: GPO, 11 July 1990), (quote from title of bill); S2370 and HR 4263, to amend the Copyright Act in order to clarify applicability of fair use standards to both published and unpublished works.

8. U.S. Congress, House Committee on the Judiciary, 100th Congress, First and Second Sessions, *Berne Convention Implementation Act of 1987: Hearings before the Subcommittee: June 17, July 23, September 16 and 30, 1987, February 9 and 10, 1988* (Washington, D.C.: U.S. GPO, 1988); U.S. Congress, Senate Committee on the Judiciary, 100th Congress, Second Session, *The Berne Convention: Hearings before the Subcommittee: February 18 and March 3, 1988* (Washington, D.C.: GPO, 1988); U.S. Congress, Senate Committee on the Judiciary, *Moral Rights in Our Copyright Laws: Hearings before the Subcommittee: June 20, September 20, and October 24, 1989* (Washington: GPO, 1990); Nimmer, David, *The Berne Convention Implementation Act of 1988* (New York: Bender, 1989).

9. Ricketson, Sam, *The Berne Convention for the Protection of Literary and Artistic Works: 1886–1986* (London: Queen Mary College, Centre for Commercial Law Studies, Kluwer, 1987); Smits, W. A., *United States Adherence to the Berne Convention: A Missed Opportunity for Moral Rights Protection?* (Ph.D. dissertation, University of California at Los Angeles, 1989).

10. *Public Sector/Private Sector Interaction in Providing Information Services: Report to the NCLIS from the Public Sector/Private Sector Task Force* (Washington, D.C.: NCLIS, 1982); Hayes, Robert M. "A Commentary on the NCLIS Public Sector/Private

Sector Task Force and Its Report," in *Minutes of the Ninety-Ninth Annual Meeting, the Association of Research Libraries* (Washington, D.C.: ARL, 1982), pp. 12–41.

11. Hayes, Robert M., "Pricing Policies of the National Library of Medicine" (editorial), *Annals of Internal Medicine* 100(4) (April 1984): 601–4; Hayes, Robert M., "Pricing of Products and Services of the National Library of Medicine and Competition with the Private Sector: A Review of Relevant Reports. A Report to the U.S. Department of Health and Human Services" (August 1983).

12. *American Library Association Comments on NTIA January 9, 1990, Proposed "Comprehensive Study of Domestic Telecommunications Infrastructure"* (Washington, D.C.: ALA Washington Office, 12 April 1990); "Associations Take Stands on Access to Information." *American Libraries*, June 1989, pp. 485–86.

13. Freeman, Harry L., "Blame Statistics for Trade Deficit," *Wall Street Journal*, October 31, 1989, p. A22 (Western edition); Fuerbringer, Jonathan, "Accuracy in Short Supply in Flood of U.S. Statistics," *New York Times* 139(48039) (30 October 1989): A1, D4; Hayes, Robert M. "Politics and Publishing in Washington," *Special Libraries* 74(4) (Oct. 1983): 322–31; Lewis, Arnold, and Powell, Margaret S., "The Silent Threat: How Federal Policy Stifles Scholarship," *Educational Record*, Winter 1987, pp. 19–24; Mann, Jim, "Valuable Window on Japan May Be Closing, Scholars Fear," *Los Angeles Times*, 24 March 1991, pp. A24–A25; U.S. Congress, Senate, 101st Congress, Session 2, *Pentagon Rules on Media Access to the Persian Gulf War: Hearing before the Committee on Governmental Affairs, 20 Feb. 1991*, Washington: United States Government Printing Office, 1992; Rich, Spencer, "Drawing the Line on Poverty: Census Bureau Measurement Sparks Criticism from Many Quarters," *Washington Post*, 30 Oct. 1989, p. A13; Rider, Robin E., "Saving the Records of Big Science," *American Libraries*, Feb. 1991, pp. 166–68; Warnow, Joan N., et al., *A Study of the Preservation of Documents at Department of Energy Laboratories* (New York: American Institute of Physics, 1982).

14. *Less Access to Less Information by and about the U.S. Government—A 1981–1987 Chronology* (Chicago: American Library Association, 1988).

15. Reagan, Ronald, "The President's Decision Memorandum: Transfer of the Civil Space Remote Sensing Systems to the Private Sector" (White House, 28 Feb. 1983).

16. "Federal Data Go Private: Vendors Repackage Public Information—At a Price That Limits Access," *Christian Science Monitor* 82(209) (24 Sept. 1990): 15.

17. "Transcript of Closed NCLIS Meeting Details FBI's Library Awareness Program," *American Libraries*, April 1988, p. 244; "FBI to Consider Release of 'Awareness Program' Material," *American Libraries*, June 1989, p. 481; Conable, Gordon, "The FBI and You," *American Libraries*, March 1990, pp. 245–48.

18. "LC MARC Subscribers Told to Sign Licensing Agreement," *American Libraries*, Sept. 1989, p. 724; "MARC Licensing Flap Lingers, LC's Avram Takes the Heat," *American Libraries*, March 1990, pp. 255–56; "LC Drops MARC Licensing Plan," *American Libraries*, Apr. 1990, p. 288; *A Proposal to Establish the Library of Congress Fee Services Fund* (Washington, D.C.: Library of Congress, 12 June 1990).

19. "ARL, Cause, Educom Form New Information Resources Coalition," *Manage IT* 1(2) (April 1990): 1–2; Cline, Nancy, "Information Resources and the National Network," *Educom Review* 25(2) (Summer 1990): 30–34; Dougherty, Richard M., "An Ideal Win-Win Situation: The National Electronic Highway," *American Libraries*, Feb. 1991, p. 182; Gore, Albert, "Remarks on the NREN," *Educom Review* 25(2) (Summer 1990): 12–16; Huray, Paul G., and Nelson, David B., "The Federal High-Performance

Computing Program," *Educom Review* 25(2) (Summer 1990): 17–24; Jul, Erik, "Project
to Analyze Internet Information Is Underway," *OCLC Newsletter*, Mar./Apr. 1992,
pp. 13–15; Lynch, Clifford A., "Library Automation and the National Network," *Educom Review* 24(3) (Fall 1989): 21–26; Lynch, Clifford, "Telecommunications and Libraries," *DLA Bulletin* 6(1) (Fall 1986): 1, 3; Roberts, Michael M., "The NREN and
Commercial Services," *Educom Review* 24(4) (Winter 1989): 10–11; Rogers, Susan M.,
"Educational Applications of the NREN," *Educom Review* 25(2) (Summer 1990): 25–
29.

    20. Kehoe, Brendan P., *Zen and the Art of the Internet* (Chester, Pa.: Widener University, January 1992).

    21. Arms, Caroline, "Libraries and Electronic Information: The Technological Context, Part Two," *Educom Review* 24(3) (Fall 1989): 34–43; Herman, James, et al.,
"Shaping the 1990s," *ComputerWorld* 23 (27 Nov. 1989): 77–85; Hockey, Susan, "The
Role of Electronic Information in Higher Education: The Faculty Perspective," in *OCLC
Academic Libraries Directors' Conference* (Dublin, Ohio: OCLC, 1992); Hyatt, Shirley,
"New Era Communications Gives Libraries New Options," *OCLC Newsletter*, May/
June 1992, pp. 15–19; Kahn, Philippe, "Forces Shaping Academic Software Development," *Educom Review* 24(4) (Winter 1989): 24–25; Kiesler, S. B., and Sproull, L. S.
(eds.), *Computing and Change on Campus* (New York: Cambridge University Press,
1987); Lancaster, F. W., "Whither Libraries? or, Wither Libraries," *College and Research Libraries* 39(5) (Sept. 1978): 345–57; Martyn, John, et al., *Information UK 2000*
(London: British Library Research, Bowker-Saur, 1990); Meadows, Jack A., "Higher
Education and the Influence of Information Technology: Research," in *The Electronic
Campus—An Information Strategy*. Proceedings of the Conference in Banbury, England,
28–30 October 1988; Neff, Raymond K., "Merging Libraries and Computer Centers:
Manifest Destiny or Manifestly Deranged?" *Educom Bulletin*, Winter 1985, pp. 8–12,
16; U.S. Department of Commerce, *NITA Information Services Report* (Washington,
D.C.: Department of Commerce, August 1988); Galvin, Thomas J., "Research Library
Performance in the Delivery of Electronic Information," *OCLC Newsletter*, Mar./Apr.
1992, pp. 20–21; Olsen, Wallace C., *Toward an Integrated Information System* (Ithaca,
N.Y.: Cornell University, April 1986); "Technology Assessment at OCLC," *OCLC
Newsletter* 179 (May/June 1989); Thompson, James, *The End of Libraries* (London:
Bingley Press, 1982).

    22. Brown, Rowland C. W., "Brushstrokes in Flight: A Strategic Overview of Trends
in Technology in Higher Education," in *The Electronic Campus—An Information Strategy*, ed. Lynn J. Brindley. Proceedings of the Conference in Banbury, England, 28–30
October 1988.

    23. Baecker, Ronald, and Buxton, William, *Readings in Human-Computer Interaction: A Multidisciplinary Approach* (Los Altos, Calif.: Morgan Kaufmann, 1987); Berger,
Mike, "The Patron Meets the Melvyl Catalog: A Short History of the Melvyl Patron
Interface," *DLA Bulletin* 12(10) (Spring 1992): 6–7, 24–26; Card, Stuart K., Moran,
Thomas P., and Newell, Allen, *The Psychology of Human-Computer Interaction* (Hillsdale, N.J.: Lawrence Erlbaum, 1983); Carroll, John M., *Interfacing Thought: Cognitive
Aspects of Human-Computer Interaction* (Cambridge, Mass.: Bradford/MIT Press, June
1987); Draper, Stephen, and Norman, Donald, *User Centered System Design* (Hillsdale,
N.J.: Lawrence Erlbaum, 1986); Ehrich, Roger W., and Williges, Robert C. *Human-Computer Dialogue Design* (New York: Elsevier Science, January 1986); Gilb, Tom,
and Weinberg, Gerald M., *Humanized Input: Techniques for Reliable Keyboard Input*
(Wellesley Hills, Mass.: QED Information Sciences, 1977); Jul, Erik, "Ben Schneider-

man Speaks on User Interface Design," *OCLC Newsletter*, May/June 1992, pp. 10–11; McGill, Michael J., "Z39.50 Benefits for Designers and Users," *Educom Review* 24(3) (Fall 1989): 27–30; "Z39.50: Lousy Sports Car, Great Library Standard," *American Libraries*, October 1990, p. 903; *OCLC Gateway Project*, Dublin, Ohio: OCLC, 15 Jan. 1992; Mosier, Jane N., and Smith, Sidney L. *Guidelines for Designing User Interface Software*, August 1986; Nickerson, Raymond, *Using Computers: Human Factors in Information Systems* (Cambridge, Mass.: Bradford/MIT Press, January 1986); Shneiderman, Ben, *Designing the User Interface: Strategies for Effective Human-Computer Interaction* (Reading, Mass.: Addison-Wesley, 1986); Tomeski, Edward A., and Lazarus, Harold, *People-Oriented Computer Systems* (New York: Van Nostrand, 1975), chapters 1–4.

24. Fogarty, James, "Dramatically Different! Hypertext," *Online Searcher* 2(2) (Winter 1990): 1, 4.

25. Hayes, Robert M., "Distributed Library Networks: Programs and Problems," in *The Responsibility of the University Library Collection in Meeting the Needs of its Campus and Local Community* (La Jolla: Friends of the University of California at San Diego Library, 1976); Kent, Allen, and Galvin, Thomas J., *The Structure and Governance of Library Networks* (New York: Marcel Dekker, 1979).

26. Kibbey, Mark, and Evans, Nancy H., "The Network Is the Library," *Educom Review* 24(3) (Fall 1989): 15–20; *Libraries and Technology: A Strategic Plan for the Use of Advanced Technologies for Library Resource Sharing in New York State* (Albany, N.Y.: New York State Library, 1987); Lynch, Clifford, "The Melvyl System: Looking Back, Looking Forward," *DLA Bulletin* 12(10) (Spring 1992): 3–5; Mosher, Paul H., "A Natural Scheme for Collaboration In Collection Development: The RLG-NCIP Effort," *Resource Sharing and Information Networks* 2 (Spring/Summer 1985): 21–35; *OLIS: Connecting People, Libraries, and Information for Ohio's Future* (Columbus, Ohio: Ohio Board of Regents, Dec. 1989); *Request for Proposal for Telefacsmile Networking* (Sacramento: California State Library, June 1989); Glitz, Beryl, "The California Multitype Library Network: An Update," *Pacific Southwest Regional Medical Library Service*, January/February 1991, pp. 1, 4.

27. Lowry, Charles B., "Resource Sharing or Cost Shifting?—The Unequal Burden of Cooperative Cataloging and ILL in Network," *College and Research Libraries*, January 1990, pp. 11–19; *Interlibrary Loan Discussion Panel: Final Report* (Dublin, Ohio: OCLC, October 1990); Stubbs, Kendon (ed.), "Introduction," in *ARL Statistics, 1990–91*, Washington, DC: ARL, 1992. (This set of statistics shows an increase in ILL borrowing of 47 percent from 1985–86 through 1990–91, a compounded rate of 8 percent. However, OCLC data showed a *doubling* of ILL borrowing from 1985–86 through 1990–91, a compounded rate of 15 percent or nearly twice the ARL figure.

28. "ARL and RLG to Study ILL Costs," *Library Hotline* 21(17) (17 April 1992): 102; *ARL/RLG Interlibrary Loan Cost Study: Worksheet* (Washington, D.C.: ARL, 1992).

29. "Research Library Directors Evaluate OCLC's Future at Conference," *Research Libraries in OCLC: A Quarterly* 309 (Spring 1989); "RLG Board Sets Organization's Course for the 1990s" (press release), Research Libraries Group, 8 March 1991; "RLG in 1992: Setting the Stage for Change," *Research Library Group News* 26 (Fall 1991): 3–4; Shurkin, Joel, "The Rise and Fall and Rise of RLG," *American Libraries*, July/August 1982, pp. 450–55.

30. Jewett, Charles Coffin, *On the Construction of Catalogues of Libraries, and Their Publication by Means of Separate, Stereotyped Titles*, 2d ed. (Washington, D.C.: Smithsonian Institution, 1853).

31. "Citadel: A Stronghold of Information," *Research Libraries Group News* 27 (Winter 1992): 15; "CitaDel previewed at Rutgers and BYU," *Research Libraries Group News* 28 (Spring 1992): 3–6; Dean, Nita, "EPIC: A New Frame of Reference for the OCLC Database," *OCLC Newsletter*, March/April 1991, p. 21; Wilson, David L., "Researchers Get Direct Access to Huge Data Base," *Chronicle of Higher Education*, 9 October 1991, pp. A24, A28; "FirstSearch Takes the Lead," *Information Today*, Feb. 1992.

32. *Guide to Using Graph-Text, a Document Retrieval System for Scientific Journals* (Dublin, Ohio: OCLC, August 1986); "New Online Journal to Speed Publication of Peer-Reviewed Reports on Clinical Trials of Medical Treatments," *OCLC Update*, October 1991; Jul, Erik, "Graph-Text Project Provides Basis for Online Journal," *OCLC Update*, October 1991.

33. Dillon, Martin, and Crook, Mark, "A Prototype Automated Collection Analysis Tool for Libraries," *OCLC Research Review*, July 1987, pp. 3–4.

34. Hardin, G., "The Tragedy of the Commons," *Science* 162(3859) (13 Dec. 1968): 1243–48; Crowe, Beryl, "The Tragedy of the Commons Revisited," *Science* 166(3909) (28 Nov. 1969): pp. 1103–7; Smith, Wayne, Comments re the "Commons" at the Research Library Director's Conference, OCLC, 1992.

35. *RLIN Rates: Rates for Services from the Research Libraries Information Network* (Appendix C to the RLIN service agreement) (Mountain View, Calif.: Research Libraries Group, 1 July 1991); WLN Pricing. Personal communication in a meeting with Washington Library Network (WLN) management, 1992.

36. Case, Donald, *Optical Disk Publication of Databases: A Review of Applications for Academic Libraries* (Los Angeles: GSLIS, 31 August 1986); Iles, Doug, "CD-ROM Enters Mainstream IS," *Computerworld*, 5 June 1989, pp. 75–80; Miller, David C., *Special Report: Publishers, Libraries, and CD-ROM* (Benicia, Calif.: DCM Associates, prepared for the Fred Meyer Charitable Trust, March 1987); Miller, David C., *The New Optical Media in the Library and the Academy Tomorrow* (Benicia, Calif.: DCM Associates, prepared for the Fred Meyer Charitable Trust, August 1986); Miller, David C., *The New Optical Media Mid–1986: A Status Report* (Benicia, Calif.: DCM Associates, prepared for the Fred Meyer Charitable Trust, August 1986); Paisley, William, and Butler, Matilda, "The First Wave: CD-ROM Adoption in Offices and Libraries," *Microcomputers for Information Management* 4(2) (June 1987): 109–27.

37. "CD-ROM Database Sales Should Hit about 2.2 Mil by 1996 vs 1.4 Mil in 1991," *Computing World*, March 1992, p. 9; "Market Share of CD-ROM Information Products Tabulated by Type of Product for 1988 and 1990," *ComputerWorld*, 30 January 1989, p. 77; "Database Vendors Revenues Projection," *Information*, pt. 1 (October 1989): 6; "Sales of Electronic Databases to Grow 20% in 1989 vs 1988," *New York Times*, 30 December 1988, p. 23.

38. "ARL Consultants' Reports Likely to Widen Serials Rift," *American Libraries*, June 1989, p. 489; "Journal Publisher Sues Author of Price Study," *American Libraries*, Sept. 1989, pp. 717–18; "Gordon & Breach Sues Again," *American Libraries*, April 1990, p. 286; "A Response from Gordon & Breach," *American Libraries*, May 1990, p. 405.

39. Seelmeyer, John, "The Anatomy of a Library School Shutdown," *American Libraries*, February 1985, pp. 95–96, 113; "State Budget Woes Threaten U. of South Fla. Library School," *American Libraries*, November 1991, p. 926; Shank, Russell (chair), et al., *Report of the ALA Special Committee on Library School Closings* (Chicago:

ALA, June 1991); Haywood, Trevor, *Changing Faculty Environments* (Birmingham, U.K.: Birmingham Polytechnic, July 1991); Marchant, Maurice P., "The Closing of the Library School at Brigham Young University," *American Libraries*, January 1992, pp. 32–36.

40. Griffiths, Jose-Marie, and King, Donald W., *New Directions in Library and Information Science Education* (White Plains, N.Y.: Knowledge Industry Publications for the American Society for Information Science, 1986); Strategic Vision Discussion Group, Steering Committee, *Strategic Vision for Professional Librarians* (December 1991); Haas, Warren J., "Library Schools in Research Universities," in *35th Annual Report 1991*, Council on Library Resources (Washington, D.C.: Council on Library Resources, 1992), pp. 27–33; Gaughan, Tom, "Taking the Pulse of Library Education," *American Libraries*, January 1992, pp. 24–25, 120; McClure, Charles R., and Hert, Carol A., "Specialization in Library/Information Science Education: Issues, Scenarios, and the Need for Action," in *Proceedings of the Conference on Specialization in Library/ Information Science Education* (Ann Arbor: University of Michigan, SLIS, 6–8 November 1991).

41. Hayes, Robert M., "Planning and Coordination of Research on Library and Information Science in the United States," in *Proceedings of the IFLA Conference in Leipzig, GDR*, 17–22 August 1981; *The Faxon Institute for Advanced Studies in Scholarly and Scientific Communication* (Westwood, Mass.: Faxon Company, Jan. 1992).

PART III

Techniques

7

Assessing the Strategic Position

In this chapter we turn to an assessment of the strategic position of the academic library with respect to the critical elements both externally and internally: effectiveness of library tactical management, the quality of the collection and of its management, operational performance, the values to the institution and the constituency served, and effects of the external environment.

INFORMATION GATHERING AND PROJECT DATA FILES

There are needs for computer-based tools and services to support library management at all three levels: strategic (i.e., concerned with response to external environment), tactical (i.e., concerned with the internal allocation of resources), and operational (i.e., concerned with the efficient use of resources). At the end of this chapter the relevant generic data management packages are summarized; in addition, two commercially available packages of value to strategic management are described.

Most central to strategic management are data files, which should be established to serve as means to maintain knowledge of the exceptionally wide range of activities involved. This requires a continual environmental scan. Some will be focused on data internal to the library:

- internal administrative structure and operational matrix;
- budgeting;
- costs of operation;
- staff;
- equipment;

- collection; and
- usage.

Given the potentially massive amount of data that can be generated from operations, though, it is essential that the scan be carefully managed so as to select only the most significant for the purposes of strategic management. Chapter 9 will provide a framework in which to identify the relevant data, organized around a model for costing library operations but encompassing the full scope of quantitative aspects.

Some of the data are institutional. Again, the scan must be selective, but there is, as yet, no model to guide the identification of what is crucial or for organizing it. Clearly, such a model needs to be developed.

- Administrative
- Faculty and students
- Academic programs
- Research activities and facilities

The external environment encompasses a wide array of contexts, so the scan must deal with a comparable array of sources. Primary among them is the literature related to each component of the environment. The data-gathering process needs to identify those literatures, extract the most important data from them, index and abstract those data according to their strategic impact, and provide for periodic assessment of their import.

- Funding sources
- Consortial contexts
- Suppliers
- Legislation
- Technological developments

Persons

A data file on persons serves as the means for the management of planning efforts, for identifying the roles of individuals, and for communication with them. Each record in the file should include data for name, title, address, telephone number, and links to all other files (Academic Programs, Facilities, Projects, and External Environment). The linkages to other files, in a relational database structure, permit bringing together relevant data for each person that is contained in them, without redundancy or inconsistency.

Among the fields that can be included in this file are assessments of political positions: identification of "players" and of the bases for their interests (including defined responsibilities, existing capital commitments, personal priorities, and interpersonal relations). These data provide the basis for assessing the technical effects of political positions with respect to design decisions and resource commitments and for assessing means for their resolution. Admittedly, this concept is sensitive and fraught with potential difficulties. If properly handled, though, it provides a most important component of strategic management.

Academic Programs

The purpose of the Academic Program data file is to provide means for identifying individual units (schools and departments, organized research units, and others). Each record should include data for name, responsibility, budget, and staff. Links with the other data files (Facilities, Projects, Persons, and External Environment) again permit the bringing together of relevant data; of special importance is the linkage to the Persons file, for the identification of the responsible manager.

Facilities

The purpose of the Facilities data file is to provide means for identifying the several information facilities (Libraries, Computers, Media centers, Archives, and Other kinds); for each, recognition of the system, department, and other categories should be provided for. The records in this file identify the name of the facility, the responsible person (by linkage to the Persons file), budget, and staff. Linkages to the other data files (Persons, Academic Programs, Projects, and External Environments) provide means for relating relevant data.

Projects

The Projects data file is to provide means of identifying relevant research projects, wherever they may have been carried out, and tie-in of possible researchers of subprojects of the strategic management project; it also provides means for the distribution of communications. Each record identifies a project by name and identifies the responsible person (linking to the Persons file), the assigned budget, and related staff (again by linkage to the Persons file). Some records in this file may be specific to subprojects within a strategic planning effort (both supporting studies and research efforts); others relate to projects funded elsewhere. Of course, links to the other files (Persons, Facilities, Academic Programs, and External Environment) provide means for relating relevant data.

At a very early stage in the strategic management effort, data should be obtained from the Office of Contracts and Grants for all funded projects on the campus that relate to information needs. It is likely that over 10 percent are either generating information files (in the specific sense, not in some generalized sense) or are acquiring them for purposes of analysis. The funding of that 10 percent or more may be an even greater percentage of the total external contract and grant funding.

External Environment

The data file on the external environment has the purpose of tying in data about relevant literature, technological forecasts, political and societal forces, the status of publishing, and similar items. The records provide both bibliographic references and technical details. Again, links to the other files provide means for relating relevant data.

ASSESSMENT OF MANAGEMENT

We turn now to the use of these data files for evaluation of the library's strategic position, first with respect to management.

Structure and Control

Chapter 2 discussed the relevant aspects in assessment of the library's structure and the means for control: management style, decision-making processes, centralized or decentralized administration, hierarchy or matrix structure, and functional or programmatic organization. For the specific situation, of course, those need to be evaluated as objectively as possible so as to identify aspects that are deficient and need change or are exemplary and need support.

Budget and Finance

The objective of financial planning models is to provide means for assessing the effects of alternative financial policies and of external environments upon the financial structure.

Historical financial data, especially for sources and uses of funds, provide the input. A budget model then permits the testing of alternative policies and alternative assumptions about the internal and external factors. Typically, such a model will consist of equations that relate variables (such as costs of processing, costs of acquisition, cash flow as a percentage of costs, means for depreciation of capital investments, liabilities, and assets).

There are two stages in the development of effective models for projection of expenditures. The first is the cost model itself; this sets a relation, usually linear, between specific operating parameters and the associated cost projection. In chapter 9 we will present a detailed model for costing of library operations and services, identifying relevant operational parameters within it.

The second is a set of management considerations, which provide the context for budget projections and for setting confidence limits on the results. The following discusses examples of such management considerations, classified into internal and external managerial elements.

Internal Managerial Elements

These include administrative categories of budget, time periods of support, and levels of funding. The resulting projections serve as the means for overall control of budget. Categories of budget are affected by internal and external policies on appropriate uses of funds and by the level of existing commitments. Time periods are affected by delays in cycle and by whether the funding is recurring or nonrecurring.

Given the projected budgets, based on the programmatic parameters and related managerial elements, library management will then allocate the totality of funds to each administrative unit. They can treat the total budget for each unit as a control figure. The following aspects affect the managerial decisions: carry-forward budgets, carry-forward liens, reimbursables, prudency in management (to avoid overruns), and accumulation of funds (to make major purchases). The freedom to use funds in these ways, or the extent to which it is circumscribed, is crucial to strategic funds management.

External Considerations

There are a number of external considerations that affect the budgeting and expenditure processes: inflation, funding delays, funding mandates, external management decisions and controls, and delays in personnel processes.

Risks

The assessment of risks—whether financial risks, programmatic risks, market risks, or administrative risks—is a necessity if strategic management is to proceed with awareness. The assessment of financial risk is relatively straightforward since the data are quantifiable, though that by no means says that it is easy. It requires that projections of costs and income be treated not as fixed quantities, but as subject to statistical variation. The financial model should incorporate distributions reflecting such variation; the appendix to this chapter describes one commercial package, an add-in to spreadsheets, that provides that kind of capability.

More difficult to assess are the nonquantifiable risks. Later in this chapter, we will discuss means for programmatic assessment of collections, collection management, and operational performance. With respect to the collections and their management, the state of embrittlement clearly is a matter of risk. Assessment of the market risks (e.g., repercussions from the affected faculty) surely are a central part of decisions concerning collection development and operations. However, making such assessments today is essentially qualitative, without evident means for modeling even in a descriptive way. In the same vein, the risks involved in administrative decisions should be assessed, but there are few models to guide their assessment.

ASSESSMENT OF MARKET AND POSITION

We turn now to a number of existing models that have been developed for the business world, first discussing them in that context and then commenting on the extent to which they are applicable to academic libraries.[1] They are descriptive matrices used to display and assess the strength of business position, market, and competition for various products and services. The purpose is to provide an objective basis for resource allocation among constituent business units.

Academic Library Context

The interpretation for their application to academic libraries will be made at the level of the organization as a whole. However, they are equally meaningful for the assessment of an individual product or service, so the reader should visualize application in that way as well. To provide a framework for doing so, let us briefly review the academic library products and services and the markets for them.

Products and Services

Academic library products include (1) acquisition and related services, (2) bibliographic control and related services, (3) management of automated information systems, (4) information management and access services, (5) document delivery services, (6) publication both in bulk and on demand, (7) information staff management and training services, (8) information analysis services, and (9) database design and management services.

Markets

The markets for those services from the academic library include faculty, organized research activities, students, administrative staff, other libraries, public service agencies, corporations, information brokers, and persons in professional practice.

Figure 7.1
Categories of Units by Growth of Market and Share of Market

Growth of Market

		High	Low
Share of Market	High	Stars	Cash Cows
	Low	Problems	Dogs

The BCG Growth-Share Matrix

This matrix model (which is identified with the Boston Consulting Group; hence, the acronym) was developed during the 1960s as a simple method for the analysis of the strategic position of companies.

The Business Interpretation

Underlying the BCG model are two assumptions: Growth in a market implies that it is desirable to invest in it, and gaining a large share of a market implies a strong position. Growth is used as the primary determinant because it is argued that in growing markets it is easier to gain market share; a given market share increases in value as the market grows; and demand is likely to exceed supply, supporting higher prices and profits. Market share is used as the measure of strength because firms with a large share enjoy advantages of size: economies of scale, dominance, and strong bargaining positions. They will gain experience faster and can therefore reduce their costs more rapidly, exploiting what is called the *experience curve*.

These rationales derive from analyses (called PIMS, for profit impact of market strategy) of a database generated by General Electric in the early 1960s; it covered over 2,000 business units in over 200 firms. One analysis showed a virtually linear relationship between market share and return on investment. Another showed that highly capital-intensive companies do not have high return on investment (because of the high capital investment, but also because of high competition).

The model shown in figure 7.1 easily divides business units into four categories, based on high or low growth versus high or low share. The most superficial strategy is to move cash from the "cows" to the "problems." A more complex strategy is to examine the "dogs" to determine whether a shift of focus might not move them into the higher share categories; generally, though, the view is that it is best to liquidate them.

There are serious problems with the BCG model. The model is sensitive to the measure used—past growth versus predicted future growth—and the basis for classification into high or low. The model is sensitive to the definitions of product and market: scope, focus, already served or newly to be served, and categories of customers. The analyses are sensitive to subjective judgments.

Academic Library Interpretation

Is it meaningful to apply the BCG model to academic libraries? On the surface, it would seem that the answer is a resounding no. Virtually every aspect seems alien and inappropriate, if not totally contrary to experience.

Specifically, markets for academic library products and services are essentially stable, at best growing at rates comparable to general population growth. The experience curve has been almost fully traversed by academic libraries; as a result, they already are efficient throughout their operations. Academic libraries are, by their very nature, exceptionally capital-intensive; indeed, the investment in collections and in the means for access represents about two-thirds of their yearly budget, a commitment dramatically greater than even the high technology industries.

The last point is especially relevant. The share of the market for academic library products and services, as measured by statistics of use, is high in comparison with that for computers and commercial services. Given the low growth rate, the BCG matrix would suggest regarding them as "cash cows," but the PIMS analysis shows that there will not be high return on investment in capital intensive industries, whatever the market share.

Industry Attractiveness/Business Position Matrix

A second descriptive matrix generalizes from the BCG model. A mix of measures is used to identify industry attractiveness: size, growth, customer satisfaction, competition, price levels, profitability, technology, governmental regulation, and economic sensitivity. These factors are all evaluated in terms of return on investment. In the same vein, a mix of measures is used to characterize business position: size, growth, share, customer loyalty, profit margins, distribution, technology skills, patents, marketing, flexibility, and organization.

The Business Interpretation

The basic model, of course, is not different. The resulting strategies are generally variants of those for the BCG model, as shown in figure 7.2.

Academic Library Interpretation

This model is far more appropriate than the BCG model, since the mix of measures begins to incorporate some that are very meaningful to academic libraries. The market size is easy to determine and can be evaluated for consistency with expenditures (as reflected in percentage of institutional budget, for example); its growth rate is easy to determine and relevant to

Figure 7.2
Categories of Units by Industry Attractiveness and Business Position

Industry Attractiveness

		High	Medium	Low
Business Position	High	Invest	Invest	Selective
	Medium	Invest	Selective	Divest
	Low	Selective	Divest	Divest

decisions. The customer satisfaction is measurable in many ways, and for most academic libraries is very high. There is little direct or indirect competition. Price levels and profitability, while not directly applicable, are representable by expenditures. Technology has been well absorbed by academic libraries in exceptionally effective and efficient ways. Government regulation is a problem in the areas that were discussed in chapter 6, but it affects any competition at least to the same extent. There is great economic sensitivity, especially in the current environment.

With respect to business positions, academic libraries are large components of the institution (usually second only to faculty in percentage of the budget). The share of the academic market and customer loyalty are both high. The means for distribution are highly effective, as are the technology skills. There is the strength of professional identity, a proprietary position virtually equivalent to a patent. The tools for marketing of services are excellent. There is strength and flexibility in organization.

In other words, the range of measures for both market and position are relevant and measurable. The current assessment for academic libraries must be high on both Industry Attractiveness and Business Position, which argues for Invest.

Directional Policy Matrix

The Business Interpretation

Another modification of the BCG adds refinements: more quantification and specificity in recommendations. For the first element, weights are developed to translate the qualitative assessments of the BCG and industry attractiveness/business position models into quantitative measures. For the second, the three alternatives (Invest, Selective, and Divest) are replaced, as shown in figure 7.3.

Academic Library Interpretation

Since this model builds on the industry attractiveness/business position model, it also can be applied to academic libraries. The use of weights to

Figure 7.3
Categories of Units by Industry Attractiveness and Business Position

Industry Attractiveness

		High	Medium	Low
Business Position	High	Leader	Grow	Generate Cash
	Medium	Try harder	Proceed Carefully	Phased Withdraw
	Low	Quit	Phased Withdraw	Withdraw

Figure 7.4
Categories of Units by Competitive Position

Market Attraction

		High			Low		
		Competition			Competition		
			High	Low		High	Low
Business Position	High		1	2	High	5	6
	Low		3	4	Low	7	8

emphasize the relative importance of the several component measures for the two dimensions of course adds greatly to the richness of representation. It does mean, though, that essentially qualitative issues will be almost artificially translated into quantitative ones. The weights of necessity will be subjective, and even political. The value, though, is that this model provides means for dealing with those kinds of issues.

Three-Dimensional Model: Attractiveness, Position, Competition

Another generalization of the BCG model adds a third dimension—the level of competition—to those of market and position. At its simplest, it presents an array of eight cells, as shown in figure 7.4.

The Not-for-Profit Interpretation

For each cell, there is traditional wisdom about the appropriate choice of options in the business community. Of more immediate importance here, though, are the interpretations that apply to not-for-profit agencies in general, since academic libraries would appear to fall into that group.[2]

In not-for-profit agencies, the competition arises from alternative agencies that either provide similar services or are in principle capable of doing so. For example, a welfare agency may provide job counseling services, but the local school district and community college may be able to do so as well; the agency may provide referral services, but the local public library may do so as well. The appropriate strategies to adopt for each of the eight cells shown above are as follows:

Cell 1: Negotiate from strength with the alternative agency, dividing programs as most appropriate to the missions of both agencies. It is of some interest to note that this strategy is *not* one generally available to commerce and industry because of the constraints of the Sherman Anti-Trust Act; indeed, it may not be available to some not-for-profit organizations.

Cell 2: This is obviously the ideal position. The imperative is to consolidate the position and to expand as aggressively as possible in order to preclude potential entry of competitors in the future.

Cell 3: Under these conditions, there really is no reason for the agency to consider the service or to continue it if already providing it. Divestment of services in which the agency is noncompetitive is usually a painful choice, but it may result in strengthening the agency in the remaining areas of service.

Cell 4: If the programs are truly attractive, the obvious strategy is to commit the resources to create strength and move the agency into cell 2. If the resources for doing so are not available, the alternative strategy is to assist other agencies in developing strengths.

Cell 5: With low market attractiveness, competing strengths become nonproductive, so the strategy is deliberately to transfer programs together with expertise to the strongest competing agency, assisting them as may be most effective.

Cell 6: This may well be the most difficult of the strategic contexts, since the agency with strength may be the only means for meeting very real needs. The strategy must be to make a most careful evaluation of mission and of the degree to which the activity is central to it.

Cell 7: The strategy is clear: Get out fast, though responsibly. The activity may be important enough to warrant assuring that it is transferred to the strong alternative agency in an orderly, effective manner.

Cell 8: What are we doing in this position? Clearly someone has failed to assess the importance of an activity, the resources needed to serve it, and the demand for it.

Academic Library Interpretation

This model looks exceptionally valuable for application to academic libraries, especially as the assessments of market and position use an enriched set of criteria for evaluation. The importance of information in the academic institution implies that the market attraction is high, and the strength of academic libraries in general implies that their business position is high. The result is that the order of priorities for consideration of alternatives should be cells 1, 2, 3, 4. Of course, the assessments of market, position, and competition will need to be made by each particular library.

ASSESSMENT OF ACADEMIC LIBRARY OPERATIONS

Collections and Collection Management

We now turn from models developed in the business world to those that are more specific to academic libraries.[3] They provide means for assessment of the relationships among products and services, missions, and markets.

The book collection of a library, the data files of an indexing or abstracting service, and the contents of an archive: these are the basic capital resource for any information system. Measurement and evaluation of the individual collection, of the policies for its development, and of its management are basic to management decisions about what will be acquired, what means are appropriate for organization of them and access to them, where the materials will be stored, and what materials need to be preserved and in what form. Assessment of the collections of groups of libraries or other information institutions are essential in large-scale management decisions.[4] There are several models for collection assessment and evaluation:

Formula Approaches

The use of formulas, the most well known of which is the Clapp-Jordan formula, is one approach.[5] It identifies variables that characterize the programmatic objectives of a collection (such as numbers of students, faculty, and degree programs for an academic library); it then uses weights for each variable, summing across the set of them to obtain a measure of desired levels of either holdings or additions.

The National Shelflist Count

This project was one of the earliest and simplest of the tools developed to provide objective, comparative information about subject collections at specific institutions.[6] It was based on work at the University of Wisconsin Library in 1966. The first count was conducted by seventeen libraries in 1973; the data were published in 1974. In 1985, forty-eight libraries, including the Library of Congress and the National Agriculture Library, participated. The count is based on a segmentation of the Library of Congress classification system into 490 subject areas. Reports from each library include: actual title count, percent of institutional collection by specific classification area, relation between holdings and the number of titles held by all participants, the sized-related group, and the Library of Congress. Completing a count is estimated to take between forty and seventy hours.

North American Collections Inventory Project/ RLG Conspectus

This project was begun in 1979 by the Research Libraries Group.[7] It is an effort to describe and compare collections qualitatively using five categories or levels as descriptors: (0) Out of Scope, (1) Minimal, (2) Basic Information, (3) Instructional Support, (4) Research, and (5) Comprehensive. Worksheets break down Library of Congress (LC) numbers into 7,000 ranges, in which the evaluator assigns levels to the current and existing collection strength; some libraries have added Desired Collection Intensity to assist in formulating collection policies.

The UNC–CH Conspectus System is a dBase III program designed to manage the local and consortia information gathered for the NCIP/RLG Conspectus project. It was created by the Collection Development staff at the University of North Carolina. It includes space for: Current Collecting Intensity, Existing Collection Strength, Desired Collecting Intensity, local notes, preservation notes, related academic disciplines, library units and selectors, primary and secondary emphases, and reliance.

Count Analysis and Faculty Research Profile

This project was undertaken at Arizona State University.[8] LC class numbers were assigned to courses offered by the university. Data collected included: LC class number, course number, course title, code representing department and the subject specialist, Library of Congress Subject Heading. Four printouts were produced: Library of Congress class, Subject, Department, and Course number. The LC class report showed overlaps and indicated demand.

National Databases

There are several nationally available databases that can serve as means for comparison of individual institutions with standard files.[9] One approach to evaluating an undergraduate collection is to compare a library's holdings to the titles listed in *Books for College Libraries* (3rd ed.), "a recommended core collection for Undergraduate libraries." Another, the OCLC/AMIGOS Collection Analysis (compact disk), is especially valuable.[10] It was developed by OCLC as a collection and acquisitions assessment tool. It provides a means for an individual library to compare its collection with those of groups of peer institutions.

User-Based Methods

These are methods of collection development that tie collections closely to users. They seek answers to questions such as: How do we know what people are looking for, but not finding? Are we really buying the best items available on a given subject? Are we covering more than one or two points of view, building balanced collections according to the interests and needs of as many people as possible, and purchasing materials that will outlive the season? Will these be items valuable next year? These methods gather information about users: through a survey, a community profile, and an in-house survey.[11]

Storage Decisions

Chapter 10 presents a formal model for assessment of this situation as well as for making decisions concerning it.

Preservation Condition

Chapter 3 of this text presents the issues relevant to this assessment, together with summarizing data from studies at several research libraries concerning it.

Operational Performance

The performance of a library or other information system is defined here to be the efficiency (i.e., cost-effectiveness) of its operation. The significant issues relate to the means for measuring effectiveness and cost. Of special importance is the distinction between those aspects of performance that can be quantified and those that are essentially qualitative.

Technical Services

Chapter 9 provides a model that can be used for assessment of technical services performance as well as costs.

Delivery of Public Services

The delivery of public services, though, is far more difficult to assess, and there currently is not even an appropriate descriptive model, much less a quantitative one, to assist.

ASSESSMENT OF INSTITUTIONAL VALUE

An academic library functions within the larger institutional context. It requires tangible expenditures in capital investments (in the collection, in the buildings to house it, and in the equipment needed for processing) and in the operating expenses for staff and services. However, the benefits are largely intangible and uncertain, accruing in the long-term future, and not at the time when expenditures are made. How does one balance these? There must be some basis for determining the value to the institution that will justify the investment it makes in providing information.[12]

Relationship to Faculty Productivity

One approach to the assessment of institutional values applies a classical econometric model relating productivity to variables for capital investment and labor.[13] Productivity for the faculty of a university is probably best measured by research publications or, perhaps, by citations to them. Publications were used in a test of this approach, with results that demonstrated a positive correlation between the size of the library's collection and the research productivity of its faculty. Such a study could easily be replicated for a given university, showing changes over time, or in comparison among peer institutions.

ASSESSMENT OF THE EXTERNAL ENVIRONMENT

Chapter 6 summarizes the current assessment of the external environments. There do not appear to be any models, even descriptive ones, for assessing the impact of each environmental factor.

APPENDIX

Generic Computing Software

Spreadsheet software is a powerful tool for making the various assessments identified in this chapter.

Database software is crucial to the maintenance of the basic data files identified at the beginning of this chapter.

Specific Commercial Computer Software

InfoMapper is a software package that provides means for maintaining databases in a manner especially appropriate to strategic management.[14] It uses an array of database structures together with means for organization of the stored data and reporting from them. The result is an exceptionally valuable tool, which is worthy of consideration by anyone with responsibility for management of strategic planning.

The reports that can be derived permit the information resource manager to identify who does or does not use materials that would be of value to their respective responsibilities. As a result, areas of lack, of overlap and duplication, or of potential sharing of information can be made evident.

Basic data about information resources, the users, and the relationships between them are entered to provide the basic record from which all other operations and results are developed. The range of resources is unlimited, encompassing internal documents (technical and administrative reports, correspondence, files, and so forth) and external sources from print publications to electronic databases and on-line services.

@RISK dramatically extends the ability to use Lotus 1–2–3 spreadsheets for "what if" analyses.[15] It does so by providing means for assessing effects on critical dependent variables of statistical variability in data from which they are derived. It thus brings to the microcomputer a powerful, even essential, tool for risk analysis.

The program provides an array of thirty-four @ functions to supplement those that are standard in Lotus 1–2–3 spreadsheets. Each @ function represents a statistical distribution for the data in the cell in which it is stored. In normal spreadsheet operation, the value delivered by the @ function is the "expected value" (or mean) for the distribution, so that the effect is identical to that resulting from storage of the expected value itself.

The power that is available, though, is spectacular. *@RISK* provides means for automatically sampling the distributions stored in cells so that the effects of their statistical variability upon a criterion variable can rapidly be determined. The commands available permit the user to control simulation of large numbers of such sampling and then to show graphically what the resulting distribution for the criterion variable or variables would be. The result is a dramatic picture of the risks implied by potential variability in source data.

Appropriate @ functions for distributions are recorded in cells of the spreadsheet. For example, they might represent the expected distributions of "SALES" and "COSTS," or of "BOND PRICE" and "PRIME RATE." The distribution of a derived value for "NET REVENUE" could then result from a calculation based on the combination of distributions for "SALES" and "COSTS," and that for determining "PRESENT VALUE" of a bond, from a calculation based on the combination of distributions for "BOND PRICE" and "PRIME RATE."

Once the appropriate distributions have been entered and *@RISK* has been attached, simulations can then be run that sample from the distributions and determine the resulting value for the dependent variable. With a single *@RISK* command specified from the *@RISK* menu (in standard Lotus 1–2–3 structure), the user can call for a simulation and specify the type of sampling, the number of samples (i.e., iterations) to be taken, and the variable or variables to be evaluated.

The results can then be viewed in graphical form as a distribution of the dependent variable together with the usual array of statistics for that distribution, including identification of the expected value, or mean, and of various percentiles. The user thus has a clear picture of the range of values and can qualitatively assess the risk implications.

NOTES

1. Each of the course textbooks listed in note 1 of chapter 1 has a section devoted to discussion of these models, as follows: Aaker, ch. 10; Boulton, chs. 4–7; Certo and Peter, ch. 4; Glueck and Jauch, ch. 5; Hax and Majluf, ch. 15; and Justis et al., ch. 3.

2. Macmillan, Ian C., "Competitive Strategies for Not-for-Profit Agencies," in *Advances in Strategic Management*, vol. 1, ed. Robert Lamb (Greenwich, Conn.: JAI Press, 1983), pp. 61–82.

3. Dougherty, Richard M., and Heinritz, Fred J. *Scientific Management of Library Operations* (Metuchen, N.J.: Scarecrow Press, 1982).

4. American Library Association, *Guidelines for Collection Development* (Chicago: American Library Association, 1979); Axford, H. W., "Collection Management: A New Dimension," *Journal of Academic Librarianship* 6 (1981): 324–29; Dowd, Sheila T., "The Formulation of a Collection Development Policy Statement," in *Collection Development in Libraries: A Treatise*, ed. Robert D. Steuart and George B. Miller, Jr. (Greenwich, Conn.: JAI Press, 1980), pp. 67–87; Faigel, Martin, "Methods and Issues in Collection Evaluation Today," *Library Acquisitions: Practice and Theory* 9(1) (1985): 21–35; American Library Association, *Guide to Evaluation of Library Collections* (Chicago: American Library Association, 1989); Kaske, N. K., "Evaluation of Current Collection Utilization Methodologies and Findings," *Collection Management* 3(2–3) (1979): 197–99; Lancaster, F. Wilfrid, *The Measurement and Evaluation of Library Services* (Washington, D.C.: Information Resources Press, 1977).

5. Clapp, Verner W., and Jordan, Robert T, "Quantitative Criteria for Adequacy of Academic Library Collections," *College and Research Libraries* 50 (March 1989): 153–63; Voigt, Melvin, "Acquisition Rates in University Libraries," *College and Research Libraries* 36 (July 1975): 263–71. (The formula presented in this article, modified somewhat and called the Voigt-Susskind Formula, has been the basis for allocations within the University of California for more than a decade.)

6. Branin, Joseph J., Farrell, David, and Tibdin, Marriann, "The National Shelflist Count Project: Its History, Limitations, and Usefulness," *Library Resources and Technical Services* 29 (October/December 1985): 333–42; Dannelly, Gay N., "The National Shelflist Count: A Tool for Collection Management," paper presented at the conference, Collection Development in Action, Toledo, Ohio, October 28, 1988; Ortopan, Leroy D., "National Shelflist Count: A Historical Introduction," *Library Resources and Technical Services* 29 (October/December 1985): 328–32.

7. Farrell, David, and Reed-Scott, Jutta, "The North American Collections Inventory Project: Implications for the Future of Coordinated Management of Research Collections," *Library Resources and Technical Services* 33 (January 1989): 15–28; Farrell, David, "The North American Inventory Project (NCIP): Phase II Results in Indiana," *Resource Sharing and Information Networks* 2 (Spring/Summer 1985): 37–48; Farrell, David, "The NCIP Option for Coordinated Collection Management," *Library Resources and Technical Services* 30 (January–March 1986): 47–56; Ferguson, Anthony W., Grant, Joan, and Rutstein, Joel S., "The RLG Conspectus: Its Uses and Benefits," *College and*

Research Libraries 49 (March 1989): 197–206; Gwinn, Nancy E., and Mosher, Paul H., "Coordinating Collection Development: The RLG Conspectus," *College and Research Libraries* 44 (March 1983): 128–40; MacEwan, Bonnie, "The North American Inventory Project: A Tool for Selection, Education and Communication," *Library Acquisitions: Practice and Theory* 13 (1989): 45–50; Reed-Scott, Jutta, *Manual for the North American Inventory of Research Collections* (Washington, D.C.: Association of Research Libraries, Office of Management Studies, 1988); Mosher, Paul H., "A Natural Scheme for Collaboration in Collection Development: The RLG-NCIP Effort," *Resource Sharing and Information Networks* 2 (Spring/Summer 1985): 21–35; Oberg, Larry R., "Evaluating the Conspectus Approach for Smaller Library Collections," *College and Research Libraries* 49 (May 1988): 187–96; Association of Research Libraries, Office of Management Studies, *Qualitative Collection Analysis: The Conspectus Methodology*, SPEC Kit 151 (Washington, D.C.: Association of Research Libraries, Office of Management Studies, 1989).

8. Palais, Elliot, "Use of Course Analysis in Compiling a Collection Development Policy Statement for a University Library," *Journal of Academic Librarianship* 1 (March 1987): 8–13.

9. Armbrister, Ann, "Library Marc Tapes as a Resource for Collection Analysis: The AMIGOS Service," *Advances in Library Automation and Networking* 2 (1988): 119–35; Sanders, Nancy P., O'Neill, Edward T., and Weibel, Stuart L., "Automated Collection Analysis Using the OCLC and RLG Bibliographic Databases," *College and Research Libraries* 49 (July 1985): 305–15.

10. *Books for College Libraries* (3rd ed.) (Chicago: American Library Association, 1988); Dillon, Martin, and Crook, Mark A., "A Prototype Automated Collection Analysis Tool for Libraries," *OCLC Research Review*, July 1987, pp. 3–4; Amigos, "Four Academic Libraries Purchase OCLC/Amigos Collection Analysis CD" (news release), 6 October 1989.

11. Aguilar, William, "The Application of Relative Use and Interlibrary Demand in Collection Development," *Collection Management* 8(1) (1986): 15–24; Broadus, Robert, "Use Studies of Library Collections," *Library Resources and Technical Services* 24(4) (1980): 317–24; Burns, Robert W., Jr., "Library Use as a Performance Measure: Its Background and Rationale," *Journal of Academic Librarianship* 4(1) (1978): 4–11; Christiansen, Dorothy E., Davis, C. Roger, and Reed-Scott, Jutta, "Guidelines to Collection Evaluation through Use and User Studies," *Library Resources and Technical Services* 27(4) (October/December 1983): 432–40; Church, Steven S., "User Criteria for Evaluation of Library Services," *Journal of Library Administration* 2(1) (1981): 35–46; Lancaster, F. Wilfrid, "Evaluating Collections by Their Use," *Collection Management* 4(1–2) (1982): 15–43; Lopez, Manuel D., "The Lopez or Citation Technique of In-Depth Collection Evaluation Explicated," *College and Research Libraries* 44(3) (1983): 251–55; Millson-Martula, Christopher, "Use Studies and Serials Rationalization: A Review," *Serials Librarian* 15(1–2) (1988): 121–36; Morse, Philip M., "Measures of Library Effectiveness," *Library Quarterly* 42(1) (Jan. 1972): 15–30; Nutter, Susan K., "Online Systems and the Management of Collections: Use and Implications," *Advances in Library Automation and Networking* 1, 125–49; Obert, Beverly, "Collection Development through Student Surveys and Collection Analysis," *Illinois Libraries* 70(1) (1988): 46–53; Osburn, Charles B., "Non-Use and User Studies in Collection Development," *Collection Management* 4(1–2) (1982): 45–53; Sarloe, Bart, "Achieving Client-Centered

Collection Development in Small and Medium-Sized Academic Libraries,'' *College and Research Libraries* 50 (May 1989): 344–53.

12. Marschak, Jacob, "Towards an Economic Theory of Organization and Information," in *Decision Processes*, ed. R. M. Thrall, C. H. Coombs, and R. L. Davis (New York: Wiley, 1954); McDonough, Adrian M., *Information Economics and Management Systems* (New York: McGraw-Hill, 1963); McLean, Neil, "The Changing Economics of Information: A Library/Information Service View," in *The Electronic Campus—An Information Strategy*, ed. Lynn J. Brindley. Proceedings of the Conference in Banbury, England, 28–30 October 1988, pp. 53–64; Nilsonger, Thomas E., "A Test of Two Citation Checking Techniques for Evaluating Political Science Collections in University Libraries," *Library Resources and Technical Services* 27(2) (1983): 163–76; Summers, David, "The Changing Economics of Information: An Industry View," in *The Electronic Campus—An Information Strategy*. Proceedings of the Conference in Banbury, England, 28–30 October 1988.

13. Hayes, Robert M., "The Management of Library Resources: The Balance between Capital and Staff in Providing Services," *Library Research* 1(2) (Summer 1979): 119–42; Hayes, Robert M., and Erickson, Timothy, "Added Value as a Function of Purchases of Information Services," *Information Society* 1(4) (Dec. 1982): 307–38; Hayes, Robert M., et al., "An Application of the Cobb-Douglas Model to the Association of Research Libraries," *Library and Information Science Research* 5(3) (Fall 1983): 291–326.

14. Hayes, Robert M., "InfoMapper," *Information Today* 9(7) (July/August 1992): 9–10.

15. Hayes, Robert M., "@RISK," *Information Today* 9(8) (Sept. 1992): 12–13.

8

Visualizing the Future

This chapter is concerned with means for visualizing the library's future environment: the market represented by the institutional setting and the needs of users, and all the external environmental contexts. In doing so, contrast is drawn between projection and forecasting versus prospective viewing and planning.

QUANTITATIVE FORECASTING

It is beyond the scope of this book to provide technical details about the rich array of mathematical techniques for quantitative forecasting. For those, the reader will need to turn to appropriate texts.[1] However, there is value in providing a brief descriptive overview of the means that are available.

Methods

Extrapolation from Past to Future

The most evident means for quantitative forecasting is Time Series Projection. It uses historical data to identify alternative models: trends, moving averages and smoothing, and seasonal variations. The appendix describes one available commercial computer package providing extensive capabilities for time series analysis. The most dramatic historic examples of application of such forecasting to academic libraries have related to projections of the patterns of growth of collections.[2]

Simulation

A simulation depends upon having a model of relationships among variables that characterize the system or situation being studied. For example, the relevant variables may include ones that represent the internal resources of the library—its collection, its staff, and its computer equipment—from which the model can derive measures of production. They may include ones that reflect the policies of the library—for collection development, for access allocation decisions, and for delivery of services—from which the model can derive effects of different policies. They may reflect the nature of the market or constituencies served, including needs, frequency of requests, and required response times, from which the model can predict the effects of differing market demands.

Chapters 9 and 10 provide bases for simulations of at least parts of the first two sets of variables: the internal or endogenous and the policy variables. The Lotus 1–2–3 add-in, @RISK (described at the end of chapter 7), provides a powerful means for implementing simulations within spreadsheets.

Sources of Data

Predicasts

This is a powerful source of data for input to models for decision making.[3] It draws on publications in which predictions are made about future events.

Co-Works Foundation Pack

The commercial package described in the appendix to this chapter provides access to a wide range of economic and demographic time series.

Reported Library Statistics

The ARL and the ACRL each provide yearly reports of representative data about their respective libraries.[4] As will be illustrated in chapters 9 and 10, these can be used both for formulation of models and for testing of them.

Statistics of Use

The most evident data are statistics derivable from actual operations of a library. There are two flaws or deficiencies. First, they represent only the users, not the nonusers. Second, they reflect the specifics of the information system rather than those of the users; as a result they embody the perceptions of the users about what they can expect rather than of what they need. Despite those deficiencies, though, statistics do provide an objective set of data on which to base estimates of user needs and characteristics.

Figure 8.1
Representative Matrix

$$
\begin{array}{ccc}
A & x = & b \\
\begin{bmatrix} 10 & 7 & 8 & 7 \\ 7 & 5 & 6 & 5 \\ 8 & 6 & 10 & 9 \\ 7 & 5 & 9 & 10 \end{bmatrix} &
\begin{bmatrix} x_1 \\ x_2 \\ x_3 \\ x_4 \end{bmatrix} &
\begin{bmatrix} b_1 \\ b_2 \\ b_3 \\ b_4 \end{bmatrix}
\end{array}
\qquad
\begin{array}{ccc}
A & x = & b \\
\begin{bmatrix} 10 & 7 & 8 & 7 \\ 7 & 5 & 6 & 5 \\ 8 & 6 & 10 & 9 \\ 7 & 5 & 9 & 10 \end{bmatrix} &
\begin{bmatrix} 1 \\ 1 \\ 1 \\ 1 \end{bmatrix} &
\begin{bmatrix} 32 \\ 23 \\ 33 \\ 31 \end{bmatrix}
\end{array}
$$

Monitoring and Analysis of Use Logs

Of special value with respect to data about use is the fact that automated systems provide easy means for monitoring operations, acquiring data in the form of usage logs (limited only by the requirements of privacy for the individual user).

Problems

Reliability of Data

All sources of data are subject to inaccuracy in measurement, inconsistency, and general unreliability. The problems with ARL and ACRL data in this respect have been thoroughly identified, but in many respects "they are the only game in town"; so if one wants to play, therefore, one has to accept the unreliability.[5]

Stability of Models

A technical problem of special importance, but one not generally recognized, is the likelihood that models will be ill-conditioned and, as a result, unstable. To illustrate the effects of such instability, consider the following simple example: Suppose the library consists of four collections (e.g., branches) and that there are four groups of users (e.g., departments), suppose we have historical data showing the level of use of each collection by each group of user. Such a situation is likely to be represented by a set of linear equations, $A(x) = b$, where A might represent the historical pattern of use, the distribution of resources among the set of libraries might be given by x, and the size of each department by b. It can then be used to determine the x that will best serve a given b (see figure 8.1). However, let us suppose that the measurement of the values for b = (32,23,33,31) is slightly in error and that b′ = (32.1,22.9,33.1,30.9) is used instead of the real values for b. The model will then produce as its answer a dramatically different result, as shown in figure 8.2.

Another problem arises from errors in the model. Let us suppose that the values in the matrix A, representing the decision model, are slightly in error (see figure 8.3). This problem is potentially even more catastrophic

Figure 8.2
Effects of Variation in Measurement of Vector Values

$$
\begin{array}{ccc}
A & x' & = \quad b'
\end{array}
$$

$$
\begin{bmatrix}
10 & 7 & 8 & 7 \\
7 & 5 & 6 & 5 \\
8 & 6 & 10 & 9 \\
7 & 5 & 9 & 10
\end{bmatrix}
\begin{bmatrix}
9.2 \\
-12.6 \\
4.5 \\
1.1
\end{bmatrix}
\begin{bmatrix}
32.1 \\
22.9 \\
33.1 \\
30.9
\end{bmatrix}
$$

Figure 8.3
Effects of Variation in Measurement of Matrix Values

$$
\begin{array}{ccc}
A'' & x'' & = \quad b
\end{array}
$$

$$
\begin{bmatrix}
10.00 & 7.00 & 8.10 & 7.00 \\
7.08 & 5.04 & 6.00 & 5.00 \\
8.00 & 5.98 & 9.89 & 9.00 \\
6.99 & 4.99 & 9.00 & 9.98
\end{bmatrix}
\begin{bmatrix}
-81 \\
137 \\
-34 \\
22
\end{bmatrix}
\begin{bmatrix}
32 \\
23 \\
33 \\
31
\end{bmatrix}
$$

than those due to error in measurement of variables, since one tends to accept the model as given and to be concerned only with assuring that variables are reliably measured.

QUALITATIVE FORECASTING

Questionnaires, Interviews, and Surveys

These are self-evident means for determining needs, independent of data about the library itself, though usually they may focus on the library as the context for assessment of needs. Typically, they will ask the user to identify and assess the relative importance of a number of alternative sources for needed information.[6] In virtually any response to such a question, the user will identify, in order of use, personal files and collections, colleagues, and current publications. Libraries will be ranked anywhere from number four to number seven. Moreover, such a result should not be surprising, though usually the librarian will be disappointed, if not shocked, to be considered so infrequently. The next section of this chapter will examine a particular approach to interview, the critical incident technique.

Future Studies

Three techniques for what are called "Future Studies"—simulations, scenarios, and Delphi studies—will be discussed later in this chapter.

CRITICAL INCIDENT TECHNIQUE

The "critical incident technique" (CIT) is an especially effective form of interview. In it, the interviewer asks the respondent to think of a *specific* incident (the critical incident) in which an information need was particularly significant. It then explores three aspects of the critical incident: the antecedent context for the need, the attempts to meet the need, and the outcome (i.e., whether the need was or was not satisfied).

A recent example of use of CIT is a study of Medline use carried out for the National Library of Medicine by American Institutes for Research, a company in Palo Alto that specializes in this kind of study.[7] It focused on physicians and identified the following kinds of need for use of Medline: (1) patient care, (2) research, (3) teaching, (4) learning, (5) administration, and (6) consulting and other business endeavors.

The Process

Demographic Data

First, the respondent is asked to supply information of a demographic nature, providing details about him- or herself, position and responsibilities, and knowledge and experience.

Antecedent Context

The CIT then involves a series of carefully structured questions designed to elicit data on which the nature of needs can be identified and classified; that provides the means for exploring antecedents or the context for the critical incident. To do so, the respondent may be given a list of typical activities that might lead to an information need and will be asked to identify which, if any, applied to the critical incident; the question will be open-ended, though, so that it is easy for the respondent to add to the list and redefine its elements. The respondent is encouraged to amplify on the anecdotal evidence with details that enrich the picture. In particular, some questions will explore the kinds of information needed, the urgency of the need, the requirements for coverage or specificity, the means for use of the information.

Means for Meeting Needs

The CIT then asks about the means for getting the needed information. Again, a list of typical sources may be provided, which are also open-ended so as to encourage additions or redefinitions. Questions will explore whether the respondent used the sources directly or used an intermediary of some kind. They will explore the various measures of effectiveness— precision, recall, response time, recency, or currency of the data provided, the forms in which the information was provided, the effort needed on the part of the respondent to use the source and to deal with the information obtained.

Assessment of Effectiveness

Finally, the CIT examines the effect of the information obtained upon resolution of the antecedent need. Did it meet the needs (if so, in what way, and if not, why not)? What was the outcome for the critical incident and what role did the information that was received play in that outcome?

Open-Ended Questions and Note-Taking

Consider a typical thirty- to sixty-minute interview in which the stimulus is a limited set of open-ended questions:

"What has been your experience with . . . ?"

"What happened on the most recent occasion of . . . ?"

"What is your assessment of the value of . . . ?"

The notes taken during such an interview (or transcribed from a recording of it) probably amount to about 1,500 words. (Notes from such an interview may run to about ten pages of twenty lines, with about 8 words per line, for example.) Beyond the anecdotal substance derived from such open-ended questions, there will also be more standardized objective data: descriptive of the interview itself (data, time, place, interviewer, etc.), demographic data (name, sex, age, organizational affiliation, position, etc.), and a priori structural data (i.e., questions for which there can be preset categories of response). These all provide the solid data for statistical analyses of their inter-relations with each other as well as with the results from the more free-form responses to the open-ended questions.

Transcription of Notes

Following the interview, transcribe the notes into a computer. If done immediately after the interview, the notes are fresh enough to serve as stimulus for remembrance of substance that may be added to the computer file. Sometimes, though, there must be a delay of some days before transcription; in such cases the computer file is usually simply a copy of the notes without additional substance. In some cases, the transcription may be done by clerical staff and then, of course, it must be simply a verbatim reproduction of the notes as taken. Input of the notes for an interview (taking them at about 1,500 words) will require about one hour of time, about the same as the interview itself.

Content Analysis of Interviews

Of course, as with any of the methods for determining user needs for information, data acquisition through the CIT interview is only the first stage. The set of interviews must then be analyzed; a taxonomy of needs must be derived. In part, the "seed" question listing alternatives provides a starting point, but the taxonomic analysis must build from it in order to accommodate the needs as actually described by the respondents. The evaluations of effectiveness of sources are of value both as means for assessing them and, more important, as means for determining the needs that serve as the basis for assessment. If response time was a problem, that serves not only to assess the responsiveness of the source but also to highlight the importance of response time to the user.

We turn now to a methodology for the analysis of open-ended questions, the kind especially effective in providing anecdotal evidence that gives richness and texture to otherwise dry and useless statistics. The result is a cognitive map (i.e., content analysis) of the range of views derived from the interviews.

Preliminary Accounting Controls

When a sufficient set of notes is available, the results of each interview are reviewed to assure that each is complete, that the standardized data are all in consistent form (usually in a database structure), and that all necessary controls have been established (for example, a count of the number of interviews included in the set to be analyzed).

Identifying "Units of Discourse"

Now, the process of content analysis can begin. The computer file for each interview is examined sequentially, with the objective of identifying units of discourse, interpreted as phrases that can be regarded as reflecting a cohesive element in the discussion. The choice should be narrow rather than broad, so that a typical sentence might involve three or four such units of discourse; however, the breadth must be sufficient to be identifiable and complete. Each unit of discourse should be placed on a single line of text, followed by a carriage return.

Operational Accounting Controls

The next step is purely mechanical. Each line is assigned a sequential number within the interview. Typically, for example, an open-ended question will itself have a number; that becomes the first digit or so, with each line within the response being a subdivision. The result is in a format such as:

"17 05 007," meaning "Interview 17, Question 5, Line 7," or
"45 20 205," meaning "Interview 45, Question 20, Line 205."

(Other variants are, of course, equally effective, and the choice of format is hardly a material issue provided it is consistently followed.) That makes it easy to reconstruct the original sequence, but more importantly it permits the unit of discourse to be related to the interviewee, to the question, and to the surrounding units of discourse.

Figure 8.4
Illustration of Coding for Units of Discourse

Sequence	Code	Text
"17 05 007,	123	This is the text of the unit of discourse"
"17 05 007,	456	This is the text of the unit of discourse"
"17 05 007,	890	This is the text of the unit of discourse"
"45 20 205,	045	Another unit of discourse"
"45 20 205,	321	Another unit of discourse"
"45 20 205,	567	Another unit of discourse"
"45 20 205,	890	Another unit of discourse"

Category Coding

The next step, though, is very substantive. Each unit of discourse is now examined both as a unit and in the context in which it is seen. A code is assigned to it to represent a conceptual category to which it relates. The result is that each line—that is, each unit of discourse—has two codes assigned to it: The first is the mechanical sequence code and the second is the conceptual category code.

At times, one might want to assign a set of category codes to a unit of discourse. To do so, a copy is made of the unit of discourse, together with its mechanical sequence code, for each category code. The result might then look as shown in figure 8.4.

Development of Category Codes

Obviously, before proceeding further in discussion, we must deal with the question, "What is the origin of the conceptual categories and the related codes?" There are two sources, reflecting the two approaches to development of any taxonomy; the important point is that the two approaches should be treated as complementary, not competitive or mutually exclusive; in other words, one can use both, in parallel and in conjunction with each other. One approach uses an a priori set of categories as the source of codes, which of course requires that there must be a theoretical structure for the area of concern in the interviews sufficient to represent the issues involved, even though perhaps only at a preliminary stage.

The second source is the set of interviews themselves. Let us suppose that there is insufficient a priori knowledge to generate a conceptual structure; at best there may be very broad categories. As each unit of discourse is examined, it is compared with others and rough distinctions are made among them. If there are broad categories already identified, we will use them; if not, we will just build as we go, but the categories rapidly become self-evident.

In the next step, which is applicable both to the development of codes and to the analysis of the interviews, the entire body of units of discourse is simply sorted on the category codes, so that all units in a given category are physically brought together, separated from their sources. The set of units in a category is now examined and subcategories identified; again, they also rapidly become self-evident. A taxonomy is developed and the category codes are made more specific to represent it; the codes assigned to individual lines are modified to reflect the more refined structure. This process is repeated at increasing levels of detail until the taxonomy of categories is sufficient for the purposes of large-scale analysis and commentary.

Analysis of Categorized Groups of Units of Discourse

At the large level of analysis—the entire set of units of discourse—the same process is applied again but now with the intent of analysis of import rather than analysis of structure. That is, the set of units of discourse within a category is examined for their interrelationships in order to determine the general nature of the set. That general nature is virtually self-evident by this stage.

At this point, one can develop text that reflects the results of analysis of each category. The crucial point, though, is that the units of discourse within a group almost speak for themselves; they provide anecdotal detail that is exceptionally rich, real, and effective.

Statistical Analysis of Relationships

The final stage in analysis is to provide a statistical analysis of the categories, of the relationships among them, of the relationships between them, and of the relationships to the objective demographic data elements.

SIMULATIONS

While simulations are essentially quantitative, they provide powerful means for qualitative study of the future. In particular, they permit one to explore hypothetical futures, determine the implications of alternative models, evaluate the effects of variation in data, and assess the effects of different policies. A spreadsheet provides a simple example of such uses in its ability to make "what if" assessments. A more powerful example with spreadsheets is represented by the use of the add-in program @RISK for risk analysis.

One important strategic management use of simulation is for contingency planning. It allows the manager to see what the effects of change, in funding or in demand, for example, will be and to explore alternative responses to them. Another is for assessment of operational effectiveness, to assess the extent to which objectives are, or are not, being met by simulating the intended performance and comparing the results with the actual outcome.

SCENARIOS

Another method for obtaining data from the persons with a stake in the design and implementation of a system is the use of scenarios.[8] While usually applied in efforts to predict the future, as is the Delphi method to be discussed later, it is equally applicable to policy-making contexts.

The objective is to identify a number of alternative systems, each of which is strategically plausible and makes good operational sense. The alternatives are not expected or intended to be mutually exclusive, but each should depict a radically different set of priorities, objectives, methods for solution, choice of technology, or other alternative factor. The effects on users, on management, and on operations would presumably be different under each system. The objective then is to determine how actions and choices made by the participants can be affected by each of them and, in the implementation, how each of them can influence the design and development of the system.

The Process

Form Teams

Teams are formed from persons who represent the groups or individuals with a stake in the outcome of the design and development process. Typically, the groups might include users, managers, operational staff, top administration, and staff functions; they might include also experts in technology (both hardware and software), educators and researchers, and politicians and professional interests. The scope is limited only by the scope of the system being considered.

In forming the teams, three different tactics can be followed, each with its own advantages and disadvantages: The teams can be formed randomly, that is, without any preconceived intent; they can be formed by putting together persons with a common focus of concern (users with users, managers with managers, etc.); or they can be formed by putting together groups with a common view of the world (high-tech enthusiasts with high-tech enthusiasts, conservatives with conservatives, etc.). The advantage of the first is that it requires no conscious process of deciding who should work together; the disadvantage is that the results cannot be calibrated with anything. The advantage of the second is that the participants in each team presumably have a common basis of understanding, thus minimizing the problems in communication at the outset, while the disadvantage is that there is little opportunity for gaining insights from other perspectives. The advantage of the third is that there is likely to be a reinforcement of perspectives, with each area of concern being represented in the process; the disadvantage is the difficulty in identifying commoness of views. On balance, the third approach seems best.

Evaluation of Needs

Each team identifies needs that are either highly likely to be important in system operations, or, at the other extreme, highly unlikely. This serves as a means for laying out the universe of choices; it aids in exchange of opinions and ideas; and it reveals the assumptions and biases of the participants. As part of this, each team is then asked to evaluate the relative importance of the array of needs. Which of them must be served by the system? Some, perhaps, must not be served.

Development of Scenarios

Each team postulates a strategy that will, in its view, meet the needs as identified in step two and identifies the events that are necessary (i.e., that must or must not happen) for the development and implementation of the postulated strategy. Each team then develops a scenario or descriptive narrative that links the necessary events into a process of development, covering to the extent imagination permits both likely successes and likely failures in achievement of the postulated strategy.

The structure of each scenario should include a perception of the current situation, a visualization of expected or desired final situations, and a description of the pathways between them, showing the process of development. It may be of value to divide the scenario into subsystems, when there are aspects that can have independent development, and then to show the resulting interactions among the subsystems. The scenario should conclude with a summary of consequences to be expected.

The scenarios should reflect the interactions among actors' strategies, the effects of changing environments, and the view of each team about long-term trends. Each team then presents its listing of needs, its postulated strategy, its set of events, and its scenario to the entire group of teams. In this way, all participants gain a wide view of the set of alternatives, of the priorities with which various aspects are viewed.

Analysis

The final stage is an analysis of the substance from the several scenarios. The array of needs and events are tabulated, with the differences in priorities shown. The result is a basis for assessment of the impact of any final choice upon each of the positions identified. There may be a final reconciliation of views, with the group as a plenary body rather than as team participants.

The process of analysis of scenarios is probably best done by construction of a database arranged around a set of internal and external variables. From them, a matrix showing dependencies among variables (both internal and external) can be created. Then co-effect matrices (i.e., powers of the original matrix) can be developed, leading to a cross-impact analysis from which hypotheses can be assessed.

The Potential Scenarios

The potential set of scenarios is limited only by the imagination of the participants, but one might expect to find one or more of the following types of emphasis, especially if the teams are chosen to reflect common views of the world.

High-Technology Emphasis

A team of high-tech enthusiasts presumably will emphasize the opportunities presented by the combination of increasing capabilities with decreasing costs of the technologies. They will identify new kinds of needs requiring new kinds of services; they may well develop a revolutionary scenario, with events involving a dramatic replacement of current methods with new ones.

Economic Emphasis

Another team may well place its emphasis on the funding implications. They will identify needs that reflect market-oriented choices in the willingness of users to pay for services that meet them; they will develop scenarios that are evolutionary, with events that utilize existing capital investments most effectively.

Operational Emphasis

Another team may focus on the operational effects. They will identify effects on staffing, both current and future, and on the tactical and operational management.

Networking Emphasis

Another team might focus on interinstitutional cooperation. They will identify the advantages in the sharing of resources, in the adoption of commonly accepted standards, and in the provision of location-independent data access.

Institutional Emphasis

Another team might focus on institutional objectives, seeing the information system in terms of its support to them and the needs of users in terms of institutional measures of performance.

THE DELPHI TECHNIQUE

The Delphi technique is a procedure using sequential questionnaires by which the opinions of experts can be brought to bear on issues that are essentially nonfactual. Its original use was for establishing predictions about the future, with the view that the opinions of experts, especially if they represented a spectrum of informed knowledge, could be combined into useful statistical consensus.[9] That use is still of value in the strategic management of academic libraries as a means for assessing the external technological and publishing environment.

It is also of value in assessment of political positions. Positions will vary in the extent to which they are supportive of the library strategic interests or resistant to them. They will differ in their effects: their basis, nature, degree of certainty, and degree of importance.

The Questionnaire Method

The use of questionnaires, rather than open forum discussion, is intended to avoid the effects of dominant personalities—of people that could sway or affect the opinions of others simply on the basis of force of argument. The underlying rationale is that experts will make valid projections from their own knowledge, but if they are affected by the immediate impact of the social environment those projections will no longer be validly based on their own experience.

Another value of a sequence of questionnaires is the possibility they provide for the experts to assimilate the view of others, rationalize their arguments, and incorporate the evidence of the results from one questionnaire in responding to the next one. The underlying rationale is that even experts are uncertain in their views when faced with nonfactual issues and will modify those views based on a rational—or perhaps even not so rational—response to what other experts appear to conclude about the same or related issues.

Role of Discussion

The process is facilitated and the effects are amplified if face-to-face discussion occurs between successive questionnaires. In that way, discussion can be based upon the statistical results from prior questionnaires, and later ones can benefit from the arguments presented during the discussion, but sufficiently removed from the impact of personality to permit the individual's own knowledge and experience to be dominant in the answers.

Convergence or Divergence?

In this kind of process, successive questionnaires may repeat questions from earlier ones to determine whether there is a convergence of views from one questionnaire to the next. The general expectation is that there will be convergence, though it is likely that questions will be of two types:

1. Questions on which there is no disagreement in principle. On such questions, one would indeed expect to see convergence in views.

2. Questions on which there is a fundamental issue of disagreement in principle. On such questions, one might expect to see divergence in views, an evident dichotomization in the response.

The assumption is that experts indeed will rationally consider the opinions of others and will modify their own judgement when doing so does not jeopardize a point of principle. However, if they consider that the possibility of a consensus will threaten something they regard as vital, they will consciously move away from what may appear to be consensus, with the view of counterbalancing it.

Nature of Questions

Typically, the kinds of nonfactual issues that have been considered in the Delphi approach have been predictions about the future, in forms like:

- What will be the crucial events?
- When will they occur?
- What will be the effects?
- What can be done to deal with the effects?

Usually, these kinds of questions have been incorporated, in about that sequence, in successive questionnaires. That is, the participant experts will first be asked, "What will be the crucial events?," and so on through the progression. The intent of that sequence is to focus not only on the views but on the relationships between the questions. Thus, in successive questionnaires one can focus on the crucial issues (as identified in prior questionnaires), significant time periods, or significant effects rather than dissipating one's efforts on less important ones.

Figure 8.5
Illustration of Graphical Display of Quartile Distributions

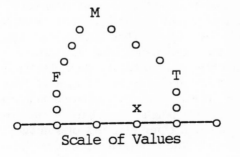

Form of Presentation

As a matter of technical detail, it is typical to present the results in the form of a quartile distribution of the illustrative form (shown in figure 8.5), where F records the "first quartile" (i.e., 25 percent of the answers are less than that value), M records the median (or middle value), and T records the "third quartile" (i.e., 25 percent of the cases are greater than that value). The picture is frequently pictured as a house, with M as the ridge-pole and F and T as the eaves. The scale of values can be temporal ("When will an event occur ?"), ordinal ("How important ?"), or a measure scale. The "x" is frequently inserted at the answer for a given respondent, so the respondent can see how his or her answer compares with the general picture.

Value in Policy Formation

With that as the general frame of reference for the Delphi process, it seems eminently suitable for dealing with issues of policy formulation, perhaps even more appropriate for them than for the more usual applications to predictions (since, in a sense, predictions become matters of fact, not opinion, while matters of policy remain forever nonfactual). Beyond that, however, it provides a means for dealing with political factors in the process of strategic management.

APPENDIX

CoWorks Time Series Library provides a source of time series data together with powerful display and analysis tools. It functions as a spreadsheet application program (operating under either Lotus 1–2–3 or Borland Quattro-Pro in 123 menu mode) for the display and analysis functions. It can draw upon associated files of over five hundred existing individual time series related to economic and demographic data for the United States and regions of the world.[10]

Among the capabilities of this program are a set of mathematical tools that permit the user to perform mathematical operations especially appropriate to time series analysis. They include the means for conversion of source data, for combination of several time series in a single analysis, for calculation of a variety of essential statistical characteristics, for evaluating standard trigonometric and exponential functions. They also provide means for extrapolation (an exceptionally seductive but dangerous process in time series analysis) and interpolation (a relatively safe process).

Of greatest importance for purposes of strategic management is the ability to incorporate time series data specific to the user and to combine them with the broad range of standard national and international time series data. This provides means for relating the experience of the individual library or institution to the larger environmental contexts.

MaxThink is an exceptionally imaginative and creative commercial program to support conceptual analysis of text. It provides a variety of means for viewing textual data and for structuring them. It can serve as a word processor, with all of the standard functions for textual input and formatting and for copying and moving textual segments. In that respect, it is similar to any other standard package and especially to typical "outliners." However, to those standard functions it adds a wide range of means for conceptual analysis: (1) prioritizing textual data (i.e., ranking items in order of importance, (2) assigning categories to textual data, (3) accumulating and gathering textual data into categories, (4) joining text from related categories or dividing text into subcategories, (5) sorting data by categories, and (6) performing operations on categories of text that are applied automatically to the entire group.

The program embodies that best qualities of hypertext, with all its philosophical objectives, and combines them with realistic objectives in application to real problems in textual analysis. The processes for analysis of interviews, as described in this chapter, are well exemplified in and supported by the capabilities of this commercial program.

NOTES

1. Makridakis, Spyros, and Wheelwright, Steven C., *The Handbook of Forecasting* (New York: Wiley, 1987); Makridakis, Spyros, and Wheelwright, Steven C., *Forecasting Methods for Management*, 5th ed. (New York: John Wiley and Sons, 1989); Roberts, Fred S., *Measurement Theory with Applications to Decision Making, Utility, and the Social Sciences* (Reading, Mass.: Addison-Wesley, 1979), volume 7 of *Encyclopedia of Mathematics and its Applications*; Saaty, Thomas L., *Mathematical Methods of Operations Research* (New York: McGraw-Hill, 1959); Saaty, Thomas L., *Thinking with Models: Mathematical Models in the Physical, Biological, and Social Sciences* (New York: Pergamon Press, 1981); Tukey, John W., *Exploratory Data Analysis* (Reading, Mass.: Addison-Wesley, 1977).

2. Drake, Miriam A., *Academic Research Libraries: A Study of Growth* (West Lafayette, Ind.: Purdue University, Libraries and Audio-Visual Center, 1977); Dunn, Oliver C., Tolliver, Don L., and Tolliver, Romona S., *The Past and Likely Future of 58 Research Libraries, 1951–1980: A Statistical Study of Growth and Change* (West Lafayette, Ind.: Purdue University, 1965–1972).

3. *Predicasts F & S Index: United States* (Cleveland, Ohio: Predicasts Inc., 1980–); *Predicasts Forecasts* (Cleveland, Ohio: Predicasts, Inc., 1980–); *Predicasts, Inc. World Casts: Product* (Cleveland, Ohio: Predicasts, Inc., 1992); *PROMT, Predicasts Overview of Markets and Technology* (Cleveland, Ohio: Predicasts, Inc., 1992).

4. Association of Research Libraries, *ARL Statistics, 1988–89* (Washington, D.C.: Association of Research Libraries, 1990); Stubbs, Kendon, and Buxton, David, (comps.), *Cumulated ARL University Library Statistics, 1962–63 through 1978–79* (Washington, D.C.: Association of Research Libraries, 1981); *ACRL University Library Statistics* (Chicago, Ill.: Association of College and Research Libraries, 1990).

5. Hayes, Robert M., et al., "An Application of the Cobb-Douglas Model to the Association of Research Libraries," *Library and Information Science Research* 5(3) (Fall 1983): 291–326; Piternick, George, "ARL Statistics—Handle with Care," *College and Research Libraries* 38 (Sept. 1977): 419–23.

6. Ackoff, Russell, *The Design of Social Research* (Chicago: University of Chicago Press, 1953); Bookstein, Abraham, "Questionnaire Research in a Library Setting," *Journal of Academic Librarianship* 1(1) (1985): 24–28; Butler, Meredith, and Gratch, Bonnie, "Planning a User Study: The Process Defined," *College and Research Libraries* 43(4) (1982): 320–30; Checkland, Peter, *Systems Thinking, Systems Practice* (Chichester, U.K.: Wiley, 1981); Colin, K., Lindsey, George N., and Callahan, Daniel, "Toward Usable User Studies," *Journal of the American Society for Information Science* 31 (1980): 347–56; Harris, Colin, "Surveying the User and User Studies," *Information and Library Manager* 5(3) (1985): 9–14; Kidston, James S., "The Validity of Questionnaire Responses," *Library Quarterly* 55(2) (1985): 133–50; Martin, Lowell, "User Studies and Library Planning," *Library Trends* 24 (January 1976): 483–95; Moran, Barbara B., "Construction of the Questionnaire in Survey Research," *Public Libraries* 24(2) (1985): 75–76; Powell, Ronald R., *The Relationship of Library User Studies to Performance Measures: A Review of the Literature* (Chicago: University of Illinois, 1985); Association of Research Libraries, *User Surveys*, SPEC Kit 148 (Washington, D.C.: Association of Research Libraries, Office of Management Studies, Systems and Procedures Exchange Center, 1988); Association of Research Libraries, *User Surveys and Evaluation of Library Services*, SPEC Kit 71 (Washington, D.C.: Association of Research Libraries, Office of Management Studies, Systems Procedures and Exchange Center, 1981); Association of Research Libraries, *User Surveys in ARL Libraries*, SPEC Kit 101 (Washington, D.C.: Association of Research Libraries, Office of Management Studies, Systems Procedures and Exchange Center, 1984).

7. Wilson, Sandra R., *Use of Critical Incident Technique to Evaluate the Impact of MEDLINE: Final Report* (Palo Alto, Calif.: American Institutes for Research, 1989).

8. Godet, Michel, *Scenarios and Strategic Management* (London: Butterworths, 1987); Herman, James, et al., "Shaping the 1990s: A New Way of Looking at the Future Helps Industry Participants Develop Their Visions of the Next Five Years," *Computer World*, 27 Nov. 1989, pp. 77–85.

9. Helmer, Olaf, *Looking Forward: A Guide to Future Research* (Beverly Hills, Calif.: Sage Publications, 1983); Helmer, Olaf, *The Delphi Method for Systematizing*

Judgements about the Future (Los Angeles: University of California at Los Angeles Institute of Government and Public Affairs, 1966).

10. Delonas, Nicholas, "The Time Series Machine," *Lotus* 7(11) (November 1991): 68–71.

9

Costing Library Operations and Services

Among the most crucial elements of strategic management is obtaining a clear picture of costs of library operations and information services.[1] Unfortunately, data reported in the literature vary widely and use widely divergent bases: units of work, inclusion or exclusion of overhead, and means for determining data (e.g., time and motion study versus full accounting).[2] The result is that there are very few solid, easily replicable methods to support this essential function. In this chapter, I attempt to deal with this lack by presenting a formal approach to the costing of library operations and services.

FUNDAMENTAL APPROACH TO COSTING

The fundamental approach used in this cost analysis is an ex post facto cost accounting.[3] That is, cost data reported in a wide variety of ways are reduced to a common cost accounting structure. This approach is in contrast to the typical time and motion study, in which careful measurements are made of the time actually taken for each of a sequence of operations, and to a total cost approach, in which reported costs for an operation are taken as a whole and simply divided by the total workload. Finally, it is in contrast to a true cost accounting, in which data are recorded and analyzed in standard cost categories at the time they are incurred.

It is important to recognize the differences among these approaches, since they result in dramatically different estimates of cost that are difficult to reconcile. The most accurate and complete is a true cost accounting based on records at the time costs are incurred and properly allocated. The most detailed will be the time and motion study, but it will usually account for only the most specific costs. At the other extreme, the total cost approach provides no detail and no means for analysis of functions; it is the least accurate of the methods and may grossly mis-estimate the costs, both under and over, in ways that make it impossible to calibrate. The ad hoc cost accounting approach presented here is an effort to establish a standard means for dealing with quoted costs that will include all components in a framework that permits analysis.

ESTIMATES OF DIRECT LABOR

Workload Factors

Table 9.1 presents workload factors providing standard estimates for direct labor in "FTE," representing the full-time equivalent of a working year of $42 \times 40 = 1,680$ hours. (The remaining 10 weeks of the calendar year provide for holidays, vacation, sick leave, and personal leave.)

It is important to note that the estimates for "Reference" are expressed in units of work different from those for other kinds of processes. "Hours of Desk Service," as shown here, may be the appropriate unit of measure, and in testing of a spreadsheet model it will be used, but with many reservations.

Data from Observation of Library Operations

The generic estimates of workload factors were the result of an iterative process, carried out over many years, in which estimates at a given point in time were matched with actual and/or reported costs for a visited library and operations within it as of that time. If estimates matched library costs to within 10 percent, they were regarded as further confirmed. However, if the estimated costs differed substantially (i.e., by more than 10 percent) from the reported ones, they were carefully examined for possible reasons for the differences. Were they caused by flaws in the means for estimation, and if so, should they result in changes in the basis for estimation? Did they reflect differences in operations rather than flaws in the means for estimation, and if so, should they result in additions to the bases for estimation? Did they reflect real differences in efficiencies, and if so, how should the efficiencies be treated?

Data Reported in the Literature

There is an extensive array of published data.[4] On the surface, they appear to be so inconsistent and unreliable as to be valueless. However, by careful evaluation of the basis on which the values are reported (units of work, basis for assessment of time, etc.), it was possible to reconcile differences and produce results that could be calibrated with those from other sources.

Table 9.1
Matrix of Workload Factors

Workload Factors (illustrative values for direct labor)			
Category	Level of Staff	Yearly FTE	Units
Acquisitions			
Selection	Professional	0.25 FTE per 1000 titles	
Ordering	Clerical	0.20 FTE per 1000 titles	
Invoicing	Clerical	0.20 FTE per 1000 titles	
Cataloging			
Original	Professional	1.60 FTE per 1000 titles	
Copy	Clerical	0.20 FTE per 1000 titles	
Maintenance	Clerical, Student	0.25 FTE per 1000 titles	
Circulation			
Records	Student	0.06 FTE per 1000 items	
Shelving	Student	0.04 FTE per 1000 items	
Serials			
Receiving	Student	0.10 FTE per 1000 serials	
Records	Student	0.10 FTE per 1000 serials	
Physical Handling			
Receiving	Student	0.02 FTE per 1000 items	
Labeling, etc.	Student	0.06 FTE per 1000 items	
Preservation & Binding			
Identification	Student	0.06 FTE per 1000 items	
Assessment	Professional	0.12 FTE per 1000 items	
Bibliographic	Clerical	0.40 FTE per 1000 items	
Preparation	Student	0.40 FTE per 1000 volumes	
Reproduction	Technician	1.50 FTE per 1000 volumes	
Treatment (3)	Technician	1.50 FTE per 1000 volumes	
Binding	Technician	0.25 FTE per 1000 volumes	
ILL Borrowing			
Bibliographic	Professional	0.20 FTE per 1000 borrows	
Handling	Student	0.10 FTE per 1000 borrows	
Records	Clerical	0.20 FTE per 1000 borrows	
ILL Lending			
Bibliographic	Professional	0.05 FTE per 1000 lends	
Handling	Student	0.10 FTE per 1000 lends	
Records	Clerical	0.20 FTE per 1000 lends	
Reference (other than ILL)			
Bibliographic	Professional	0.50 FTE per 1000 hours	
Ready	Clerical	0.50 FTE per 1000 hours	

Time and Motion Study

One basis for published data is time and motion studies, but to use such data requires recognition of the difference between those results and direct labor time (which the workload factors represent). The crucial point is that the usual time and motion study will not include the wide range of times that are not specifically related to the process under study. A rule of thumb was finally derived for determining direct time from time and motion study data: 1.5/1. That is, if the time and motion time for an operation was measured at thirty minutes, the direct time was taken at forty-five minutes.

Analogy

Another means used for developing workload factors was analogy, with the view that comparable tasks should take comparable times. This permits several different sources of data to be compared, even though they may seem to deal with different functions.

Rules of Thumb for Manual Operations

Underlying the workload factors also were a number of rules of thumb for manual operations.[5] However, they are separable from the workload factors and have application in much broader contexts.

Keyboarding

One manual operation is *keyboarding* (which years ago we called typing, and then keypunching). How much time does it take to keyboard a given amount of data? As a base rate, we have estimates for typing: 60 to 100 words per minute as a time and motion study rate, but sustainable for fairly long periods of time. That would imply rates of keyboarding (counting a word as 6 characters plus a space) of 25,000–42,000 keystrokes per hour. Using the factor of 1.5 for conversion from time and motion study to direct time, that is equivalent to 17,000–28,000 keystrokes per hour for eight hours of direct time. That rate assumes keyboarding of straight text, from clean copy, without any decision making or interpretation.

However, typing turns out to be a poor basis for estimating data entry into computer systems, whether by punched cards or cathode ray tube (CRT) terminals. Here, the experience is more on the order of 10,000 to 13,000 key strokes per hour of direct time. Again, that rate assumes straight text, from clean copy, without decision making or interpretation. It also assumes a production context rather than a start-and-stop situation. For a start-and-stop context, the rate is on the order of 3,000 to 5,000 key strokes per hour. Similar reductions will be experienced if there are problems with the source data, if many decisions need to be made, if the data is largely numerical or tabular.

Figure 9.1
Graph for Sorting as a Function of Batch Size

log(Time per Item) = .25 + .25*log {(Batch Size)}

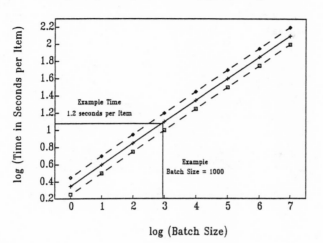

log (Batch Size)

Error Rates

People make errors in keyboarding data. Some errors will be detected at the time they are made and will be corrected immediately; the rule of thumb for keyboarding rates indicated above includes time for such immediate correction. The rate of such immediately detected errors probably varies widely from individual to individual and depends upon context.

For errors that must be detected by proofing (i.e., errors that are not corrected during the original typing), the rule of thumb is 1/1,000 (one error per thousand keystrokes). There have been studies of the nature of such errors for different kinds of data, both numerical and textual. A typical error is interchange; another is doubling one character rather than an adjacent double. (Incidentally, a separate kind of error, not represented in the rule of thumb, is spelling error or grammatical error.) Data from OCLC suggests that the error rate after proofing is on the order of 1/3,000 (i.e., normal proofing will pick up about two errors in three).

Sorting and Filing

Storage of records into manual files usually involves a two-stage process in which a batch of records is sorted into filing sequence and the batch is then merged into the file. For these operations, the two graphs shown in figures 9.1 and 9.2 provide bases for estimation. The primary content of these graphs is provided by the following equations:

Sorting $\log(T_1) = .2 + .2 \times \log(B) + \log(B)$, or $T_1 = 1.6 \times B^{.2} \times B$

Filing $\log(T_2) = .8 + .2 \times \log(F/B) + \log(B)$, or $T_2 = 6.3 \times (F/B)^{.2} \times B$

Figure 9.2
Graph for Filing as a Function of the Ratio of File Size to Batch Size

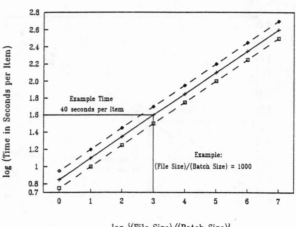

log (Time per Item) = .75 + .25*log {(File Size)/(Batch Size)}

log {(File Size)/(Batch Size)}

where T_1 and T_2 are total times, in seconds, respectively, to sort and file a batch of size B into a file of size F. To illustrate, consider the task of filing 100 cards into a catalog of 100,000 cards: B = 100, F/B = 1000.

T_1 = 400 seconds, T_2 = 1,000 seconds

Actual times are subject to wide variation around these nominal values, by a factor from .8 to 1.2; for the example, the range of likely times would be from 320 to 480 seconds for sorting and from 800 to 1,200 seconds for filing.

The logarithmic relation between time and batch size for sorting is well recognized in machine sorting; the logarithmic relation between time and the ratio of file size to batch size for filing is not recognized and may not be valid. However, these rules of thumb have served well for estimating time for these kinds of tasks.

Searching Time

The time for searching a file for an item whose identification is known (i.e., whose position in the file is known) is taken as the equivalent of filing a batch of one item:

Searching $\log(T_2)$ = .8 + .2 × log(F), or T_2 = 6.3 × (F)$^{.2}$

Thus, for the example of a catalog of 100,000 cards, the time to find one item would be about sixty-three seconds, or one minute (ranging from fifty to seventy-five seconds).

Table 9.2
Alternative Methods for Overhead Allocation

Category	Percentage of Total Salaries	Non-profit Allocation	Commercial Allocation
Total Salaries	1.00 T		
Direct Salaries	0.67 T	1.00 T	0.67 T = 1.00 D
Indirect Salaries . . .	0.33 T		0.67 T = 1.00 D
Salary Benefits	0.14 T	0.14 T	
Overhead Expenses . . .	0.20 T	0.20 T	
Sub-Total		S = 1.34 T	1.34 T = 2.00 D
General & Administrative	0.10 S =	0.13 T	0.13 T = 0.20 D
Total		1.47 T	1.47 T = 2.20 D

OVERHEAD

The next major component of the cost accounting model is overhead. In general, overhead, or, as it is frequently called, *indirect*, includes those costs that cannot be directly attributed to productive work. That in no way means that such costs are not necessary or significant. It simply means that it would be difficult or irrational to attempt to associate them directly with productive work. Supervision, for example, is clearly necessary, but it in no way in itself produces catalog entries, binds volumes, films pages, or does the actual work, whatever it may be. Holidays, vacation, and sick leave are necessary components of a compensation package, but usually no productive work is accomplished during such time.

The purpose of overhead or indirect costs is to account for these kinds of costs. A typical rule for doing so is making estimates proportional to direct labor costs, and that is used here. The resulting generic values for overhead are presented in table 9.2.

This table provides two alternative means for presentation of the overhead accounts. It is important to recognize both the differences between the two and the essential equivalence of them. One, which treats "total salary" as the foundation, is typically used in not-for-profit institutions; the other, which treats "direct salary" as the foundation, is typically used in commercial contexts. Whichever is used, the total costs (leaving aside allocation of profit or amortization of capital costs) must be the same, if efficiencies are the same. Moreover, with all due respect to the much vaunted efficiency of private enterprise, there is nothing inherent in the tasks here that implies greater efficiency as a result of different means for accounting for costs. For a variety of reasons, though, the commercial accounting model seems to provide a firmer basis for control of operations. It there is the one used here.

In the following subsections, each of the major categories of overhead will be described, and then the relevant data from various site visits will be summarized. It is to be noted that the functions of overhead are as necessary and important to production as are the direct functions.

Personnel Indirect Time

Supervision and Clerical Support

Clearly, any operation must have supervision, and that usually implies clerical support (not clericals as part of direct labor, but in administrative functions). Even a one-person operation requires planning and scheduling of work, reporting and evaluation of performance, correspondence, and record keeping; in such contexts, supervision and clerical support must be treated as a portion of the single person's time. In multiple-person contexts, however, these overhead items are critical and should be carefully and separately accounted for.

What is the portion of time required for the functions of supervision? Military and industrial experience, over centuries, has established a standard "span of control," represented at the simplest level by the squad: a group of eight to twelve persons under a noncommissioned officer as supervisor. That ratio, of 1/8 to 1/12, appears to be quite common and, given no other data, was the original basis for the hypothetical overhead rates, as presented above. The experience in examination of libraries generally confirmed the validity of that ratio of supervisors to direct staff FTE.

However, the data from several libraries visited can be used to obtain more immediate factual estimates, both for supervision in general and specific preservation tasks. Except for the smallest of groups, the ratio was uniformly 12 percent (plus or minus 0.5 percent); a ratio of roughly one supervisor to eight staff, which is close to the military and industrial experience in span of control. In the very small groups, the description of duties clearly shows that persons identified as "supervisors" spend a high portion of time in direct, productive labor, and there is no reason to treat the ratio of supervision time to direct labor time in such circumstances as substantially different from 1/8.

That ratio, though, does not recognize the fact that the supervisors are universally paid higher salaries. As a result, the proportion of salary dollars is dramatically different, being nearly twice: about 20 percent. Again, the proportion was quite uniform, differing by at most 0.5 percent either way from 20 percent.

The difference between the ratios for FTE and for salaries is so dramatic that it is valuable to look more closely at the underlying structure. It turns out to be largely a result of the high percentage of library FTE that are students. In fact, university libraries are quite similar, almost uniform, in using students for about 25 percent of their staff FTE. But those FTE cost

Table 9.3
Distribution of Overhead among Staff and Students

Category	FTE Distribution	Salary Distribution
Direct		
Full time	50% of the FTE	55% of the salaries
Student	25%	10%
Indirect: Supervision and Clerical		
Full time	11%	18%
Indirect: Benefit days		
Full time	14% (i.e., .187*75%)	17% (i.e., .187*90%)
Totals	100% of the FTE	100% of the salaries

only about 10 percent of the salary dollars, and they carry minimal benefits such as days off with pay. The result is the following comparison of distributions for FTE and for salary dollars (see table 9.3).

Unallocated Time

In every operation there is time of staff, who may be in principle assigned to direct work, which should be assigned to indirect or overhead time—here called *unallocated time* (i.e., time that is not allocated to direct, productive work). For example, staff attend meetings; they also participate in orientation, deal with visitors who ask for data about operations and costs, attend union and professional society meetings, and participate in training programs. There are innumerable demands on staff time that fall into this category.

Unfortunately, there are no practices in libraries to account for it. The kinds of activities involved may or may not be recognized as reducing the time for direct, productive work. Surely, some, such as time to attend professional society meetings, are recognized; even for these activities, however, there is no evident record of the total time commitment. Others, such as time for training and for internal meetings, appear simply to be accepted as part of the workload, even though they clearly are not specific to the workload tasks.

Of all of the categories of overhead, this is the one most likely to result in dramatic increases in indirect costs and in reduction in productivity. Given that, it would seem valuable to establish at least some benchmarks for acceptable ranges of values.

Benefit Days

A major set of benefits, of course, are the days for holiday, vacation, sick leave, personal leave, and sabbatical. There are wide variations among these categories, but the modal cluster is clear and narrow. First, the range for holidays is typically from 10 to 13 days, but the evident mode is 11 days per year. Given 260 days total per year (fifty-two weeks at 5 days per week) as the total salary period, at 11 days per year, holidays represent 4.2 percent of total salary.

Second, a likely range for vacation time is from 15 to 25 days per year, with a mean at 22 days (about four weeks). For 260 days total per year, that represents 8.4 percent of total salary.

Third, sick leave and personal leave are usually treated as part of a combined package by most, if not all, institutions even though in principle they should not be substitutable. Combined, they cluster around 16 days per year, which, for 260 days total, represents 6.1 percent of total salary. Of course, the extent to which these are in fact used varies much more than holidays and vacations, so the actual cost of sick leave and personal leave may be different from the started policies.

Fourth, sabbatical leave or some equivalent leave with pay is frequently a perquisite for professional positions, especially when they have faculty status. Typically, a sabbatical might be accumulated at the rate of half a year to one year every seven years. If sabbaticals were taken at that rate, the benefit days would be the equivalent of 7 percent to 14 percent. The fact, however, is that sabbaticals seem to be rarely taken, even in institutions where librarians have faculty status. The result is that this benefit has negligible addition to overhead.

As table 9.4 shows, adding all of these together produces a total of 18.7 percent of total salary that must be paid for benefit days for full-time employees. However, again the high percentage of FTE filled by students has a dramatic effect on benefit days, since vacations are not accumulated by them and they are not likely to be paid for holiday time, unless they actually work on those days. Given that about 25 percent of the staff FTE are students, the result is a significant reduction from the total of 18.7 percent to a net total of 14.0 percent (i.e., the 18.7 percent applies only to the 75 percent of staff who are full-time).

Benefits

The total range for salary-related benefits is very wide, but the modal cluster is clearly defined at just about 25.5 percent of total salary as the average. Furthermore, the basis for the quoted values varies from statements in documents on benefits policy to ratios of expenditures. The latter will result, as will be demonstrated below, in substantially lower actual percentages because of the lessened benefits for students and other hourly employees. In any event, the average of 25.5 percent is most representative of the benefits policies, especially in university contexts.

The categories of benefits (and representative percentages of total salary), though not all of them were necessarily defined by any one institution

Table 9.4
Summary of Benefit Days

Category	Days	Percentage of Year
Holidays	11	4.2 %
Vacation	22	8.4 %
Sick Leave	16	6.1 %
Total	49	18.7 %

Table 9.5
Categories of Benefits

Social Security	7.50 % salary
Disability	1.00 % salary
Unemployment	0.50 % salary
Fica	3.00 % salary
Life insurance	0.50 % salary
Medical insurance	4.00 % salary
Tuition	1.00 % salary
Retirement	8.00 % salary
Total	25.50 % salary

as part of their benefits package, were as shown in table 9.5 (in each case, the figures reflect the employer's contribution, not that of the employee).

It is important to note that the use of student FTE has the same kind of effect upon the actual cost of benefits as it does on the distribution of salaries, though not as dramatic. Specifically, only the legally mandated benefits (Social Security, FICA, etc.) will apply to their salary—about 10 percent of their salaries. The result is a reduction in the overall cost of the benefits. It can be roughly calculated as: $(.10)(10\%) + (.90)(25.5\%) = 24\%$.

Overhead Supplies

This overhead item is difficult to estimate. Supplies and expenses are treated as a central budget in libraries and not allocated to individual departments in any manner that permits association with either functional activities or even general costs. The result is that there is no basis for estimation of their contribution to overhead, so the model uses a nominal 5 percent of total salary for this category.

Space, Maintenance, Utilities

These overhead items are exceptionally difficult to account for. The cost for construction is uncertain, the time period for amortization is undefined, and the space that is allocable to specific functions is uncertain. The cost for maintenance depends upon the nature of the space occupied but is never clearly defined, the basis for quoting the cost of maintenance varies widely among institutions, and the extent to which it in fact is provided is uncertain. The charges for utilities are usually buried in institutional budgets; they vary widely and unaccountably by the type of space occupied.

However, estimates for construction are quite focused around a modal value of $150.00 per square foot. If we use an amortization period of twenty years, that equals $7.50 per square foot per year. Estimates of the costs of maintenance are quite narrowly clustered around $5.00 per square foot per year. Finally, data for space occupied by various functions suggests that each person requires about 250 square feet (including both space actually occupied and the necessary "public space"). The result is a cost per year, per person, of $3,125.00. That is about 14 percent of the average current salary.

University Overhead

A final potential overhead item is the university overhead.[6] However, important though it is, there are great variabilities in it, great dependence upon the basis for allocation and institutional specifics, and much overlap with the library's own budget. As a result, no effort has been made to estimate either the magnitude of institutional overhead or the basis for allocation of it.

GENERAL AND ADMINISTRATIVE (G&A)

Functions

The operation of a major research library requires central administration of a high order, covering a wide range of responsibilities that, by their nature, make no direct contribution to the production of library services or to operations. They are nevertheless essential functions, without which the library could not operate. To be specific, the following functions are typically included as general and administrative:

Leadership

This clearly is the most significant function in research library administration. It sets objectives, the priorities, the style for the library. It determines how and where resources are needed and will be committed. It creates the working relation with the institution served by the library.

Personnel Administration

The functions of hiring, evaluating, promoting, maintaining records on, and, in general, providing all that is necessary for personnel administration are a fundamental G&A responsibility. To some extent, the research library may call on the larger institutional administration for assistance, but in all of the research libraries visited the library itself provided for all significant aspects of personnel administration.

Budgeting and Accounting

As multimillion-dollar operations, the research libraries must maintain complete and dedicated services for financial management. Book funds, personnel funds, and project funds must all be carefully and completely accounted for. These must be handled at the G&A level.

Public Relations and Publicity

Every major library maintains an extensive program of communications, publicity, and public relations. This kind of G&A activity is essential for development of financial support of the library, but it is even more essential to the university because of the central role of the research library in institutional reputation.

Collection Development

The central library administration plays a substantive role with respect to collection development. This reflects the importance given to that function, especially with respect to gifts from major donors, in which the tasks of collection development are inseparable from those of financial development. There is almost no rational means for separating these productive functions from the general and administrative ones.

Other Kinds of Support

None of the libraries visited included any legal counsel services within the library's administration. Instead, each depended on the legal counsel of the institution. Nor were any other specific functions identified as a part of G&A.

Should G&A Be Included in Costing?

With this definition of general and administrative functions, the question of whether their costs should be included in the cost assessment must be considered. Some would argue that these are costs that will be incurred by the library whether a new system was involved or not. They see G&A costs as fixed and would treat system management costs as marginal costs, without any allocation of G&A.

The position of this chapter is that G&A costs must be considered and properly allocated, proportionally to the direct and indirect costs involved. The rationales are as follows.

First, a new systems project will almost certainly involve a disproportionate time of the central library administration. Initiatives must be developed, proposals must be prepared, funds must be obtained, accounts must be established to manage the funds, personnel must be added, projects must be managed. Moreover, all of these take time from the most expensive staff in the library's operation. They are all add-on tasks, diverting those staff from other priority responsibilities. Those costs are not marginal but rather are real diversions of costs, and should be clearly and carefully accounted for.

Second, if independent operations—such as regional or national centers—are established to carry out any of the tasks involved, G&A costs will be incurred and will need to be paid for, not as marginal costs but as operational costs. If such alternatives are to be properly evaluated and properly budgeted, they should be compared with equivalent G&A costs in current library operations.

G&A Costs

Among the categories of information this is the most difficult to obtain as unequivocal, uniform data. In some cases, the central administration is defined to include heads of branches or operational departments in ways impossible to separate out. In other cases, the central administration, as defined, may not include all of the G&A functions; however, it may not be clear where those functions were provided.

Nonetheless, available data show that G&A—the university librarian's office, to be specific—averages about 15 percent of total operating costs (not counting costs of acquisitions), and the range was fairly narrow.

IMPLEMENTATION OF THE COSTING MODEL AS A SPREADSHEET

The costing model described in this chapter can very easily be put into a spreadsheet for use by individual libraries needing to assess their costs for strategic management purposes. The data involved fall into four categories:

1. Data measuring the workload for each function and subfunction: These data presumably would be derived from operating statistics for acquisitions, cataloging, circulation, and similar functions. They would then be entered in the spreadsheet for multiplication by the associated workload factors.

Table 9.6
Assumed Values for Parameters

Volumes per monographic title:	1.5
Volumes per serial title:	1.5
Titles per Order:	1.5
Proportion of Original Cataloging:	(Holdings/20,000,000)
Reshelving:	(Holdings)
Circulation:	(Holdings)/3
Reference Stations:	(Holdings/100,000) + .015*(Faculty)
Yearly Hours per Reference Station:	3000

2. Data measuring costs: These would relate to salaries and wages of the several levels of staff, acquisitions, and direct expenses.

3. Data measuring elements of overhead: These would include percentages for supervisory staff, clerical support, estimated unallocated time, benefit time, other benefits, space and utility costs, and other indirect expenses.

4. Data representing changes in the values for workload factors. These may be needed to reflect the specifics for the particular library.

Testing the Implementation

Such a spreadsheet has been prepared, incorporating the data presented in this chapter as default values for categories (3) and (4). It has been tested against data reported for ARL libraries and ACRL libraries (for 1988/89) and similar data obtained directly from a dozen smaller colleges.[7] The reported data (such as Holdings, Volumes Added, Current Serials, etc.) provide specifics for estimating workloads on some functions but by no means all; they also provide some bases for estimating average costs (for salaries, wages, acquisitions, and direct expenses). However, there are many functions not covered by the reported data (such as Circulation, Reference Stations, division between Original and Copy Cataloging, etc.).

For the functions not directly reported, therefore, one must estimate the workloads. To that end, uniform assumptions were made (see table 9.6). For purposes of comparison of costs with the reported ARL and ACRL data, the estimates for benefits and for overhead expenses were subtracted from the total from the model, since the reported data explicitly do not include those elements of cost. The results from applying the costing model, with these assumptions, were as shown in table 9.7.

Overall, these results for average or composite libraries seem to provide a remarkable confirmation of the validity of the costing model, given the range of sizes for the institutions and the degree of match between the results from the model and the actual. For the set of institutions taken individually, of course, the differences between the results from the model and the actual figures varied widely, but the great majority were within plus or minus 20 percent, as illustrated in figure 9.3 (for the ratio of the

Table 9.7
Application of Costing Model to Composite Libraries

ARL - 1988/89	Professional FTE Model Actual		Total FTE Model Actual		Total Expenses Model Actual	
1 Average 107 Univ. ARL	81	83	321	322	11425	12003
2 Large-14	172	160	727	587	24456	22632
3 Med-Large-15	94	100	381	376	13507	13488
4 Med-Small-15	75	79	301	299	10292	11332
5 Small-14	63	63	246	261	8310	9008
6 Added-37	58	63	216	241	8080	9155
7 Canadian-12	72	66	283	301	10380	10986
8 Non-University-11	52	120	147	296	7351	15571
9 Library of Congress	553	968	1992	1703	57671	86000

ACRL - 1988/89	Professional FTE Model Actual		Total FTE Model Actual		Total Expenses Model Actual	
1 Average 114 ACRL	25	26	76	101	3008	3518
2 Largest 20	43	40	149	164	5427	5734
3 Med-Large 16	32	36	104	137	3990	4725
4 Middle 20	29	29	92	114	3674	4142
5 Med-Small 19	22	24	66	91	2616	3125
6 Smaller 24	15	17	42	63	1732	2171
7 Smallest 15	9	10	24	36	953	1095

Colleges - 1988/89	Professional FTE Model Actual		Total FTE Model Actual		Total Expenses Model Actual	
1 Average	25	24	75	86	2877	4004
2 Smallest	4	4	11	13	524	603

differences between the model and the actual to the actual, for the ARL libraries), which is quite representative of the results for each of the criteria.

It will be noted that the results for nonuniversity research libraries do not match well, but that is to be expected since the nature of their operations is quite different. For the Library of Congress, though, the comparisons are within interesting ballparks. To make those comparisons, the budget data from LC were restricted to just "collection services" (eliminating the staff and expenditures that relate to a wide range of other statutory functions, far beyond those encompassed by the costing model); furthermore, all aspects of cost—benefits and overhead as well as G&A— were included in the comparison because the LC budget clearly includes those components.[8]

Figure 9.3
ARL Libraries 1988–1989, Professional Staff FTE: Rank Order of Difference Ratios (Actual − Model)/(Smaller of Actual and Model)

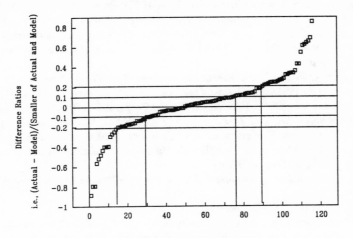

Rank Order of Difference Ratios

Table 9.8
Unit Costs for Various Operations

	ARL Libraries	ACRL Libraries
Acquisitions	$23.47/title = $16/volume	$21.40/title = $14/volume
Cataloging	$26.06/title = $17/volume	$14.51/title = $10/volume
Circulation	$2.06/circulation	$1.80/circulation
Serials	$4.15/serials title	$3.60/serials title
Physical Handling	$1.95/volume	$1.68/volume
ILL–Borrowing	$19.75/borrow	$18.00/borrow
ILL–Lending	$10.15/lend	$9.00/lend
Reference	$23.00/station-hour	$21.00/station-hour

Average Costs for Each Function

From the spreadsheet, it is easy to derive unit costs for each function in the library. Table 9.8 shows the results for the tests on the average ARL and ACRL libraries in 1988–1989.

NOTES

1. Baumol, William, and Marcus, Matihyahu, *Economics of Academic Libraries* (Washington, D.C.: American Council on Education, 1973); Cummings, Martin M., *The Economics of Research Libraries* (Washington, D.C.: Council on Library Resources, 1986); Kelly, Lauren, "Budgeting in Nonprofit Organizations," *Drexel Library Quarterly*

21(3) (Summer 1985): 3–18; Kent, Allen, et al., (eds.), "The Economics of Academic Libraries," *Library Trends* 28(1) (Summer 1979): 3–24; Palmour, Vernon E., et al., *A Study of the Characteristics, Costs, and Magnitude of Interlibrary Loans in Academic Libraries* (Westport, Conn.: Greenwood Press, 1972); Prentice, Ann, "Budgeting and Accounting: A Selected Bibliography," *Drexel Library Quarterly* 21(3) (Summer 1985): 106–12; Williams, Gordon, et al., *Library Cost Models: Owning versus Borrowing Serial Publications* (Washington, D.C.: Office of Science Information Service, National Science Foundation, 1968).

2. Bourne, Charles P., and Kasson, Madeleine, *Preliminary Report on the Review and Development of Standard Cost Data for Selected Library Technical Processing Functions* (Palo Alto, Calif.: Information General Corp., 1969); *Pre/Post Implementation Time and Methods Study of Library Public Catalog File Maintenance* (Long Beach, Calif.: California State University and College System [CSUC], 15 March 1982).

3. Hayes, Robert M., and Becker, Joseph, *Handbook of Data Processing for Libraries*, 2nd ed. (New York: Wiley, 1972), ch. 4.

4. Bourne and Kasson, *Preliminary Report*; *Pre/Post Implementation Time and Methods Study*.

5. Hayes and Becker, *Handbook of Data Processing*.

6. *Indirect Costs* (Ann Arbor: University of Michigan, 23 December 1988).

7. Association of Research Libraries, *ARL Statistics, 1988–89* (Washington, D.C.: Association of Research Libraries, 1990); Stubbs, Kendon, and Buxton, David, (comps.), *Cumulated ARL University Library Statistics, 1962–63 through 1978–79* (Washington, D.C.: Association of Research Libraries, 1981); *ACRL University Library Statistics* (Chicago, Ill.: ACRL, 1990).

8. U.S. Congress, 102nd Congress, Second Session, *Legislative Branch Appropriations for 1992. Hearings before a Subcommittee of the Committee on Appropriations. Part 1: Justification of the Budget Estimates*, Washington, D.C.: United States Government Printing Office, 1992, pp. 785–1168.

10

Making Access
Allocation Decisions

The most central strategic decision faced today by the academic library is determining what materials to acquire and where to store them.[1] The decision involves weighing costs and benefits of local access versus network access, browsability versus compact storage, rapid versus delayed response, and capital investment in buildings and collections versus operating costs in interlibrary loan or document delivery. It is especially significant in the choice between acquisition and access.[2] It must reconcile the conflict between what heretofore have been two complementary imperatives of the library profession. In this chapter, we present a formal model of the cost basis for that decision.

ACCESS ALLOCATION ALTERNATIVES

Branch or Central Library Storage

The most accessible alternative to be considered is acquisition with storage in open-access shelving of a local branch library. It provides the traditional library accessibility at the closest possible point and usually is the alternative preferred by users. Acquisition and open-access shelving elsewhere on campus, at a centralized main library or at other branches, provides traditional library accessibility but at a more remote location, requiring either that the patron go to the facility or that the library provide access and delivery service; in either event, there will be added costs incurred, a longer time for response, and a likelihood of reduced use compared to that within the given branch library.

Remote Facility Storage

Acquisition with storage at a remote facility, probably with some form of compact storage, provides reduced accessibility, as a result of both remoteness and reduced browsability; it also incurs appreciably greater costs for either the patron or the library in access to and delivery of materials, involves substantially increased time for response, and is likely to result in reduced use. To acquire but discard at some early time if the level of use does not warrant continued storage differs from the next alternative only in providing a time period during which local access is expected.

Access from Elsewhere

Dependence on access from elsewhere—through a cooperative network or from a document delivery system—is represented by traditional interlibrary loan, more formal cooperative agreements, centralized cooperative facilities, or the use of commercial services. In each case, access is subject to delay and involves significantly greater costs. Within this alternative, there are obviously subalternatives representing layers of agreement, but they all partake of essentially the same process, incur the same kinds of costs, and have comparable response times.

VARIABLES ENCOMPASSED BY THE MODEL FOR DECISION MAKING

Number of Volumes Being Considered

The first variable in the model is the population being considered for decision. That might be the set of unique volumes currently being acquired each year by the research libraries of the country (not counting duplicates); that will be taken at about 300,000 per annum. In the context of disposition of an existing collection, it will be the size of that collection.

Scope of Collection

In either context, though, a crucial variable is the scope of collection to be considered. Consider two positions in a spectrum: (1) The library has objectives to support research across the broad range of academic disciplines; or (2) the library has objectives only to support instruction at the undergraduate level. Between these two extremes lie mixes between research and instruction as well as different breadths of coverage of the disciplines and different time periods encompassed. Clearly, any library will, through decisions made either internal to the library or by the institution, arrive at a balance of relative importance among them.

Amount of Use

The next variable is the amount of use, both overall and in each category of use: circulation, in-house use, and ILL lending.[3]

Distribution of Use

The model used for the distribution here is essentially the Bradford model:[4] Let N be the total annual use over the entire set of books considered in the allocation decision, sequence the set of books in rank order of their expected level of use within the given library, and divide the sequence of volumes into groups of K volumes each.

Model: The total annual use for volumes beyond the group with rank order X will be given by $N/2^{(X)}$.

Note that in this model, the rank order X in the sequence of groups is expressed in "K volumes," K being a key parameter in the distribution, a number to be determined for the specific library context. It reflects the breadth of demand by the users of a given library. Presumably, the more diverse the needs and thus the wider the range of materials of interest, the larger K would be. It will be assumed that K is a linear function of V, the number of volumes being considered, which is the measure presented above for the scope of collection.

To illustrate the determination of K, consider the data, shown in the appended two tables in the appendix to this chapter.[5] The first shows the distribution of use of the 1969 acquisitions at the Hillman Library of the University of Pittsburgh (about 15 percent of the total collection) during seven years; the second shows the distribution of use for the total Hillman Library collection, during the same seven years. Based on those data, $K = .12 \times V$ is a reasonable value for the key parameter in the model.

Of course, this J-shaped distribution implies that the usage of volumes beyond even a small value for X is quite minimal, but that certainly reflects the reality. To illustrate, consider the total use per annum at the Hillman Library of the University of Pittsburgh, estimated above at 589,000. The model, with $K = .12 \times 553,000$, would then imply total use for all volumes ranked beyond Hillman's holdings (553,000 volumes) as follows:

$$589,000/2^{(553,000/(.12 \times 553,000))} = 589,000/2^{(8.33)} = 1,830$$

Thus, if Hillman acquisitions were of the 553,000 volumes expected to be the most frequently used, there would need to be 1,830 uses of ILL or other networks for access to other potential materials. Pitt data, as reported in ARL statistics (Stubbs, 1981), shows a total of 6,249 ILL borrows in 1976–1977 for the entire university collection; the ratio of 553,000 (holdings at the Hillman Library) to 2,175,000 (total university holdings in 1976–1977) would imply that perhaps 1,588 ILL transactions were attributable to Hillman.

Effects of Time upon Use

To this point, the use and its distribution have been measured in terms of total use or annual averages without regard for the effects of time from the original year of acquisition. Circulation data, however, suggest that at least for that use of books there is a general decay over time, perhaps settling asymptotically to some nonzero minimum.[6] It is not at all clear that there is a similar effect on in-house use, but for the moment let us suppose there is.

The decay will be taken as exponential, with a constant term to provide for steady state residual use independent of age after some number of years of exponential decay; that is, the exponential decay drops to the steady state residual use level. The rate of decay was taken at about .8 per annum; the time to steady state at seven years; the steady-state period, another seven years. The result would be total use over the fourteen years of about 5.77 times that in the initial year. In subsequent illustrations, those will be the figures used to represent the effects of time on usage.

Capital Costs in Acquisition, Processing, and Storage

To illustrate costs, figures based on the model presented in chapter 9 will be used. Note that they include all elements of cost, without regard to the source for funding them. Specifically, overhead, fully accounted for, is included as part of all costs presented.

Costs of Acquisition

These costs are incurred by the library whenever it acquires the book instead of depending upon network availability. The average cost to acquire a volume obviously includes the purchase price (or for journals, the present value of the continuing annual subscription, per volume), but it also includes the costs in selection, ordering, invoicing, and receipt. Average purchase price is identifiable from published statistics, though they need to be treated with care since the materials acquired by a research library tend to be much more expensive than reflected in general averages. The

Table 10.1
Annual Costs of Storage of 1000 Volumes

```
In a branch library,                $1000 per annum
In a browsable central library,     $ 500 per annum
In compact storage,                 $ 200 per annum
In remote storage,                  $ 100 per annum
In access from other libraries,     $   0 per annum
```

data from Seibert et al. (1987, 1990) shows "Expend for Materials"; if those are divided by volumes acquired, the range is about $50 to $75 per volume. For illustration, the cost for purchase will be taken at $60 per volume.

Costs of Processing

The book, once received, must be cataloged and physically processed for shelving. From chapter 9, these costs are about $15 per title or $10 per volume.

Costs of Storage

The cost of storage is best considered as a present value of the future expense stream for the time period of storage. (While one could take the present costs of construction, one would need still to add to them the present value of the future expenses for maintenance, so it is easiest to place the entire burden upon the future expense stream.) To do so, one needs two parameters: the assumed interest rate (or combination of interest and inflation) and the yearly cost for storage (including space, utilities, and maintenance). For illustration, the interest rate will be taken at 5 percent.

The annual cost for storage is more complicated, though, since it depends on the choice of alternative. For illustration, the cost for storage of 1,000 volumes in the several alternatives will be taken as shown in table 10.1.

If C_J is the cost of storage for one year at alternative J, and I is the assumed interest rate, then the present value of the future expense stream is given by:

$$C_J/I$$

Thus, for the hypothetical value of 0.05 for I, the present value is $20 \times C_J$. For open shelving at a central library, for example, the present value of costs will be $10 per volume ($10,000 per 1,000 volumes).

Table 10.2
Effect of Time on Use and Present Value of Access Costs

Year	1	2	3	4	5	6	7	8	9	10	11	12	13	14	Total
Relative Use	1	.80	.64	.51	.41	.33	.26	.26	.26	.26	.26	.26	.26	.26	5.77
Present Value	1	.95	.91	.86	.82	.78	.75	.71	.68	.64	.61	.58	.56	.53	
Net Cost	1	.78	.58	.44	.34	.26	.20	.18	.18	.17	.16	.15	.15	.14	5.06

Operating Costs in Access and Use

Costs of Access

For several of the alternatives, the costs of access are substantial, although they are frequently underestimated. For use of materials already in the library, the costs are incurred by the patron if we assume an open access stack system, so discussion of them will be deferred until later. For the other alternatives, though, the library will incur real costs.

For the sake of argument, assume that access from the branch library costs the library nothing but that access from the central library will involve paging at a cost of $3. For access to closed stacks, such as compact storage, or to depository facilities, the costs involve staff time and some kind of accounting system (which is likely to be a counterpart of circulation control but additional to that for the patron's circulation). For illustration, hypothesize a cost of $10 per volume for such access.

For access through interlibrary loan, the libraries incur a wide range of costs. Historic data supports as reasonable a hypothetical value of $30 for each such access (incurred in the borrowing and lending library, combined, and including allocation for overhead).

It is important to note that in making the current decision as to whether or not to acquire a volume, we must deal not only with the "present value" of the costs incurred for access over the lifetime of a given volume but with the decay in use over time. If we take figures as presented above to represent the exponential decay, the calculations in table 10.2 would serve to identify the seven-year estimated present value for costs of access.

Note that the total use over the entire collection is thus 5.77 that of first-year use; the total cost, 5.06 that of first-year costs.

Costs of Use

Of course, the major costs in use are those of the patron, which will be discussed later, but there are some costs incurred by the library. In particular, for circulation use, the library must maintain records and must reshelve; for in-house use, the library will incur some degree of costs in reshelving. For illustration, the costs for circulation, including reshelving, will be taken at $1.00 per use, the costs of reshelving alone at $0.10 per in-house use.

OTHER RELEVANT VARIABLES, THOUGH NOT INCLUDED IN THE CURRENT MODEL

Effects of Alternatives upon Use

The effect of alternative locations upon the kinds of use of books is an important variable. It is best represented by the many kinds of in-house use that simply will not be satisfied through interlibrary loan access from other libraries and thus will not be requested; they may not even be satisfied or requested from remote or compact storage.

To illustrate, browsing use clearly requires direct contact with the material; borrowing from another library simply does not even apply. Instead, the faculty member will probably travel to the host library for that kind of usage. This is the reason why faculty become so adamant about the browsability of depository facilities.

Similar effects surely are seen for each of the alternatives. There are in-house uses of branch libraries that will be much less frequent at central libraries, uses at central libraries that will not happen at depository facilities, and uses of depositories that will not happen in ILL.

The crucial point is that the reduction in such uses is not an unalloyed saving of the costs of access but instead is a reduction in the effectiveness of the total investment in the collection, as measured by use of it, as well as the effectiveness of the users (the ultimate measure of effectiveness).

User Needs and Costs in Access and Use

Aspects relevant to user needs and costs include financial costs (in cases in which the user must pay for the access), the effect of distance (an inverse function, either exponential or quadratic, depending on the cost of travel), and response time. Each of those can be more or less accurately measured. Less clear are the kinds of use (circulation versus in-house, in particular).

THE ACCESS ALLOCATION MODEL

The access allocation model simply expresses total costs as a combination of costs for each alternative, weighted by the number of volumes stored at each alternative, and recognizing the effects of distribution of use, time, and patron choices.

Relevant Variables

Let the relevant variables be symbolized as follows:

C_i—present value of capital costs (acquisition, processing, and storage) for alternative (i);

A_i—present value of operating costs (access and use) for alternative (i);

V—the total number of volumes in the collection being considered;

N—the total usage (circulation and in-house) of the V volumes; and

K—the controlling parameter for distribution of use (taken as $.12 \times V$).

Set of Volumes and Their Allocation

Let the set of V volumes being considered be sequenced in rank order of expected frequency of use, and group them into successive groups of K volumes each. Assume that the total use for volumes in groups greater than or equal to group X is given by $N/2^{(X)}$, where N is the total annual use over all V volumes. Allocate the volumes among a set of L alternative locations as follows:

Store volumes from group X_i up to X_{i+1} at alternative i. The number of volumes stored there is then $Y_i = K \times (X_{i+1} - X_i)$. The total usage of those Y_i volumes is then

$$N/2^{X}i - N/2^{X}i+1$$

Total Cost

For the purposes of this chapter, consideration will be limited to the case of two alternatives, in which group $X = X_1$ (containing $Y = K \times X_1$ volumes) are stored at alternative 1, and the remainder at alternative 2.

The total cost, S, for the access allocation decision will be given by:

(1) $S = C_2 \times (V - K \times X) + A_2 \times N/2^{(X)} + C_1 \times Y + A_1 \times (N - N/2^{(X)})$

$\quad\quad = C_2 \times V + (C_1 - C_2) \times K \times X + A_1 \times N + (A_2 - A_1) \times N/2^{(X)}$

Optimization on Cost

The optimum value for X is then given by taking the derivative of S with respect to X and setting it to zero:

(2) $dS/dX = (C_1 - C_2) \times K - (A_2 - A_1) \times N \times \ln_e 2/2^{(X)} = 0$

Hence, the optimum value for X (the one which minimizes S) is given by

(3) $X = \log_2 \dfrac{(A_2 - A_1 \times N \times \ln_e 2}{(C_1 - C_2) \times K}$

and the number of volumes to be stored at alternative 1 is then $Y = K \times X$.

Table 10.3
Seibert's Composite Libraries, 1985

Composite Libraries	Total Holdings	Volumes Added	Expend for Materials	Expend for Staff
Large	5,689,574	155,128	$4,827,351	$9,545,830
Medium-Large	3,156,717	98,464	$3,691,349	$5,394,226
Medium-Small	2,150,096	64,009	$2,635,159	$4,125,410
Small	1,794,540	59,524	$2,532,280	$3,483,838

ILLUSTRATIVE EXAMPLES

Simply to illustrate the application of equation (3), a few allocation decision problems will be examined.

Bases for Hypothesized Values

The statistics reported by the Association of Research Libraries, fraught with problems though they are, can be used to establish representative values. Seibert (Seibert et al., 1987, 1990) identifies ARL "composite libraries" at four levels of size—large, medium-large, medium-small, and small—and reports data for them for 1985 as shown in table 10.3.[7] These data will be used, in part, to derive values hypothesized in this chapter. For staff costs, though, the data from chapter 9 on "workload factors" and "overhead" will be used to extend the ARL "Expend for Staff" data to "full cost" estimates, since the ARL data do not include many significant components of costs (such as salary benefits, in particular). Data presented in the study at the University of Pittsburgh (Kent et al., 1979, and Hayes, 1981) will be used as a basis for estimates on distribution of use.

Both N and V will be taken as proportionate to total holdings (with N at about 1 use per volume held and V at total nonduplicative acquisitions, taken at 300,000 volumes, for the large ARL libraries, as national resources). With N taken at "one times holdings" divided by 5.77; V at 300,000 times holdings divided by 5,689,574; and $K = .12 \times V$, equation (3) reduces to simply 5.04, so $Y = 5.04 \times K$.

Hypothetical Values for Costs

Consider the following alternatives and related hypothetical values for the relevant cost variables:

Alternative 1   Branch Library $C_1 = 70 + 20, \quad A_1 = 0,$
Alternative 2   Central Library $C_2 = 70 + 10, \quad A_2 = 3,$

Table 10.4
Illustrative Values for Optimum Yearly Acquisitions

	N	K	Y	Acquis.	Y/Acquis.
Large ARL Library	986,000	36,000	181,270	155,128	1.17%
Medium-Large ARL Library	547,000	20,000	100,800	98,464	1.02%
Medium-Small ARL Library	372,000	14,000	70,560	64,009	1.10%
Small University Library	310,000	11,000	55,440	59,524	0.93%

Table 10.5
Acquisitions in 1989–1990 by Large ARL Libraries

Harvard	261,000	Columbia	148,872	Indiana	103,279
UCLA	246,737	Yale	147,841	Washington	102,887
Texas	202,338	Stanford	144,450		
UC Berkeley	202,202	Michigan	141,606		
Cornell	189,070	Wisconsin	139,194		
Illinois	187,489	Chicago	132,437		

Alternative 3	Compact Shelving	$C_3 = 70 + 5$,	$A_3 = 5$,
Alternative 4	Depository Facility	$C_4 = 70 + 2$,	$A_4 = 10$,
Alternative 5	Network Access	$C_5 = 0$,	$A_5 = 30$

Acquisition versus Access

The choice between acquisition and access is represented by alternatives 2 and 5. The calculation will be illustrated by a national resource (one of Seibert et al.'s "large" ARL libraries), with the application of equation (3) as follows:

$$Y = 36,000 \times \log_2\{(30-3) \times 5.06 \times (5,689,754/5.77) \times 0.69/((80-0) \times 36,000)\}$$

$$= 181,270 \qquad \text{versus actual } 155,128 \ (1.17\% \text{ of actual})$$

Table 10.4 shows the results for all four of Seibert et al.'s groups of libraries.

It is interesting to note that the ARL Statistics for 1989–90 acquisitions reported for Seibert et al.'s group of "large" ARL libraries were as shown in table 10.5. The average was 167,736 "volumes added" over all fourteen, but the top six averaged 214,700 and the top 12 averaged 178,500.

Branch Library versus Central Library

This choice is represented by alternatives 1 and 2. For a large research library acquiring 155,128 volumes, application of equation (3) would yield:

$$Y = 18,615 \times \log_2\{(3-0) \times 5.06 \times 155,128 \times .69/((90-80) \times 18,615)\}$$

$$= 58,451$$

That is, about one-third of total acquisitions should be in the branches and two-thirds in the central library.

Central Library versus Depository Facility

This choice is represented by alternatives 2 and 4. For a medium-large research library with a collection of V = 3,156,717 volumes (so K = .12 × V = 378,806, and N = V), application of equation (3) would be as follows:

$$Y = 378,806 \times \log_2\{(10-3) \times 5.06 \times 3,156,717 \times .69/((80-72) \times 378,806)\}$$
$$= 1,777,113$$

That is, about 60 percent of the collection should be stored in the browsable central library (and/or branch libraries) and 40 percent in the depository.

IMPLEMENTATION OF THE ALLOCATION MODEL AS A SPREADSHEET

The allocation model described in this chapter can very easily be put into a spreadsheet for use by individual libraries needing to assess allocation decisions for strategic management purposes. The data involved fall into three categories:

1. Data measuring the population of materials involved in the decision: For choice between acquisition and borrowing, the data would be derived from national and international statistics concerning publications; for choice about local allocation, they would be derived from statistics on the current collection. They would then be entered in the spreadsheet for inclusion in the model.

2. Data measuring costs: These would relate to operational data about costs of acquisition, technical processing, and storage within the library and charges from the sources of materials.

3. Data measuring volumes of activity: These would include data on the distributions of use both among categories of materials and over time.

Testing of the Implementation

Such a spreadsheet has been prepared, incorporating the data presented in this chapter as default values for categories (1) through (3). It has been tested against data reported for ARL libraries and ACRL libraries (for 1988–89) and similar data obtained directly from a dozen smaller colleges.[8] The reported data for holdings provide a basis for estimating various parameters. For other parameters in the model, the following uniform assumptions were made:

1. Total use is taken as equal to holdings; use of serials is taken at 40 percent of holdings.

Table 10.6
Application of Allocation Model to Composite Libraries

ARL - 1988/89	Current Serials		Volumes Added		ILL Borrowing	
	Model	Actual	Model	Actual	Model	Actual
1 Average 107	27748	27654	88236	79891	13089	10725
2 Large–14	64160	62821	203058	164834	28855	22986
3 Med–Large–15	34302	31719	109103	94964	16219	7913
4 Med–Small–15	24720	23319	78377	68836	11322	9956
5 Small–14	20292	20295	64479	53727	9504	8549
6 Added–37	17812	20598	56905	58066	8788	9029
7 Canadian–12	23074	17645	73245	74847	10699	8011
ACRL - 1988/89	**Current Serials**		**Volumes Added**		**ILL Borrowing**	
	Model	Actual	Model	Actual	Model	Actual
1 Average 114	6201	6775	20194	23286	3825	5063
2 Largest 20	13103	10830	42506	41017	7066	6562
3 Med–Large 16	8666	9605	28170	30932	5040	5992
4 Middle 20	7079	8187	23005	29121	4083	5778
5 Med–Small 19	5169	5821	16850	20258	3306	4987
6 Smaller 24	3021	4003	9894	13412	2225	4380
7 Smallest 15	1353	2111	4447	6891	1085	2311
Colleges–1988/89	**Current Serials**		**Volumes Added**		**ILL Borrowing**	
	Model	Actual	Model	Actual	Model	Actual
1 AVERAGE	6175	6900	20079	21621	3623	5609

2. The population of serials (in 1988–89) is taken at 105,000 (equal to that of the university library with the largest number of current serials at the time); the population of total potential acquisitions—monographs and current serials combined—is taken at 300,000 volumes.

3. The number of volumes per title (for both serials and monographs) is taken at 1.5.

4. Average cost for a serial title (selection, purchase, processing, binding, and storage) is taken at $107 for ARL libraries, $86 for ACRL libraries, and $80 for colleges; the cost for a monograph title is taken at $62 for all academic libraries.

5. Cost for borrowing any material is taken at $30.

6. ILL is estimated at 25 percent of unmet uses.

The results from applying the allocation model, with these assumptions, appear in table 10.6.

Overall, these results for average or composite libraries seem to provide a remarkable confirmation of the validity of the allocation model, given the range of sizes for the institutions and the degree of match between the results from the model and the actual. For the set of institutions taken

Figure 10.1
ILL Borrowing: Rank Order of Difference Ratios (Actual − Model)/(Lesser of Actual, Model)

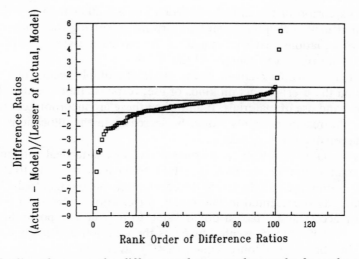

individually, of course, the differences between the results from the model and the actual figures varied widely, but the great majority were within plus or minus 20 percent, as illustrated in figure 10.1 (for the ratio of the differences, between the model and the actual, to the actual, for the ARL libraries), which is quite representative of the results for each of the criteria.

Composite Libraries

It is worth noting that using composite libraries has the virtue of balancing out decisions made in individual libraries and therefore is likely to produce results that are closer to optimum than those of the individual libraries. That is, individual libraries may overacquire or underacquire, but the composite library will have balanced those and lies closer to the optimum.

CONCLUSIONS AND COMMENTARY

Conclusions

The use distribution model fits the data from the University of Pittsburgh closely enough to warrant consideration of it for the purposes of allocation decisions. Further testing of it against data from other libraries is obviously necessary, however.

The access allocation model provides a relatively simple equation for optimum decision making that incorporates the relevant variables in rational ways. When the model is applied to representative data for the several composite libraries, the results appear to be reasonably consistent with the decisions actually being made in practice over a broad range of decision contexts.

The extension of the model to several levels, rather than just the two presented in this chapter, is straightforward, involving the solution of a series of equations, each representing the partial derivative of the total cost, S, with respect to the one of the X_i.

The major missing element in the model is suitable recognition of the effects on the user: impact on kinds of use, response times, and real costs in access and use of materials. If and when these are incorporated into the model, the results certainly would be increases in the allocations to the more accessible levels of access.

There would seem to be two nonexclusive means to deal with the variables relating to the user. One, clearly, is to measure the costs to the user in dollar terms and add them into the cost equation in parallel to the library costs already represented in the model; for example, one could take the time for access and attach a dollar value to it. Another possibility is to replace "Cost" (as represented by S) as the criterion-dependent variable by "Cost" times "Response Time" $(S \times T)$, averaging the response time over the alternatives, weighted by the uses resulting from the allocation choices.

While the illustrations have all been in the context of decisions about allocation of library materials, the model and the results equation (3) for optimal allocation should be applicable to other kinds of information records and access allocation alternatives. For computer-based contexts, though, the response time is likely to be a variable of far greater significance than cost alone, so the measure $S \times T$ should be the necessary one to use.

Commentary

A major motivation for creating the model presented in this chapter was concern that the rhetoric of access (meaning "access to materials held elsewhere") as a replacement for acquisition has failed to recognize the fact that access is not free but indeed is expensive, potentially even bankrupting, if acquisitions were to be reduced to levels such that much more than the current 1 percent (approximately) of uses required such access.

To deal with that concern, a model needed to be available to provide means by which relevant costs could be balanced and the costs of alternatives rationally compared. The fact that the model as it developed provided a simple equation for determining the decision is a valuable result.

Underlying development of the model was the belief that academic library managers are exceptionally effective in making decisions about allocation of resources, without needing formal equations to do so. That the results in application of the model match so closely the decisions made in actual practice can be interpreted both as substantiation of the model and as endorsement of the quality of academic library management decision making.

There is one subsidiary result from the model and its application to ARL, ACRL, and college libraries that is worth emphasis. The match between the results from the model and the actual ILL usage is remarkably close with the assumption that only 25 percent of the missed uses result in ILL requests. That could have potentially catastrophic implications if the level of acquisition is substantially reduced. The problem is not only the increases in costs for ILL that would be incurred, but the effects of the loss of 75 percent of the missed uses of the library that never even result in ILL requests. Those missed uses will result in a dramatic loss of importance of the library to the academic community.

APPENDIX

A problem, of course, is measurement of the amount of in-house use of a collection, especially in contrast to circulation use, for which there are readily available data. Most studies have used "sweeps," in which the books on tables or at collection points are reviewed and counted; reshelving statistics have been used to provide a limited measure. A couple of studies (Fussler and Simon, 1968; Kent et al., 1979) have concluded that it is not necessary to obtain data on in-house use.[9] However, in each case there are dramatic contradictions:

Fussler and Simon:

"Non-recorded use is roughly proportional to recorded use" (p. 115);

"Low use books get proportionally more browsing" (p. 114).

Kent:

"Circulation use is a . . . reliable index of all use" (p. 28);

Nearly a quarter (24.6 percent) of the books used in-house had never circulated (p. 31).

In the same vein, Hindle and Buckland (1978) stated, "circulation and in-house use are similar *except at the lowest levels of circulation*" (emphasis added).[10] These all strongly suggest that there are substantial differences between the distribution of circulation use and that of in-house use; though each will exhibit the same J-shaped curve, the position of groups of volumes will be different. In fact, typically 15 percent to 20 percent of in-house use will involve books that rarely if ever circulate; that hardly confirms the view that circulation use characterizes all use of a collection (Kent, 1979, pp. 28–31; Lawrence, 1980, pp. 27, 38; Thompson, 1978, p. 9; Hindle, 1978, p. 268).[11]

Tables 10.7 and 10.8 show the application of the Bradford model to data from the University of Pittsburgh (Kent, 1979).

Table 10.7
Distribution of Use of 1969 Acquisitions at Hillman Library

$$K = 4423 = 0.12*36860, \; V(X) = 36860 - K*X$$

X	V(X)	Circ(V(X))	N/2^(X)	Rel. Diff.
0	36860	149110	149110	0.00
1	32437	74522	74555	0.00
2	28014	37568	37278	−0.01
3	23590	18744	18639	−0.01
4	19167	9778	9319	−0.05
5	14744	4661	4660	0.00
6	10321		2330	
7	5898		1165	
8	1474		582	
9			291	
10			146	
Sum for X > 5		4535	4514	−0.00

Source: Allen Kent, p. 17, table 3, and Robert M. Hayes, "The Distribution of Use of Library Materials," *Library Research* 3 (Fall 1981): 215–60.

Notes Regarding These Computations

The variable V(X) is calculated by subtracting $K \times X$ successively from N = 36,860 (the 1969 acquisitions at Hillman) and from N = 542,552 (the total Hillman collection in 1976), respectively.

Circ(X), for X between 0 and 5, is determined from the respective tables in Kent (1979) by calculations that are best seen by illustration: V(1) = 32,437 for the 1969 data. The closest cumulative volumes (derived from table 3, p. 17, of Kent, 1969), is 32,381, covering frequency of use from 0 through 10, and the associated cumulative circulations are 73,906; the difference of 56 must be drawn from a frequency of 11; the resulting 616 circulations are added to 73,906, for the total of 74,522. Similar calculations were used for other values of V(X) for both table 3 and table 23 (Kent, 1979).

Circ(X), for X greater than 5, cannot be directly derived from table 3 of Kent (1979), since for volumes less than 14,698, the circulation was zero. The analysis in Hayes (1981), however, provides some basis for estimating the *potential* circulation (and therefore in-house use) by identifying components of a mixture of Poisson distributions that may underlie the data in Kent's table 3. Among them is one consisting of 12,752 volumes with .762 as the a priori likelihood of circulation. That would result in 5,952 volumes with a zero circulation but the potential of 4,535 circulations;

Table 10.8
Distribution of Use of Hillman Library Holdings

$$K = 65106 = 0.12*542552, \quad V(X) = 542552 - K*X$$

X	V(X)	Circ(V(X))	N/2^(X)	Rel. Diff.
0	542552	1403367	1403367	0.00
1	477446	745703	701684	-0.06
2	412340	340655	350842	0.03
3	347233	184376	175421	-0.05
4	282127	90857	87710	-0.04
5	217021	44000	43855	-0.00
6	151915		21928	
7	86808		10964	
8	21702		5482	
9			2741	
10			1370	
Sum for X > 5		41814	42485	0.02

Source: Allen Kent, p. 40, table 23, and Robert M. Hayes, "The Distribution of Use of Library Materials," *Library Research* 3 (Fall 1981): 215–60.

those 4,535 circulations are shown in the table in parallel with the sum of the related values for the model.

In the same vein, the data directly derived from Kent's table 23 are limited to X from 0 through 5, since table 23 shows 257,613 volumes with zero circulations. Again, components of a mixture of Poisson distributions were identified in Hayes (1981), among them one consisting of 130,000 volumes with .64 as the a priori likelihood of circulation. The would result in 68,548 volumes from that component that have zero circulation but with the potential of 41,814 circulations; those 41,814 circulations again are shown in the table in parallel with the sum of related values for the model.

NOTES

1. Stayner, Richard A., and Richardson, Valerie E., *The Cost-Effectiveness of Alternative Library Storage Programs* (Melbourne, Australia: Monash University, Graduate School of Librarianship, 1983); Jain, A. K., et al., "A Statistical Model of Book Use and Its Application to the Book Storage Problem," *Journal of the American Statistical Association* 64 (December 1969): 1211–24; Leimkuhler, F. F., "Storage Policies for Information Systems," Paper presented at the Joint National Meeting of the American Astronautical Society and the Operations Research Society, Denver, Colorado, June 1969; Lister, W. C., *Least-Cost Decision Rules for the Selection of Library Materials for Compact Storage* (Ph.D. thesis, Purdue University, 1967).

2. Werking, Richard Hume, "Allocating the Academic Library's Book Budget: Historical Perspectives and Current Reflections," *Journal of Academic Librarianship* 14(3) (July 1988): 140–44; Werking, Richard Hume, "Collection Growth and Expenditures in Academic Libraries: A Preliminary Inquiry," *College and Research Libraries* 109(2) (Jan. 1991): 5–23.

3. Bookstein, Abraham, "Comments on the Morse-Chen Discussion of Noncirculating Books," *Library Quarterly* 45(2) (1975): 195–98; Bowen, Alice, "Nonrecorded Use of Books and Browsing in the Stacks of a Research Library" (M.A. thesis, University of Chicago, 1961); Burrell, Q., "A Simple Stochastic Model for Library Loans," *Journal of Documentation* 36 (1980): 115–132; Burrell, Q., "Alternative Models for Library Circulation Data," *Journal of Documentation* 38 (1982): 1–13; Harris, C., "A Comparison of Issues and In-Library Use of Books," *Aslib Proceedings* 29(3) (Mar. 1977): 118–26; Jain, A. K., *A Statistical Study of Book Use* (Ph.D. thesis, Purdue University, 1967); Lazorick, Gerald J., "Patterns of Book Use Using the Binomial Distribution," *Library Research* 1 (1979): 171–88; Morse, Philip M., "Measures of Library Effectiveness," *Library Quarterly* (42)1 (Jan. 1972): 15–30; Morse, Philip M., and Chen, Chingchih, "Using Circulation Data to Obtain Unbiased Estimates of Book Use," *Library Quarterly* 45(2) (1975): 179–94.

4. Bradford, S. C., "Sources of Information on Specific Subjects," *Engineering* 137(3549) (1934): 85–86; Buckland, Michael K., *Book Availability and the Library User* (New York: Pergamon, 1975), 14–21.

5. Kent, Allen, et al., (eds.), *Use of Library Materials: The University of Pittsburgh Study* (New York: Marcel Dekker, 1979). See especially Bulick, Stephen, et al., "Circulation and In-House Use of Books," ch. 2.

6. Hayes, Robert M., "The Distribution of Use of Library Materials: Analysis of Data from the University of Pittsburgh," *Library Research* 3 (Fall 1981): 215–60; Buckland, *Book Availability*, 12–13; Line, M. B., and Sandison, A., "Obsolescence and Changes in the Use of Literature with Time," *Journal of Documentation* 30 (1974): 283–350; Morse, P. M., and Elston, C., "A Probabilistic Model for Obsolescence," *Operations Research* 17(1) (1969): 36–47.

7. Dunn, Oliver C., et al., *The Past and Likely Future of 58 Research Libraries, 1951–1980: A Statistical Study of Growth and Change* (West Lafayette, Ind: Purdue University, 1965–1972); Seibert, Warren, et al., *Research Library Trends, 1951–1980 and Beyond* (Bethesda, Md.: Lister Hill Center for Biomedical Communications, March 1987); Seibert, Warren, et al., *Research Library Trends II: 35 Libraries in the 1970s and Beyond* (Bethesda, Md.: Lister Hill Center for Biomedical Communications, January 1990).

8. Stubbs, Kendon, and Buxton, David, (comps.), *Cumulated ARL University Library Statistics: 1962–63 through 1978–79* (Washington, D.C.: Association of Research Libraries, 1981); Association of Research Libraries, *ARL Statistics, 1988–89* (Washington, D.C.: Association of Research Libraries, 1990); Association of College and Research Libraries, *ACRL University Library Statistics* (Chicago: Association of College and Research Libraries, 1990); Piternick, George, "ARL Statistics—Handle with Care," *College and Research Libraries* 38 (Sept. 1977): 419–423.

9. Fussler, Herman H., and Simon, J. L., *Patterns in the Use of Books in Large Research Libraries* (Chicago: University of Chicago Press, 1969); Kent et al., *Use of Library Materials*; University of Pittsburgh, Senate Library Committee, *Report on the Study of Library Use at Pitt by Professor Allen Kent, et al.*, July 1979.

10. Hindle, A., and Worthington, D., "Simple Stochastic Models for Library Loan,"

Journal of Documentation 36(3) (Sept. 1980): p. 2; Hindle, Anthony, and Buckland, Michael, "In-Library Book Usage in Relation to Circulation," *Collection Management* 2(4) (Winter 1978): 265–77 (quotation on p. 276).

11. Lawrence, Gary S., "A Cost Model for Storage and Weeding Programs," *College and Research Libraries* 42(1981): 138–47; Lawrence, Gary S., and Oja, Anne R., *The Use of the General Collections at the University of California* (Berkeley: University of California, Library Studies and Research Division, 30 January 1980); Thompson, Donald D., *In-House Use and Immediacy of Need: The Riverside Pilot Studies* (Berkeley: University of California, November 1978); *Reader Failure at the Shelf* (Loughborough, Leicestershire, U.K.: Loughborough University, Department of Library and Information Studies, Centre for Library and Information Management, 1982), fig. 10.1.

References

Aaker, David A. *Developing Business Strategies*. 2nd ed. New York: Wiley, 1988.

Abelson, Philip H. "Information Exchange Groups" (editorial). *Science* 154(3750) (11 November 1966): 727.

Ackoff, Russell. *The Design of Social Research*. Chicago: University of Chicago Press, 1953.

ACRL University Library Statistics. Chicago: Association of College and Research Libraries, 1990.

"Agreement Near on Changes in Faculty Rewards Structure." *Notice, Academic Senate of UC* 16(8) (June 1992): 1, 5–6.

Aguilar, William. "The Application of Relative Use and Interlibrary Demand in Collection Development." *Collection Management* 8(1) (1986): 15–24.

Akers, John F. "Two Visions and the Challenge for Higher Education." *Educom Review* 24(4) (Winter 1989): 12–18.

Albritton, Errett C. "NIH's Former 'IEG' Program of Quick Communication." *Bulletin of the American Physical Society* ser. 2, 13(1) (29 January 1968): 31.

American Foundation on Automation and Employment. *Automation and the Middle Manager: What Has Happened and What the Future Holds*. New York: American Foundation on Automation and Employment, 1966.

American Library Association. *Guide to Evaluation of Library Collections*. Chicago: American Library Association, 1989.

American Library Association. *Guidelines for Collection Development*. Chicago: American Library Association, 1979.

American Library Association (ALA). Washington, D.C., Office. *American Library Association Comments on NTIA January 9, 1990, Proposed "Comprehensive Study of Domestic Telecommunications Infrastructure."* Washington, D.C.: ALA Washington Office, 12 April 1990.

Amigos. "Four Academic Libraries Purchase OCLC/Amigos Collection Analysis CD" (news release). 6 October 1989.

"ARL and RLG to Study ILL Costs." *Library Hotline* 21(17) (17 April 1992): 102.

"ARL, Cause, Educom Form New Information Resources Coalition." *Manage IT* 1(2) (April 1990): 1–2.

"ARL Consultants' Reports Likely to Widen Serials Rift." *American Libraries*, June 1989, p. 489.

Armbrister, Ann. "Library Marc Tapes as a Resource for Collection Analysis: The AMIGOS Service." *Advances in Library Automation and Networking* 2 (1988): 119–35.

Arms, Caroline. "Libraries and Electronic Information: The Technological Context, Part Two." *Educom Review* 24(3) (Fall 1989): 34–43.

Association of American Medical Colleges. *The Management of Information in Academic Medicine*, vol. 2. Washington, D.C.: Association of American Medical Colleges, 1982.

Association of American Publishers. *AAP Electronic Manuscript Series: Standard for Electronic Manuscript Preparation and Markup: An SGML Application Conforming to International Standard ISO 8879—Standard Generalized Markup Language*. Version 2.0, rev. ed. Washington, D.C.: Association of American Publishers, 1989.

Association of American Universities. *The Ph.D. Shortage*. Washington, D.C.: Association of American Universities, 1990.

Association of Research Libraries (ARL). *ARL Preservation Statistics, 1990–91*. Washington, D.C.: ARL, 1992.

Association of Research Libraries. *ARL/RLG Interlibrary Loan Cost Study: Worksheet*. Washington, D.C.: ARL, 1992.

Association of Research Libraries. *ARL Statistics, 1988–89*. Washington, D.C.: Association of Research Libraries, 1990.

Association of Research Libraries. *The Changing System for Scholarly Communication*. Washington, D.C.: ARL, 1966.

Association of Research Libraries. Office of Management Studies. Systems and Procedures Exchange Center. *Copyright Policies in ARL Libraries*, SPEC kit 102. Washington, D.C.: Association of Research Libraries, 1984.

Association of Research Libraries. Office of Management Studies. *Qualitative Collection Analysis: The Conspectus Methodology*. SPEC kit 151. Washington, D.C.: Association of Research Libraries, 1989.

Association of Research Libraries. Office of Management Studies. *University Copyright Policies in ARL Libraries*. SPEC kit 138. Washington, D.C.: Association of Research Libraries, 1987.

Association of Research Libraries. Office of Management Studies. Systems Procedures and Exchange Center. *User Surveys and Evaluation of Library Services*. SPEC kit 71. Washington, D.C.: ARL, 1981.

Association of Research Libraries. Office of Management Studies. Systems Procedures and Exchange Center. *User Surveys in ARL Libraries*. SPEC kit 101. Washington, D.C.: ARL, 1984.

"Associations Take Stands on Access to Information." *American Libraries*, June 1989, pp. 485–86.

Astone, Barbara. *Pursuing Diversity: Recruiting College Minority Students*. Washington, D.C.: George Washington University, 1990.

Avram, Henriette D. "Copyright in the Electronic Environment." *Educom Review* 24(3) (Fall 1989): 31–33.

Axford, H. W. "Collection Management: A New Dimension." *Journal of Academic Librarianship* 6 (1981): 324–29.

Baecker, Ronald, and William Buxton. *Readings in Human-Computer Interaction: A Multidisciplinary Approach*. Los Altos, Calif.: Morgan Kaufmann, 1987.

Bair, James H. "The Integrated Future of Image Management." *Imaging and Information Consultant* 1(2) (March/April 1991): 3–5.

Balestri, Diane. "Educational Uses of Information Technology." *Educom Review* 24(4) (Winter 1989): 7–9.

Battin, Patricia. "The Electronic Library—A Vision for the Future." *Educom Bulletin*, Summer 1984, pp. 12–17, 34.

Baumol, William, and Matihyahu Marcus. *Economics of Academic Libraries*. Washington, D.C.: American Council on Education, 1973.

Berger, Mike. "The Patron Meets the Melvyl Catalog: A Short History of the Melvyl Patron Interface." *DLA Bulletin* 12(10) (Spring 1992): 6–7, 24–26.

Bok, Derek. "Looking into Education's High-Tech Future." *Harvard Magazine*, May/June 1985, pp. 29–38. Reprinted in *Educom Bulletin*, Fall 1985, pp. 2–17.

Books for College Libraries, 3rd ed. Chicago: American Library Association, 1988.

Bookstein, Abraham. "Comments on the Morse-Chen Discussion of Non-Circulating Books." *Library Quarterly* 45(2) (1975): 195–98.

———. "Questionnaire Research in a Library Setting." *Journal of Academic Librarianship* 1(1) (1985): 24–28.

Bosseau, Don L. *After the OPAC, CD-ROM, Hypermedia, and Networking—What Lies Ahead for Libraries and Librarians?* San Diego: California State University at San Diego, 1991.

Boulton, William R. *Business Policy: The Art of Strategic Management*. New York: MacMillan, 1984.

Bourne, Charles P., and Madeleine Kasson. *Preliminary Report on the Review and Development of Standard Cost Data for Selected Library Technical Processing Functions*. Palo Alto, Calif.: Information General Corp., 1969.

Bowen, Alice. "Nonrecorded Use of Books and Browsing in the Stacks of a Research Library." M.A. Thesis, University of Chicago, 1961.

Bowen, Howard R., and Jack H. Schuster. *American Professors—A National Resource Imperiled*. New York: Oxford University Press, 1986.

Bradford, S. C. "Sources of Information on Specific Subjects." *Engineering* 137(3549) (1934): 85–86.

Branin, Joseph J., David Farrell, and Marriann Tibdin. "The National Shelflist Count Project: Its History, Limitations, and Usefulness." *Library Resources and Technical Services* 29 (October/December 1985): 333–42.

Brindley, Lynne J. *Libraries and the Wired-up Campus: The Future Role of the Library in Academic Information Handling*. Birmingham, U.K.: BLR&D, 1988.

Broadus, Robert. "Use Studies of Library Collections." *Library Resources and Technical Services* 24(4) (1980): 317–24.

Brown, Rowland C. W. "Brushstrokes in Flight: A Strategic Overview of Trends in Technology in Higher Education." In *The Electronic Campus—An Information Strategy*, ed. Lynn J. Brindley. Proceedings of the Conference in Banbury, England, 28–30 October 1988, pp. 22-41.

Buckland, Michael K. *Book Availability and the Library User*. New York: Pergamon, 1975.

"Budget-Struck Stanford Library Merged with Computer Center." *American Libraries*, October 1990, p. 830.

Burns, Robert W., Jr. "Library Use as a Performance Measure: Its Background and Rationale." *Journal of Academic Librarianship* 4(1) (1978): 4–11.

Burrell, Q. "A Simple Stochastic Model for Library Loans." *Journal of Documentation* 36 (1980): 115–32.

———. "Alternative Models for Library Circulation Data." *Journal of Documentation* 38 (1982): 1–13.

Butler, Meredith, and Bonnie Gratch. "Planning a User Study: The Process Defined." *College and Research Libraries* 43(4) (1982): 320–30.

California State Library. *Request for Proposal for Telefacsimile Networking*. Sacramento: California State Library, June 1989.

"Cal. State's Leviathan II Is a Whale of a Project." *American Libraries*, Oct. 1989, p. 839.

Card, Stuart K., Thomas P. Moran, and Allen Newell. *The Psychology of Human-Computer Interaction*. Hillsdale, N.J.: Lawrence Erlbaum Associates, 1983.

Carroll, Bonnie, and Donald W. King. "Value of Information." *Drexel Library Quarterly* 21 (Summer 1985): 39–60.

Carroll, John M. *Interfacing Thought: Cognitive Aspects of Human-Computer Interaction*. Cambridge, Mass.: Bradford/MIT Press, June 1987.

Case, Donald. *Optical Disk Publication of Databases: A Review of Applications for Academic Libraries*. Los Angeles: GSLIS, 31 August 1986.

"CD-ROM Database Sales Should Hit about 2.2 Mil by 1996 vs 1.4 Mil in 1991." *Computing World*, March 1992, p. 9.

Center for Research Libraries. *Center for Research Libraries Handbook*. Chicago: CRL, n.d.

Certo, Samuel C., and J. Paul Peter. *Strategic Management*. New York: Random House, 1988.

Checkland, Peter. *Systems Thinking, Systems Practice*. Chichester, U.K.: Wiley, 1981.

Chen, Ching-Chih. "CD-Interactive: What Is Coming Out from the Pipeline?" *Microcomputer Information Management* 7 (Sept. 1990): 243–52.

Christiansen, Dorothy E., C. Roger Davis, and Jutta Reed-Scott. "Guidelines to Collection Evaluation through Use and User Studies." *Library Resources and Technical Services* 27(4) (October/December 1983): 432–40.

Church, Steven S. "User Criteria for Evaluation of Library Services." *Journal of Library Administration* 2(1) (1981): 35–46.

"CIO-Type Positions Meeting Higher Ed Needs for Consolidation." *Manage IT* 1(5) (October 1990): 1, 3–4.

"Citadel: A Stronghold of Information." *Research Libraries Group News* 27 (Winter 1992): 15.

"CitaDel Previewed at Rutgers and BYU." *Research Libraries Group News* 28 (Spring 1992): 3–6.

Clapp, Verner W., and Robert T. Jordan. "Quantitative Criteria for Adequacy of

Academic Library Collections." *College and Research Libraries* 50 (March 1989): 153–63.

Cleland, David I. *Matrix Management Systems Handbook.* New York: Van Nostrand Reinhold Co., 1984.

Cline, Nancy. "Information Resources and the National Network." *Educom Review* 25(2) (Summer 1990): 30–34.

Colin, K., George N. Lindsey, and Daniel Callahan. "Toward Usable User Studies." *Journal of the American Society for Information Science* 31 (1980): 347–56.

"Colleges and Universities Are Forced to Make Cuts and Adjustments Due to Harsh Economic Realities." *New York Times*, 3 Feb. 1992, p. A1.

Commission on Preservation and Access. *Preserving the Illustrated Text: Report of the Joint Task Force on Text and Image.* Washington, D.C.: Commission on Preservation and Access, 1992.

Conable, Gordon. "The FBI and You." *American Libraries*, March 1990, pp. 245–48.

Conatser, Kelly R. "In or Out?—A Simple 1–2–3 Model Reveals whether Outsourcing Is for You." *Lotus* 8(8) (Aug. 1992): 36–40.

Connors, J. L., and T. A. Romberg. "Middle Management and Quality Control." *Human Organization* 50(1) (Spring 1991): 61–65.

Council on Library Resources. Committee on Preservation and Access. *Brittle Books: Reports of the Committee on Preservation and Access.* Washington, D.C.: Council on Library Resources, 1986.

Crews, Kenneth D. *Copyright Policies at American Research Universities: Balancing Information Needs and Legal Limits.* Ph.D. dissertation, University of California at Los Angeles, 1990.

———. *Copyright at the Research University: A Select Bibliography of Secondary Literature, 1967–1986.* Los Angeles: GSLIS, 31 October 1986.

Crowe, Beryl. "The Tragedy of the Commons Revisited." *Science* 166(3909) (28 Nov. 1969): 1103–7.

Cummings, Martin M. *The Economics of Research Libraries.* Washington, D.C.: Council on Library Resources, 1986.

Cyert, Richard M. "The Role of Electronic Information in Higher Education." *OCLC Newsletter*, Mar./Apr. 1992, pp. 18–19.

Dannelly, Gay N. "The National Shelflist Count: A Tool for Collection Management." Paper presented at Collection Development in Action Conference, Toledo, Ohio, October 28, 1988.

"Database Vendors Revenues Projection." *Information* (part 1) (October 1989): 6.

Dean, Nita. "EPIC: A New Frame of Reference for the OCLC Database." *OCLC Newsletter*, March/April 1991, p. 21.

DeGennaro, Richard. *Libraries, Technology, and the Information Marketplace.* Boston: G.K. Hall, 1987.

Delonas, Nicholas. "The Time Series Machine." *Lotus* 7(11) (November 1991): 68–71.

Dillon, Martin, and Mark Crook. "A Prototype Automated Collection Analysis Tool for Libraries." *OCLC Research Review*, July 1987, pp. 3–4.

Dougherty, Richard M. "An Ideal Win-Win Situation: The National Electronic Highway." *American Libraries*, Feb. 1991, p. 182.

Dougherty, Richard M., and Fred J. Heinritz. *Scientific Management of Library Operations*. Metuchen, N.J.: Scarecrow Press, 1982.

Dowd, Sheila T. "The Formulation of a Collection Development Policy Statement." In *Collection Development in Libraries: A Treatise*, ed. Robert D. Steuart and George B. Miller, Jr. Greenwich, Conn.: JAI Press, 1980, pp. 67–87.

Drake, Miriam A. *Academic Research Libraries: A Study of Growth*. West Lafayette, Ind.: Libraries and Audio-Visual Center, Purdue University, 1977.

Draper, Stephen, and Donald Norman. *User Centered System Design*. Hillsdale, N.J.: Lawrence Erlbaum Associates, 1986.

Dunn, Oliver C., et al. *The Past and Likely Future of 58 Research Libraries, 1951– 1980: A Statistical Study of Growth and Change*. West Lafayette, Ind.: Purdue University, 1965–1972.

Ehrich, Roger W., and Robert C. Williges. *Human-Computer Dialogue Design*. New York: Elsevier Science, January 1986.

The Electronic Campus—An Information Strategy. Proceedings of the Conference in Banbury, England, 28–30 October 1988.

Ess, Charles. "Intermedia." *Computers and the Humanities* 24(4) (August 1990): 324–30.

Faigel, Martin. "Methods and Issues in Collection Evaluation Today." *Library Acquisitions: Practice and Theory* 9(1) (1985): 21–35.

Farmington Plan Newsletter, nos. 1–31. Washington, D.C.: Association of Research Libraries, March 1949–May 1970.

Farrell, David. "The North American Inventory Project (NCIP): Phase II Results in Indiana." *Resource Sharing and Information Networks* 2 (Spring/Summer 1985): 37–48.

———. "The NCIP Option for Coordinated Collection Management." *Library Resources and Technical Services* 30 (January-March 1986): 47–56.

Farrell, David, and Jutta Reed-Scott. "The North American Collections Inventory Project: Implications for the Future of Coordinated Management of Research Collections." *Library Resources and Technical Services* 33 (January 1989): 15–28.

Faxon Company. *The Faxon Institute for Advanced Studies in Scholarly and Scientific Communication*. Westwood, Mass.: Faxon Company.

"FBI to Consider Release of 'Awareness Program' Material." *American Libraries*, June 1989, p. 481.

"Federal Data Go Private: Vendors Repackage Public Information—At a Price that Limits Access." *Christian Science Monitor* 82(209) (Monday, 24 September 1990): 15.

Ferguson, Anthony W., Joan Grant, and Joel S. Rutstein. "The RLG Conspectus: Its Uses and Benefits." *College and Research Libraries* 49 (March 1989): 197–206.

Final Report on the Project for Strategic Planning for Information Resources in the Research University. Los Angeles: GSLIS, December 1990.

The First Emperor of China (video disk). Santa Monica, Calif.: The Voyager Company, 1991.

"FirstSearch Takes the Lead." *Information Today*, Feb. 1992.

Flanders, Bruce. "Spectacular Systems!" *American Libraries*, Oct. 1989, pp. 915–22.

———. "NREN: The Big Issues Aren't Technical." *American Libraries*, June 1991, pp. 572–74.

Fogarty, James. "Dramatically Different! Hypertext." *Online Searcher* 2(2) (Winter 1990): 1, 4.

Ford, Kenneth W. (executive director, American Institute of Physics). "Refuting Gordon & Breach" (letter). *American Libraries*, March 1990, p. 192.

Frand, Jason. *The Microcomputerization of Business Schools*. Los Angeles: UCLA Graduate School of Management, 1987.

Frand, Jason, and Julia A. Britt. *Seventh Annual UCLA Survey of Business School Computer Usage, September 1990*. Los Angeles: UCLA, John E. Anderson Graduate School of Management, 1990.

Freeman, Harry L. "Blame Statistics for Trade Deficit." *Wall Street Journal* (Oct. 31, 1989): A22 (Western edition).

Fuerbringer, Jonathan. "Accuracy in Short Supply in Flood of U.S. Statistics." *New York Times* 139(48039) (30 October 1989): A1, D4.

Fulop, L. "Middle Managers—Victims or Vanguards of the Entrepreneurial Movement?" *Journal of Management Studies* 28(1) (1991): 25–54.

Fussler, Herman H., and J. L. Simon. *Patterns in the Use of Books in Large Research Libraries*. Chicago: University of Chicago Press, 1969.

Galvin, Thomas J. "Research Library Performance in the Delivery of Electronic Information." *OCLC Newsletter*, Mar./Apr. 1992, pp. 20–21.

Gardner, Nigel. "Bringing the Electronic Campus to Reality: Opportunities and Challenges in Teaching." In *The Electronic Campus—An Information Strategy*, ed. Lynn J. Brindley. Proceedings of the Conference in Banbury, England, 28–30 October 1988, pp. 5–12.

Garrett, Nina, et al. "Computers in Foreign Language Teaching and Research; A 'New Humanism': Part One." *Educom* 25(1) (Spring 1990): 36–49.

———. "Computing in Foreign Language Teaching and Research: Part Two." *Educom Review* 25(2) (Summer 1990): 39–45.

Gaughan, Tom. "Taking the Pulse of Library Education." *American Libraries*, January 1992, pp. 24–25, 120.

Gherman, Paul M. "Setting Budgets for Libraries in the Electronic Era." *Chronicle of Higher Education*, 14 August 1991, p. A36.

Gilb, Tom, and Gerald M. Weinberg. *Humanized Input: Techniques for Reliable Keyboard Input*. Wellesley Hills, Mass.: QED Information Sciences, 1977.

Gilbert, Steven W. "Information Technology, Intellectual Property, and Education." *Educom* 25(1) (Spring 1990): 14–20.

Gilbert, Steven W., and Kenneth C. Green. "New Computing in Higher Education." *Change*, May/June 1986, pp. 33–50.

Glick, Milton D. "Integrating Computing into Higher Education." *Educom Review* 25(2) (Summer 1990): pp. 35–38.

Glitz, Beryl. "The California Multitype Library Network: An Update." *Pacific Southwest Regional Medical Library Service*, January/February 1991, pp. 1, 4.

Glueck, William F., and Lawrence R. Jauch. *Business Policy and Strategic Management*. New York: McGraw-Hill, 1984.

Godet, Michel. *Scenarios and Strategic Management*. London: Butterworths, 1987.

"Gordon & Breach Sues Again." *American Libraries*, April 1990, p. 286.

Gore, Albert. "Remarks on the NREN." *Educom Review* 25(2) (Summer 1990): 12–16.

Greenberger, Martin, ed. *Technologies for the 21st Century: On Multimedia*. Santa Monica, Calif.: Voyager Co., 1990.

Griffiths, Jose-Marie, and Donald W. King. *Intellectual Property Rights in an Age of Electronics and Information*. Washington, D.C.: U.S. Congress, Office of Technology Assessment, 1986.

————. *New Directions in Library and Information Science Education*. White Plains, N.Y.: Knowledge Industry Publications for the American Society for Information Science, 1986.

Guide to Using Graph-Text, A Document Retrieval System for Scientific Journals. Dublin, Ohio: OCLC, August 1986.

Gwinn, Nancy E., and Paul H. Mosher. "Coordinating Collection Development: The RLG Conspectus." *College and Research Libraries* 44 (March 1983): 128–40.

Haas, Warren J. "Library Schools in Research Universities." In Council on Library Resources, *35th Annual Report 1991*. Washington, D.C.: Council on Library Resources, 1992, pp. 27–33.

Hake, R. R. "PhD Supply and Demand." *Science* 249 (1969): 611–12.

Hardin, G. "The Tragedy of the Commons." *Science* 162(3859), 13 Dec. 1968, pp. 1243–48.

Harris, C. "A Comparison of Issues and In-Library Use of Books." *Aslib Proceedings* 29(3) (Mar. 1977): 118–26.

Harris, C. L. "Columbia University Library's Staff Development Seminar." *Journal of Academic Librarianship* 17(2) (3 May 1991): 71–73.

Harris, Colin. "Surveying the User and User Studies." *Information and Library Manager* 5(3) (1985): 9–14.

Hax, Arnoldo C., ed. *Readings on Strategic Management*. Cambridge: Ballinger, 1984.

Hax, Arnoldo C., and Nicolas S. Majluf. *Strategic Management: An Integrative Perspective*. Englewood Cliffs, N.J.: Prentice-Hall, 1984.

Hayes, Robert M. "Distributed Library Networks: Programs and Problems." In *The Responsibility of the University Library Collection in Meeting the Needs of Its Campus and Local Community*, ed. Friends of the UCSD Library. La Jolla: Friends of the UCSD Library, 1976.

————. "The Management of Library Resources: The Balance between Capital and Staff in Providing Services." *Library Research* 1(2) (Summer 1979): 119–42.

————. "The Distribution of Use of Library Materials: Analysis of Data from the University of Pittsburgh." *Library Research* 3 (Fall 1981): 215–60.

————. "Planning and Coordination of Research on Library and Information Science in the United States." Proceedings of the IFLA Conference in Leipzig, GDR, 17–22 August 1981.

————. "A Commentary on the NCLIS Public Sector/Private Sector Task Force and Its Report." In Association of Research Libraries, *Minutes of the Ninety-*

Ninth Annual Meeting, Association of Research Libraries. Washington, D.C.: ARL, 1982, pp. 12–41.

———. "Politics and Publishing in Washington." *Special Libraries* 74(4) (Oct. 1983): 322–31.

———. "Pricing of Products and Services of the National Library of Medicine and Competition with the Private Sector: A Review of Relevant Reports." A Report to the U.S. Department of Health and Human Services, August 1983.

———. "Pricing Policies of the National Library of Medicine" (editorial). *Annals of Internal Medicine* 100(4) (April 1984): 601–4.

———. "Strategic Planning for Information Resources in the Research University." *RQ* 25(4) (Summer 1986): 427–31.

———. "Desktop Publishing: Problems of Control." *Scholarly Publishing* 21(2) (Jan. 1990): 117–23. Also published as "Who Should Be in Control?" in *Desktop Publishing in the University*, ed. Joan N. Burstyn. Syracuse, N.Y.: Syracuse University, 1991.

———. "@RISK." *Information Today* 9(8) (September 1992): 12–13.

———. "InfoMapper." *Information Today* 9(7) (July/August 1992): 9–10.

———. "Long-Range Strategic Planning for Information Resources in the Research University." In *Advances in Library Administration and Organization*, ed. Gerard B. McCabe and Bernard Kreissman. New York: JAI Press, 1992.

———., ed. *Universities, Information Technology, and Academic Libraries: The Next Twenty Years. The Report of the CLR Sponsored Frontiers Conference, Lake Arrowhead, December 1981*. Norwood, N.J.: Ablex Press, 1986.

———., and Joseph Becker. *Handbook of Data Processing for Libraries*, 2nd ed. New York: Wiley, 1972, ch. 4.

———., and Timothy Erickson. "Added Value as a Function of Purchases of Information Services." *Information Society* 1(4) (Dec. 1982): 307–38.

———., and Susan Palmer. "The Effects of Distance upon Use of Libraries." *Library and Information Science Research* 5(1) (Spring 1983): 67–100.

———. et al. "An Application of the Cobb-Douglas Model to the Association of Research Libraries." *Library and Information Science Research* 5(3) (Fall 1983): 291–326.

Haywood, Trevor. *Changing Faculty Environments*. Birmingham, U.K.: Birmingham Polytechnic, July 1991.

Helmer, Olaf. *The Delphi Method for Systematizing Judgements about the Future*. Los Angeles: UCLA Institute of Government and Public Affairs, 1966.

———. *Looking Forward: A Guide to Futures Research*. Beverly Hills, Calif.: Sage Publications, 1983.

Herman, James, et al. "Shaping the 1990s: A New Way of Looking at the Future Helps Industry Participants Develop Their Visions of the Next Five Years." *Computer World*, 27 Nov. 1989, pp. 77–85.

Hindle, A., and D. Worthington. "Simple Stochastic Models for Library Loan." *Journal of Documentation* 36(3) (Sept. 1980): 209–13.

Hindle, Anthony, and Michael Buckland. "In-Library Book Usage in Relation to Circulation." *Collection Management* 2(4) (Winter 1978): 265–77.

Hockey, Susan. "The Role of Electronic Information in Higher Education: The

Faculty Perspective." *OCLC Academic Libraries Directors' Conference*. Dublin, Ohio: OCLC, 1992.

Hodge, Stanley P., and Marilyn Ivins. "Current International Newspapers: Some Collection Management Implications." *College and Research Libraries* 48(1) (1987): 50–61.

Hofer, Charles W., and Dan Schendel. *Strategy Formulation: Analytical Concepts*. St. Paul, Minn.: West Publishing, 1978.

Holt, Brian G. F., and Stephen Hanger. *Conspectus in the British Library*. London: British Library, 1986.

Huray, Paul G., and David B. Nelson. "The Federal High-Performance Computing Program." *Educom Review* 25(2) (Summer 1990): 17–24.

Hyatt, Shirley. "New Era Communications Gives Libraries New Options." *OCLC Newsletter*, May/June 1992, pp. 15–19.

"Hypertext Update." *SIGOMET Education and Training Newsletter* 1(7) (August 1989): 1, 3.

Iles, Doug. "CD-ROM Enters Mainstream IS." *Computerworld*, 5 June 1989, pp. 75–80.

The ILIAD Newsletter: ILIAD—The Telelibrary Pilot Project at the Royal Melbourne Institute of Technology. Melbourne: Royal Melbourne Institute of Technology, 1992.

Indirect Costs. Ann Arbor: University of Michigan, 23 December 1988.

"Information Technology: Video Disks Offer a Detailed Portrait of Qin, the First Chinese Emperor." *Chronicle of Higher Education* 38(22) (Feb. 5, 1992).

Intellectual Property Rights and Fair Use: Strengthening Scholarly Communication in the 1990s. Proceedings of the 9th Annual Conference of Research Library Directors. Dublin, Ohio: OCLC, 1991.

Interlibrary Loan Discussion Panel: Final Report. Dublin, Ohio: OCLC, October 1990.

"International Statement on 'Information Exchange Groups' " (letter). *Science* 155(3767) (10 March 1967): 1195–96.

Ito, Russell. "Big Media on Campus." *MacUser* 5(9) (Sept. 1989): 50 (concerning Intermedia).

Jain, A. K. *A Statistical Study of Book Use*. Ph.D. Thesis, Purdue University, 1967.

Jain, A. K., et al. "A Statistical Model of Book Use and Its Application to the Book Storage Problem." *Journal of the American Statistical Association* 64 (December 1969): 1211–24.

Jewett, Charles Coffin. *On the Construction of Catalogues of Libraries, and their Publication by Means of Separate, Stereotyped Titles*. 2d ed. Washington, D.C.: Smithsonian Institution, 1853.

"Joint Project Sends Images at High Speed." *Australian*, 21 May 1991.

"Journal Publisher Sues Author of Price Study." *American Libraries*, Sept. 1989, pp. 717–18.

Jul, Erik. "Graph-Text Project Provides Basis for Online Journal." *OCLC Update*, October 1991.

————. "Project to Analyze Internet Information Is Underway." *OCLC Newsletter*, Mar./Apr. 1992, pp. 13–15.

————. "Ben Schneiderman Speaks on User Interface Design." *OCLC Newsletter*, May/June 1992, pp. 10–11.

Justis, Robert T., et al. *Strategic Management and Policy*. Englewood Cliffs, N.J.: Prentice-Hall, 1985.

Kahn, Philippe. "Forces Shaping Academic Software Development." *Educom Review* 24(4) (Winter 1989): 24–25.

Kaske, N. K. "Evaluation of Current Collection Utilization Methodologies and Findings." *Collection Management* 3(2–3) (1979): 197–99.

Kehoe, Brendan P. *Zen and the Art of the Internet*. Chester, Pa.: Widener University, January 1992.

Kelly, Lauren. "Budgeting in Nonprofit Organizations." *Drexel Library Quarterly* 21(3) (Summer 1985): 3–18.

Kent, Allen, et al., eds. "The Economics of Academic Libraries." *Library Trends* 28(1) (Summer 1979): 3–24.

———. *Use of Library Materials: The University of Pittsburgh Study*. New York: Marcel Dekker, 1979.

Kent, Allen, and Thomas J. Galvin. *The Structure and Governance of Library Networks*. New York: Marcel Dekker, 1979.

Kibbey, Mark, and Nancy H. Evans. "The Network Is the Library." *Educom Review* 24(3) (Fall 1989): 15–20.

Kidston, James S. "The Validity of Questionnaire Responses." *Library Quarterly* 55(2) (1985): 133–50.

Kiesler, S. B., and L. S. Sproull, eds. *Computing and Change on Campus*. New York: Cambridge University Press, 1987.

Kirwin, William D. *Personal Computing: A Gartner Group Briefing—August 10–12, 1992*. Stamford, Conn.: GartnerGroup, 1992. (Page 2 shows total expenses, divided 19 percent for capital and 81 percent for labor.)

Kniffel, Leonard. "Books Made to Order: Libraries as Publishers." *American Libraries*, September 1989, pp. 735–39.

Knight, Kenneth, ed. *Matrix Management*. New York: PBI, 1977.

Kolitsky, Michael A. "Constructing a Science Center in the Age of Hypermedia." *Computers in Life Science Education* 8(2) (February 1991): 9–13.

Konopasek, Katherine, and Nancy Patricia O'Brien. "Undergraduate Periodical Usage: A Model of Measurement." *Serials Librarian* 9(2) (1984): 65–74.

Koteen, Jack. *Strategic Management in Public and Nonprofit Organizations*. New York: Praeger, 1989.

Lamb, Robert, and Paul Shrivastava, eds. *Advances in Strategic Management*, vols. 1–3. Greenwich, Conn.: JAI Press, 1982–1988.

Lambert, Richard D. *Beyond Growth: The Next Stage in Language and Area Studies*. Washington, D.C.: Association of American Universities, 1984.

Lancashire, Ian, and Willard McCarty. *The Humanities Computing Yearbook, 1988*. Oxford: The Clarendon Press, 1988.

Lancaster, F. W. "Whither Libraries? or, Wither Libraries." *College and Research Libraries* 39(5) (Sept. 1978): 345–57.

Lancaster, F. Wilfrid. *The Dissemination of Scientific and Technical Information: Toward a Paperless System*. Champaign: University of Illinois, Graduate School of Library Science, 1977.

———. *The Measurement and Evaluation of Library Services*. Washington, D.C.: Information Resources Press, 1977.

————. "Evaluating Collections by Their Use." *Collection Management* 4(1–2) (1982): 15–43.

————. "The Paperless Society Revisited." *American Libraries*, Sept. 1985, pp. 553–55.

Lancaster, F. W., and Linda C. Smith, eds. *Artificial Intelligence and Expert Systems: Will They Change the Library?* Urbana-Champaign: University of Illinois at Urbana-Champaign, GSLIS, 1992.

Lawrence, Gary S. "A Cost Model for Storage and Weeding Programs." *College and Research Libraries* 42 (1981): 138–47.

Lawrence, Gary S., and Anne R. Oja. *The Use of the General Collections at the University of California*. Berkeley: University of California, Library Studies and Research Division, 30 January 1980.

Lazorick, Gerald J. "Patterns of Book Use Using the Binomial Distribution." *Library Research* 1 (1979): 171–88.

"LC Drops MARC Licensing Plan." *American Libraries*, Apr. 1990, p. 288.

"LC MARC Subscribers Told to Sign Licensing Agreement." *American Libraries*, Sept. 1989, p. 724.

Leeuwenburg, Jeff, et al. "Electronic Imaging: Systems R&D, and Collection Building at RMIT." *Australian Academic and Research Libraries*, September 1991.

Leimkuhler, F. F. "Storage Policies for Information Systems." Paper presented at the Joint National Meeting of the American Astronautical Society and the Operations Research Society, Denver, June 1969.

Lesk, M. "Image Formats for Preservation and Access." *Information Technology in Libraries* 9(4) (1991): 300–308.

Less Access to Less Information by and about the U.S. Government—A 1981–1987 Chronology. Chicago: American Library Association, 1988.

Lewis, Arnold, and Margaret S. Powell. "The Silent Threat: How Federal Policy Stifles Scholarship." *Educational Record*, Winter 1987, pp. 19–24.

Lewis, D. W. "8 Truths for Middle Managers in Lean Times." *Library Journal* 116(14) (1 September 1991): 315–16.

Line, M. B., and A. Sandison. "Obsolescence and Changes in the Use of Literature with Time." *Journal of Documentation* 30 (1974): 283–350.

Lister, W. C. *Least-Cost Decision Rules for the Selection of Library Materials for Compact Storage*. Ph.D. thesis, Purdue University, 1967.

Lohman, C. K. "Retrenchment, Retirement Benefits, and the Faculty Role." *Academe* 77(3) (May–June, 1991): 18–21.

Lopez, Manuel D. "The Lopez or Citation Technique of In-Depth Collection Evaluation Explicated." *College and Research Libraries* 44(3) (1983): 251–55.

Loughborough University. Department of Library and Information Studies. Centre for Library and Information Management. *Reader Failure at the Shelf*. Loughborough, Leicestershire: Loughborough University, 1982.

Lowry, Charles B. "Resources Sharing or Cost Shifting?—The Unequal Burden of Cooperative Cataloging and ILL in Network." *College and Research Libraries*, January 1990, pp. 11–19.

————. *Comparative Study of Periodical Literature Indexing: Print versus Electronic Access*. Arlington, Tex.: University of Texas, 31 July 1992.

MORTON COLLEGE LIBRARY
CICERO, ILLINOIS

Lozier, G. G. "Projecting Faculty Retirement." *American Economic Review* 81(2) (May 1991): 101–5.

Lunden, Elizabeth. "The Library as a Business." *American Libraries*, July/Aug. 1982, pp. 471–72.

Lynch, Clifford. "Telecommunications and Libraries." *DLA Bulletin* 6(1) (Fall 1986): 1, 3.

———. "The Melvyl System: Looking Back, Looking Forward." *DLA Bulletin* 12(10) (Spring 1992): 3–5.

———. "Library Automation and the National Network." *Educom Review* 24(3) (Fall 1989): 21–26.

McClure, Charles R., and Carol A. Hert. "Specialization in Library/Information Science Education: Issues, Scenarios, and the Need for Action." *Proceedings of the Conference on Specialization in Library/Information Science Education*. Ann Arbor: University of Michigan, 6–8 November 1991.

McDonough, Adrian M. *Information Economics and Management Systems*. New York: McGraw-Hill, 1963.

MacEwan, Bonnie. "The North American Inventory Project: A Tool for Selection, Education and Communication." *Library Acquisitions: Practice and Theory* 13 (1989): 45–50.

McGill, Michael J. "Z39.50 Benefits for Designers and Users." *Educom Review* 24(3) (Fall 1989): 27–30.

Machovec, George S. "Locally Loaded Databases in Arizona State University's Online Catalog Using the CARL System." *Information Technology and Libraries* 8(2) (June 1989): 161–69.

McLean, Neil. "The Changing Economics of Information: A Library/Information Service View." In *The Electronic Campus—An Information Strategy*, ed. Lynn J. Brindley. Proceedings of the Conference in Banbury, England, 28–30 October 1988, pp. 53–64.

Macmillan, Ian C. "Competitive Strategies for Not-For-Profit Agencies." In *Advances in Strategic Management*, vol 1., ed. Robert Lamb. Greenwich, Conn.: JAI Press, 1982, pp. 61–82.

MacMillan, Ian C., and Patricia E. Jones. *Strategy Formulation: Power and Politics*. St. Paul, Minn.: West Publishing, 1986.

McNamee, Patrick B. *Tools and Techniques for Strategic Management*. Oxford: Pergamon, 1985.

Maguire, Carmel, et al. *Image-Based Information and the Future of Academic and Research Libraries*. Sydney, Australia: University of New South Wales, 1991.

Makridakis, Spyros, and Steven C. Wheelwright. *Forecasting Methods for Management*, 5th ed. New York: John Wiley, 1989.

———. *The Handbook of Forecasting*. New York: Wiley, 1987.

Mann, Jim. "Valuable Window on Japan May be Closing, Scholars Fear." *Los Angeles Times*, 24 March 1991, pp. A24–A25.

"Many Views, but Little Consensus on Pister Report as Time Nears to Make Decision." *Notice, Academic Senate of UC* 16(7) (March 1992).

"MARC Licensing Flap Lingers, LC's Avram Takes the Heat." *American Libraries*, March 1990, pp. 255–56.

Marchant, Maurice P. "The Closing of the Library School at Brigham Young University." *American Libraries*, January 1992, pp. 32–36.

"Market Share of CD-ROM Information Products Tabulated by Type of Product for 1988 and 1990." *ComputerWorld*, 30 January 1989, p. 77.

Marschak, Jacob. "Towards an Economic Theory of Organization and Information." In *Decision Processes*, ed. R. M. Thrall, et al. New York: Wiley, 1954.

Martin, Lowell. "User Studies and Library Planning." *Library Trends* 24 (Jan. 1976): 483–95.

Martyn, John, et al. *Information UK 2000*. London: British Library Research, Bowker-Saur, 1990.

Matheson, Nina W. "Academic Information in the Academic Sciences Center: Roles for the Library in Information Management." *Journal of Medical Education* 57(10) (1982): part 2.

Meadows, Jack A. "Higher Education and the Influence of Information Technology: Research." In *The Electronic Campus—An Information Strategy*, ed. Lynn J. Brindley. Proceedings of the Conference in Banbury, England, 28–30 October 1988, pp. 13–21.

Merrill-Oldham, Jan, et al. *Preservation Program Models: A Study Project and Report*. Washington, D.C.: ARL, 1991.

Michalak, Thomas J. "An Experiment in Enhancing Catalog Records at Carnegie-Mellon University." *Library Hi-Tech* 31(3) (1990): 33–41.

Miller, David C. *The New Optical Media in the Library and the Academy Tomorrow*. Benicia, Calif.: DCM Associates, prepared for the Fred Meyer Charitable Trust, August 1986.

———. *The New Optical Media Mid–1986: A Status Report*. Benicia, Calif.: DCM Associates, prepared for the Fred Meyer Charitable Trust, August 1986.

———. *Moving Information: Graphic Images on CD-ROM*. Benicia, Calif.: DCM Associates, prepared for the Fred Meyer Charitable Trust, March 1987.

———. *Special Report: Publishers, Libraries, and CD-ROM*. Benicia, Calif.: DCM Associates, prepared for the Fred Meyer Charitable Trust, March 1987.

Millson-Martula, Christopher. "Use Studies and Serials Rationalization: A Review." *Serials Librarian* 15(1–2) (1988): 121–36.

Mooers, Calvin. *Zator Technical Bulletin 136*, December 1959.

Moran, Barbara B. "Construction of the Questionnaire in Survey Research." *Public Libraries* 24(2) (1985): 75–76.

Morse, P. M., and C. Elston. "A Probabilistic Model for Obsolescence." *Operations Research* 17(1) (1969): 36–47.

Morse, Philip M. "Measures of Library Effectiveness." *Library Quarterly* 42(1) (Jan. 1972): 15–30.

Morse, Philip M., and Ching-chih Chen. "Using Circulation Data to Obtain Unbiased Estimates of Book Use." *Library Quarterly* 45(2) (1975): 179–94.

Morton, Herbert C., and Anne Jamieson Price. "The ACLS Survey of Scholars: Views on Publications, Computers, Libraries." *Scholarly Communication*. Washington, D.C.: Office of the Scholarly Communication and Technology, 1986.

Mosher, Paul H. "A Natural Scheme for Collaboration in Collection Development:

The RLG-NCIP Effort." *Resource Sharing and Information Networks* 2 (Spring/Summer 1985): 21–35.

Mosier, Jane N., and Sidney L. Smith. *Guidelines for Designing User Interface Software.* August 1986.

National Commission on Preservation and Access. *Annual Report.* Washington, D.C.: National Commission on Preservation and Access.

National Research Council (NRC). *Biomedical and Behavioral Research Scientists: Their Training and Supply.* Washington, D.C.: NRC, 1989.

Naylor, Thomas H. *Corporate Planning Models.* Reading, Mass.: Addison-Wesley, 1979.

Neff, Raymond K. "Merging Libraries and Computer Centers: Manifest Destiny or Manifestly Deranged?" *Educom Bulletin*, Winter 1985, pp. 8–12, 16.

Nelson, Theodor H. *Literary Machines: The Report on, and of, Project Xanadu Edition 87.1.* San Antonio, Tex.: T. H. Nelson, 1987.

"New Online Journal to Speed Publication of Peer-Reviewed Reports on Clinical Trials of Medical Treatments." *OCLC Update*, October 1991.

New York State Library. *Libraries and Technology: A Strategic Plan for the Use of Advanced Technologies for Library Resource Sharing in New York State.* Albany, N.Y.: New York State Library, 1987.

———. *Technology and the Research Environment of the Future.* Albany, N.Y.: New York State Library, February 1989.

Nickerson, Raymond. *Using Computers: Human Factors in Information Systems.* Cambridge, Mass.: Bradford/MIT Press, January 1986.

Nilsonger, Thomas E. "A Test of Two Citation Checking Techniques for Evaluating Political Science Collections in University Libraries." *Library Resources and Technical Services* 27(2) (1983): 163–76.

Nimmer, David. *The Berne Convention Implementation Act of 1988.* New York: Bender, 1989.

1991 OCLC Preservation Needs Assessment Study: Detailed Report. Dublin, Ohio: OCLC, February 1991.

1992 All-University Faculty Conference on Undergraduate Education. Berkeley: University of California, February 1992.

Nutter, Susan K. "Online Systems and the Management of Collections: Use and Implications." *Advances in Library Automation and Networking* 1, pp. 125–49.

Oberg, Larry R. "Evaluating the Conspectus Approach for Smaller Library Collections." *College and Research Libraries* 49 (May 1988): 187–96.

Obert, Beverly. "Collection Development through Student Surveys and Collection Analysis." *Illinois Libraries* 70(1) (1988): 46–53.

OCLC Gateway Project, 15 Jan. 1992. Dublin, Ohio: OCLC, 1992.

Ohio Board of Regents. *OLIS: Connecting People, Libraries, and Information for Ohio's Future.* Columbus, Ohio: Ohio Board of Regents, Dec. 1989.

Okerson, Ann, and Kenneth Stubbs. "The Library 'Doomsday Machine.' " *Publishers Weekly* 236(8) (8 Feb. 1991): 36–37.

Okerson, Ann L. "Periodical Prices: A History and Discussion." In *Advances in Serials Management*, ed. Jean G. Cook and Marcia Tuttle. Greenwich, Conn.: JAI Press, 1986, pp. 101–34.

———. "Report on the ARL Serials Project." *Serials Librarian* 17(3–4) (1990): 111–19.

Olsen, Wallace C. *Toward an Integrated Information System*. Ithaca, N.Y.: Cornell University, April 1986.

Ortopan, Leroy D. "National Shelflist Count: A Historical Introduction." *Library Resources and Technical Services* 29 (Oct./Dec. 1985): 328–32.

Osburn, Charles B. "Non-Use and User Studies in Collection Development." *Collection Management* 4(1–2) (1982): 45–53.

Paisley, William, and Matilda Butler. "The First Wave: CD-ROM Adoption in Offices and Libraries." *Microcomputers for Information Management* 4(2) (June 1987): 109–27.

Palais, Elliot. "Use of Course Analysis in Compiling a Collection Development Policy Statement for a University Library." *Journal of Academic Librarianship* 1 (March 1987): 8–13.

Palmour, Vernon E., et al. *A Study of the Characteristics, Costs, and Magnitude of Interlibrary Loans in Academic Libraries*. Westport, Conn.: Greenwood, 1972.

Pelikan, Jaroslav. "The Storm Breaking upon the University: The University in Crisis." *Key Reporter* 57(4): 2–6.

Perrault, Anna H. "Humanities Collection Management—An Impressionistic/Realistic/Optimistic Appraisal of the State of the Art." *Collection Management* 5(3–4) (1983): 1–23.

Pettigrew, Andrew M. *The Management of Strategic Change*. Oxford: Blackwell, 1987.

The PhD Shortage: The Federal Role. Washington, D.C.: Association of American Universities, 11 January 1990.

"Ph.D. Supply" (letters). *Issues in Science and Technology* 7(4) (Summer 1991): 22–29.

" 'Pister' Report Calls for Broader Definition of What Constitutes Proper Work of Faculty." *Notice, Academic Senate of UC* 16(1) (Oct. 1991): 1, 4.

Piternick, George. "ARL Statistics—Handle with Care." *College and Research Libraries* 38 (Sept. 1977): 419–23.

Pitkin, Gary M. "CARL's Latest Project: Access to Articles through the Online Catalog." *American Libraries*, Oct. 1988, pp. 769–70.

Platenic, Suzanne. "Should I or Shouldn't I?" *Beyond Computing* 1(1) (1992): 26–33.

Powell, Ronald R. *The Relationship of Library User Studies to Performance Measures: A Review of the Literature*. Chicago: University of Illinois. *User Surveys*. SPEC Kit 148. Washington, D.C.: Association of Research Libraries, 1988.

Pre/post Implementation Time and Methods Study of Library Public Catalog File Maintenance. Long Beach, Calif.: CSUC, 15 March 1982.

Predicasts Inc. *Predicasts*. Cleveland, Ohio: Predicasts, 1980–.

———. *Predicasts F & S Index: United States*. Cleveland, Ohio: Predicasts, 1980–.

———. *Predicasts Forecasts*. Cleveland, Ohio: Predicasts, 1980–.

———. *Predicasts, Inc. World Casts: Product*. Cleveland, Ohio: Predicasts, 1992.

————. *PROMT, Predicasts Overview of Markets and Technology*. Cleveland, Ohio: Predicasts, 1992.

Prentice, Ann. "Budgeting and Accounting: A Selected Bibliography." *Drexel Library Quarterly* 21(3) (Summer 1985): 106–12.

"The Preservation Challenge: A Sampling of Efforts to Save the Nation's Heritage." *Scholarly Communication* 1 (June 1985): 3.

"Progress toward National Research and Education Network." *Manage IT* 1(1) (Feb. 1990): 4.

"A Proposal for More Informative Abstracts of Clinical Articles." *Annals of Internal Medicine* 106 (1987): 598–604.

Public Sector/Private Sector Interaction in Providing Information Services: Report to the NCLIS from the Public Sector/Private Sector Task Force. Washington, D.C.: NCLIS, 1982.

"Publishing in Valid Media" (letter). *Science* 155(3769) (24 March 1967): 1497.

"Publishing Without Review" (letter). *Science* 155(3758) (6 Jan. 1967): 34.

Reagan, Ronald. "The President's Decision Memorandum: Transfer of the Civil Space Remote Sensing Systems to the Private Sector." White House, 28 Feb. 1983.

Reed-Scott, Jutta. *Manual for the North American Inventory of Research Collections*. Washington, D.C.: Association of Research Libraries, Office of Management Studies, 1988.

Reimann, Bernard C. *Managing for Change*. Oxford, Ohio: Planning Forum, 1987.

Research Associates. *State Profiles: Financing Public Higher Education*. Washington, D.C.: Research Associates, September 1991.

Research Libraries Group. *RLIN Rates: Rates for Services from the Research Libraries Information Network*. Appendix C to the RLIN service agreement. Mountain View, Calif.: Research Libraries Group, 1 July 1991.

"Research Library Directors Evaluate OCLC's Future at Conference." *Research Libraries in OCLC: A Quarterly* 309 (Spring 1989).

"A Response from Gordon & Breach." *American Libraries*, May 1990, p. 405.

Rice, James G. "The Dream of the Memex." *American Libraries*, January 1988, pp. 14–17.

Rich, Spencer. "Drawing the Line on Poverty: Census Bureau Measurement Sparks Criticism from Many Quarters." *Washington Post*, 30 Oct. 1989, p. A13.

Richardson, John, Jr. "Toward an Expert System for Reference Service: A Research Agenda for the 1990s." *College and Research Libraries*, March 1989, pp. 233–48.

Ricketson, Sam. *The Berne Convention for the Protection of Literary and Artistic Works: 1886–1986*. London: Queen Mary College, Centre for Commercial Law Studies, Kluwer, 1987.

Rider, Fremont. *The Scholar and the Future of the Research Library*. New York: Hadham Press, 1944.

Rider, Robin E. "Saving the Records of Big Science." *American Libraries*, Feb. 1991, pp. 166–68.

"RLG Board Sets Organization's Course for the 1990s" (press release). 8 March 1991.

"RLG Contributes to National Preservation Effort." *Research Library Group News* 20 (Fall 1989): 3–8.

"RLG in 1992: Setting the Stage for Change." *Research Library Group News* 26 (Fall 1991): 3–4.

"RLIN Citations File plus Document Delivery Tapped for Major Expansion." *Research Library Group News* 26 (Fall 1991): 6–7.

Roberts, Fred S. *Measurement Theory with Applications to Decision Making, Utility, and the Social Sciences*. Volume 7 in the series *Encyclopedia of Mathematics and Its Applications*. Reading, Mass.: Addison-Wesley, 1979.

Roberts, Michael M. "The NREN and Commercial Services." *Educom Review* 24(4) (Winter 1989): 10–11.

Rogers, Susan M. "Educational Applications of the NREN." *Educom Review* 25(2) (Summer 1990): 25–29.

Saaty, Thomas L. *Mathematical Methods of Operations Research*. New York: McGraw-Hill, 1959.

————. *Thinking with Models: Mathematical Models in the Physical, Biological, and Social Sciences*. New York: Pergamon Press, 1981.

"Sales of Electronic Databases to Grow 20% in 1989 vs 1988." *New York Times*, 30 December 1988, p. 23.

Sanders, Nancy P., Edward T. O'Neill, and Stuart L. Weibel. "Automated Collection Analysis Using the OCLC and RLG Bibliographic Databases." *College and Research Libraries* 49 (July 1985): 305–15.

Sarloe, Bart. "Achieving Client-Centered Collection Development in Small and Medium-Sized Academic Libraries." *College & Research Libraries* 50 (May 1989): 344–53.

Sedelow, Sally Yeates, and Walter A. Sedelow, Jr. "Artificial Intelligence, Expert Systems, and Productivity." In *Psychology and Productivity*, ed. Paul Whitney. New York: Plenum, 1989, pp. 51–66.

Seelmeyer, John. "The Anatomy of a Library School Shutdown." *American Libraries*, February 1985, pp. 95–96, 113.

Seibert, Warren, et al. *Research Library Trends, 1951–1980 and Beyond*. Bethesda, Md.: Lister Hill Center for Biomedical Communications, March 1987.

————. *Research Library Trends II: 35 Libraries in the 1970s and Beyond*. Bethesda, Md.: Lister Hill Center for Biomedical Communications, January 1990.

Self, John, ed. *Artificial Intelligence and Human Learning: Intelligent Computer-Aided Instruction*. London: Chapman and Hall, 1988.

"Serials Survey Linked to Gordon & Breach." *American Libraries*, March 1990, p. 173.

Shank, Russell (chair), et al. *Report of the ALA Special Committee on Library School Closings*. Chicago: ALA, June 1991.

Shneiderman, Ben. *Designing the User Interface: Strategies for Effective Human-Computer Interaction*. Reading, Mass.: Addison-Wesley, 1986.

Shurkin, Joel. "The Rise and Fall and Rise of RLG." *American Libraries*, Jul./Aug. 1982, pp. 450–55.

Sidgreaves, Ivan. "The Electronic Campus: Organization Issues." In *The Electronic Campus—An Information Strategy*, ed. Lynn J. Brindley. Proceedings of the Conference in Banbury, England, 28–30 October 1988, pp. 65–80.

Siegel, Donald, and Zvi Griliches. *Purchased Services, Outsourcing, Computers, and Productivity in Manufacturing*. Working paper no. 3678. Cambridge, Mass.: National Bureau of Economic Research, April 1991.

"Simmons Project Tracks Treasures of Qin Dynasty with New Technology." *American Libraries*, March 1986, p. 215.

Smith, Joan M. *The Standard Generalized Markup Language and Related Issues*. Dover, N.H.: Longwood Publishing Group, 1986.

Smith, Page. *Killing the Spirit: Higher Education in America*. New York: Viking, 1990.

Smith, Wayne. Comments re the "Commons" at the Research Library Directors' Conference, OCLC, 1992.

Smits, W. A. *United States Adherence to the Berne Convention: A Missed Opportunity for Moral Rights Protection?* PhD. Dissertation, University of California at Los Angeles, 1989.

"Stanford 'Repositions,' Library Faces Major Cuts." *American Libraries*, May 1990, p. 391.

"State Budget Woes Threaten U. of South Fla. Library School." *American Libraries*, November 1991, p. 926.

State Profiles: Financing Public Higher Education. Washington, D.C.: Research Associates, September 1991.

"Statewide Senate Cool to 'Pister' Report Proposal." *Notice, Academic Senate of UC* 16(7) (May 1992).

Stayner, Richard A., and Valerie E. Richardson. *The Cost-Effectiveness of Alternative Library Storage Programs*. Melbourne, Australia: Monash University, Graduate School of Librarianship, 1983.

Strategic Vision Discussion Group. Steering Committee. *Strategic Vision for Professional Librarians*. December 1991.

Stubbs, Kendon (ed.). "Introduction." *ARL Statistics, 1990–91*. Washington, D.C.: ARL, 1992.

Stubbs, Kendon, and David Buxton, comps. *Cumulated ARL University Library Statistics: 1962–63 through 1978–79*. Washington, D.C.: Association of Research Libraries, 1981.

Summers, David. "The Changing Economics of Information: An Industry View." In *The Electronic Campus—An Information Strategy*. Proceedings of the Conference in Banbury, England, October 28–30, 1988.

Survey Report on the Literature of Digital Image Management and Administration to Preserve the Sense of Earth from Space. Washington, D.C.: National Commission on Libraries and Information Science (NCLIS), August 1984.

"Technology Assessment at OCLC." *OCLC Newsletter* 179 (May/June 1989).

Terwiliger, Gloria. "Evaluating the Role of the Learning Resource Centre." *Community and Junior College Libraries* 1(4) (1983): 23–32.

Thompson, Donald D. *In-House Use and Immediacy of Need: The Riverside Pilot Studies*. Berkeley: University of California, Institute of Library Research, November 1978.

———. *Use of Library Services, by Category of Patron and/or Funding Source*. Berkeley: University of California, 15 June 1979.

Thompson, James. *The End of Libraries*. London: Bingley Press, 1982.

Toffler, Alvin. *Power Shift*. New York: Bantam Books, 1990, esp. pp. 172–77, 221–22.

———. "Toffler's Next Shock." *World Monitor*, November 1990, pp. 34–44.

Tomeski, Edward A., and Harold Lazarus. *People-Oriented Computer Systems*. New York: Van Nostrand, 1975, chs. 1–4.

"Transcript of Closed NCLIS Meeting Details FBI's Library Awareness Program." *American Libraries*, April 1988, p. 244.

Tukey, John W. *Exploratory Data Analysis*. Reading, Mass.: Addison-Wesley, 1977.

"UC Adopts Policy to Place More Emphasis on Teaching." *Los Angeles Times*, 17 July 1992, p. A3.

United States Code, 1988 Edition. Washington, D.C.: United States Government Printing Office, 1989.

University of California at Berkeley. Task Force on Faculty Rewards. *The Report of the Universitywide Task Force on Faculty Rewards*. Berkeley: University of California, Academic Senate, October 1991.

University of Michigan. School of Information and Library Studies (SLIS). *Information and People: A Campus Dialogue on the Challenges of Electronic Information*. Ann Arbor: University of Michigan, SLIS, 1991.

University of Pittsburgh. Senate Library Committee. *Report on the Study of Library Use at Pitt by Professor Allen Kent, et al*. July 1979.

U.S. Congress. 102nd Congress, Second Session. *Legislative Branch Appropriations for 1992. Hearings before a Subcommittee of the Committee on Appropriations. Part 1: Justification of the Budget Estimates*. Washington, D.C.: United States Government Printing Office, 1992, 785–1168.

U.S. Congress. House Committee on the Judiciary. *Berne Convention Implementation Act of 1987*. Hearings before the Subcommittee, June 17, July 23, September 16 and 30, 1987, February 9 and 10, 1988. Washington, D.C.: GPO, 1988.

U.S. Congress, Senate. *Fair Use and Unpublished Works*. S521–34. Washington, D.C.: G.P.O., 11 July 1990.

U.S. Congress. Senate Committee on Governmental Affairs. 101st Congress, Second Session. *Pentagon Rules on Media Access to the Persian Gulf War*. Hearing before the Committee on Governmental Affairs, U.S. Senate, 20 Feb. 1991.

U.S. Congress. Senate Committee on the Judiciary. *Moral Rights in Our Copyright Laws*. Hearings before the Subcommittee, June 20, September 20, and October 24, 1989. Washington, D.C.: GPO, 1990.

U.S. Congress. Senate Committee on the Judiciary. 100th Congress, Second Session. *The Berne Convention*. Hearings before the Subcommittee, February 18 and March 3, 1988. Washington, D.C.: GPO, 1988.

U.S. Department of Commerce. *NITA Information Services Report*. Washington, D.C.: U.S. Department of Commerce, August 1988.

U.S. Library of Congress. *A Proposal to Establish the Library of Congress Fee Services Fund*. Washington, D.C.: Library of Congress, 12 June 1990.

Van Houweling, Douglas E. "The Information Technology Environment of Higher Education." *Conference on Information Resources for the Campus of the Future*. Dublin, Ohio: OCLC, 1986.

Van Orden, Richard. "Content-Enriched Access to Electronic Information: Summaries of Selected Research." *Library Hi-Tech* 31(3) (1990): 27–32.

Van Tuyl, Laura. "To Ancient Greece via Computer (Perseus Database, an Electronic Library)." *Christian Science Monitor* 83(101) (19 April 1991): 13.

Vaughn, Robert C., and Robert M. Rosenzweig. "Heading off a Ph.D. Shortage." *Issues in Science and Technology* 7(2) (Winter 1991): 66–73.

Voigt, Melvin. "Acquisition Rates in University Libraries." *College and Research Libraries* 36 (July 1975): 263–71.

Voigt, Melvin J. *Case Study of the California Experience in Library Collection Building*. San Diego, Calif.: University of California Library, 1969.

Vosper, Robert. *The Farmington Plan Survey: A Summary of the Separate Studies of 1957–1961*. Urbana: University of Illinois, Graduate School of Library Science, 1965.

Walz, T. "Social Work Faculty in Retirement." *Journal of Education for Social Work* 27(1) (1991): 60–72.

Warnow, Joan N., et al. *A Study of the Preservation of Documents at Department of Energy Laboratories*. New York: American Institute of Physics, 1982.

Werking, Richard Hume. "Allocating the Academic Library's Book Budget: Historical Perspectives and Current Reflections." *Journal of Academic Librarianship* 14(3) (July 1988): 140–44.

———. "Collection Growth and Expenditures in Academic Libraries: A Preliminary Inquiry." *College and Research Libraries* 109(2) (Jan. 1991): 5–23.

White, Anthony G. *Matrix Management/Public Administration: A Selected Bibliography*. Monticello, Ill.: Vance Bibliographies, 1982.

Williams, Edwin Everitt. *Farmington Plan Handbook, with a Bibliography of the Farmington Plan, 1953–1961*. Ithaca, N.Y.: Association of Research Libraries, 1961.

Williams, Gordon, et al. *Library Cost Models: Owning versus Borrowing Serial Publications*. Washington, D.C.: Office of Science Information Service, National Science Foundation, 1968.

Wilson, David L. "Researchers Get Direct Access to Huge Data Base." *Chronicle of Higher Education*, 9 October 1991, pp. A24, A28.

———. "Model Proposed for Management of Information." *Chronicle of Higher Education*, 6 Nov. 1991.

Wilson, Sandra R. *Use of the Critical Incident Technique to Evaluate the Impact of MEDLINE: Final Report*. Palo Alto, Calif.: American Institutes for Research, 1989.

"With a Large Budget Cut on the Way, UC Weighs All Options for Making Ends Meet." *Notice* (Academic Senate of UC) 16(8) (June 1992).

WLN Pricing. Personal communication in a meeting with Washington Library Network (WLN) management, 1992.

Young, Charles. "Unmasking the Budget Crisis." *UCLA Magazine* 4(2) (Summer 1992): 6–7.

Zaleznik, Abraham. *The Managerial Mystique*. New York: Harper & Row, 1989.

"Z39.50: Lousy Sports Car, Great Library Standard." *American Libraries*, Oct. 1990, p. 903.

Index

About the Author

ROBERT M. HAYES recently retired from being Dean of the Graduate School Library and Information Science at UCLA. He holds a doctorate in mathematics and has published several books on libraries and automated information systems. In addition to a number of academic appointments, he has worked for the National Bureau of Standards, Hughes Aircraft, National Cash Register, and Magnavox Research Laboratories.